Fishamble: The New Pl

ABOUT FISHAMBLE

The company was founded in 1988 and, since 1990, has been dedicated to the discovery, development and production of new work for the Irish stage. Formerly known as Pigsback, the company was renamed Fishamble in 1997. The name is inspired by Dublin's Fishamble Street and, in particular, its playhouse which, in 1784, became the first Irish theatre to pursue a policy of producing new Irish work. Fishamble: The New Play Company has produced many plays by first-time and established playwrights in Dublin and throughout Ireland.

FISHAMBLE FIRSTS

The *Fishamble Firsts* scheme focuses on producing first plays by new writers. This includes recent productions such as *Noah and the Tower Flower* by Sean McLoughlin (2007), which won the *Irish Times* Best New Play Award and the Stewart Parker Trust Award, *The Gist of It* by Rodney Lee (2006), which was staged in New York by Origin/Fishamble, and *Monged* by Gary Duggan (2005), which won the Stewart Parker Trust Award, toured to Liverpool and was also staged in New York by Origin/Fishamble. Gavin Kostick, Deirdre Hines, Mark O'Rowe and Pat Kinevane also won a BBC/Stewart Parker Trust Award for their first plays, which were commissioned and produced by the company.

INTERNATIONAL TOURING

Fishamble has brought its work to the US, England, Scotland, Canada, Czech Republic, Romania, France and Germany. Recent touring includes bringing *The Pride of Parnell Street* by Sebastian Barry to the Tricycle Theatre (London), the Centre Culturel

Irlandais (Paris), Neue Stücke Aus Europa (Wiesbaden) and Festival of Arts & Ideas (New Haven), and touring *Forgotten* by Pat Kinevane to the Centre Culturel Irlandais (Paris), Kostel Na Pradle (Prague), International Theatre Festival (Sibiu) and Dance Base (Edinburgh). Fishamble's international touring is supported by Culture Ireland.

AWARDS

The company's work has won a number of awards including *Irish Times* Theatre Awards, BBC/Stewart Parker Trust Awards, Dublin City Council Awards and *In Dublin* Theatre Awards. It has also been nominated or shortlisted for *Irish Times* Theatre Awards, Entertainment and Media Awards, *Irish Times* Living Dublin Awards, ZeBBie Awards and Allianz Business to Arts Awards. Recent awards include *Irish Times* Theatre Awards for *Whereabouts* (2006 Special Judges' Award) and for *Noah and the Tower Flower* (2007 Best New Play Award), as well as nominations for *Forgotten* and *The Pride of Parnell Street* and Jim Culleton and Fishamble being shortlisted for Allianz Business to Arts Awards in 2008.

PUBLICATIONS

Fishamble frequently works with publishers, including New Island Books, Nick Hern Books, Faber & Faber and Methuen, in order to extend the life of plays beyond production. In recent years, Fishamble has published every play it premieres. For further details of publications, see www.fishamble.com.

PARTNERSHIPS

Fishamble often works in partnership with arts and non-arts organisations. Recent and current partners include development agencies, venues and festivals throughout Ireland, as well as festivals, theatres and cultural centres in the UK, the US and Europe. Other partners include Amnesty International, RTÉ lyric fm, British Council Ireland, TNL Canada, Ireland Newfoundland Partnership, The Gaiety School of Acting, Business to Arts, Origin

'In order to keep vibrant, theatre requires constant transfusions of new plays. This life-providing role is fulfilled enthusiastically and with wonderful results by Fishamble. Without them, Irish theatre would be anaemic.' BRIAN FRIEL

'Fishamble is to be congratulated on bringing original material to the public. It is ploughing a risky furrow to produce fresh, innovative and modern Irish writing for the theatre. I wish the company continuing success.'
MARY MCALEESE, PRESIDENT OF IRELAND

'A truly alive company like Fishamble puts electricity into the National grid of dreams.' SEBASTIAN BARRY

'Jim Culleton's work with new playwrights at Fishamble has detonated a controlled explosion of fresh talent.' FINTAN O'TOOLE

'Fishamble is dedicated to the pursuit of new work and the realisation of that work. Thus far the writing has been second to none, and I certainly hope it continues in that vein for years to come. It has been my great pleasure to be associated with them.' BRIAN COX

'I've worked with Fishamble twice, and those experiences have been among the happiest and most memorable of my writing career. Fishamble are a pleasure to work with and deserve every congratulation, in our glitz-obsessed age, for quietly keeping faith with the notion of an Irish-based theatre that can be new, fun, challenging and strange. We would all be very much poorer without the stories Fishamble have to tell.' JOE O'CONNOR

'New writing is the life-blood of theatre and Fishamble's work has been a vital source in Irish theatre. I was lucky enough to have Jim Culleton's support when I was starting out. Since then he's been a constant supporter both in terms of encouragment and commission. I know he has given a lot of new writers, including myself, a chance but he also commissions and produces our established writers. Jim Culleton – top man!' STELLA FEEHILY

'I am full of admiration and support for Fishamble's energy and magic.'
MAEVE BINCHY

'For years now, Fishamble have tackled the dangerous problem of new writing. They are to be greatly admired for their courage and persistence.'
JENNIFER JOHNSTON

'For twenty years now, Fishamble has been doing much more than presenting fresh and exciting new plays. They have discovered and nurtured a generation of playwrights. They deserve limitless praise for their continuing role as the driving force of Irish theatre.' MICHAEL COLLINS

'I congratulate Fishamble on an outstanding twenty years of achievement and dedication. A theatre company devoted to new work is a difficult endeavour to sustain. It is all the more remarkable that Jim Culleton and his colleagues have done so with notable success and with great acclaim. The contribution Fishamble has made to Irish theatre is a lasting testament to their courage and talents.' JOE DOWLING

'Fishamble and Jim Culleton were part of my introduction to theatre: their production of Pat Kinevane's *The Nun's Wood*, which toured to my local theatre in the late 1990s, was an eye-opener for my teenage self. It was one of the reasons I came to be deeply interested in theatre, one of the reasons I wanted both to write about it and to write for it. In both endeavours – as a critic and as a playwright – my subsequent experience of Fishamble has always been extremely stimulating. The company's work has continued to be an eye-opener for me in the best possible way. Working with Jim and the company on my short play for *Whereabouts* was one of the most satisfying learning experiences a beginning playwright could have.' BELINDA MCKEON

'The most important thing about Fishamble is the fact that they understand the fundamental need for new writing in Ireland. While other theatre companies bemoan the lack of new writing here, Fishamble are active in seeking it out and supporting it. They understand that not every writer emerges fully formed like some kind of a butterfly and are willing to do what some won't – take a bloody chance. The weight of expectation on new writers in this country is horrendous and Fishamble are invaluable in providing a buffer zone for, let's face it, pretty fragile emerging talent.' ABBIE SPALLEN

'For the last 20 years, Fishamble has had a strict policy of producing solely new Irish work so, unlike other companies, they do not have the luxury of reverting to the past. This in my opinion makes Fishamble the most courageous and innovative theatre company in the country because, without new plays, Irish contemporary theatre cannot survive.' SEAN MCLOUGHLIN

FISHAMBLE FIRSTS

Fishamble Firsts

An Anthology of First Plays by New Playwrights

Edited by Jim Culleton

Fishamble Firsts
First published 2008
by New Island
2 Brookside
Dundrum Road
Dublin 14

www.newisland.ie

ISBN 978-1-84840-020-7

The publishers would like to thank Casarotto Ramsey & Associates for permission to reproduce *Game* by Stella Feehily, Nick Hern books for their kind permission to reproduce *The Gist of It* by Rodney Lee, and Mary Kelly for her kind permission to reproduce 'For What Died the Sons of Róisín'.

A CIP catalogue record for this book is available from the British Library.

Printed and bound in the UK by CPI Mackays, Chatham ME5 8TD

New Island Books receives financial assistance from
The Arts Council (An Comhairle Ealaíon), Dublin, Ireland

10 9 8 7 6 5 4 3 2 1

CONTENTS

Theatre Company (New York), Accenture, Allianz, National Association of Youth Drama, Liverpool Irish Festival, The Irish Council for Bioethics and Temple Bar Cultural Trust.

TRAINING & DEVELOPMENT

Fishamble runs many developmental initiatives and training projects, such as play development workshops, dramaturgical support, discussions, seminars, special events and readings of commissioned and unsolicited work. The company runs a programme of ongoing playwriting courses which are open to the public. These courses often form links with other new play companies in Ireland, the UK, Europe and the US.

This strand of work also includes a mentoring scheme for Youth Theatre directors run in partnership with the National Association of Youth Drama, internships run with institutions including NUI and IES, off-site playwriting courses for literary, arts and theatre festivals nationwide, corporate training initiatives delivered in partnership with Business to Arts, and the *Fishamble New Writing Award*, launched in 2007, awarded to the best new writing in the Dublin Fringe Festival.

FUTURE PRODUCTIONS

New work currently in development includes plays by Sebastian Barry, Gary Duggan, Gavin Kostick, Sean McLoughlin, Elizabeth Moynihan and Abbie Spallen, as well as innovative projects with Tinderbox, ODOS Architects, St Francis Hospice and Temple Bar Cultural Trust.

STAFF

Artistic Director	Jim Culleton
General Manager	Orla Flanagan
Acting General Manager	Marketa Puzman
Literary Officer	Gavin Kostick

FISHAMBLE WISHES TO THANK THE FOLLOWING FRIENDS OF FISHAMBLE FOR THEIR INVALUABLE SUPPORT:

Robert & Lillian Chambers, Helen Cunningham, Brian Friel, Marian Keyes, Jo Mangan, Vincent O'Doherty, Andrew & Delyth Parkes, Michael & Mary O'Connor, John McColgan & Moya Doherty, David and Veronica Rowe, Dearbhail Ann Shannon.

Thank you also to those who do not wish to be credited.

For details on how to become a Friend of Fishamble, please see www.fishamble.com or contact info@fishamble.com.

Fishamble: The New Play Company
Shamrock Chambers
1/2 Eustace Street
Dublin 2
Ireland

Tel: +353-1-670 4018
Fax: +353-1-670 4019
E-mail: info@fishamble.com
Website: www.fishamble.com

Fishamble is funded by The Arts Council and Dublin City Council.

Previous World Premiere Productions

2008

Rank by Robert Massey
The Pride of Parnell Street by Sebastian Barry (revival)
Forgotten by Pat Kinevane (revival)
My Name is Rachel Corrie reading of play by Rachel Corrie, Alan Rickman and Katherine Viner

2007

The Pride of Parnell Street by Sebastian Barry
Noah and the Tower Flower by Sean McLoughlin*
Forgotten by Pat Kinevane

2006

Monged by Gary Duggan (revival)
Whereabouts – a series of short, site-specific plays by Shane Carr*, John Cronin*, John Grogan*, Louise Lowe, Belinda McKeon*, Colin Murphy*, Anna Newell*, Jack Olohan*, Jody O'Neill*, Tom Swift and Jacqueline Strawbridge*
Forgotten by Pat Kinevane (work-in-progress)
The Gist of It by Rodney Lee*

2005

Monged by Gary Duggan*
She Was Wearing… by Sebastian Barry, Maeve Binchy, Dermot Bolger, Michael Collins, Stella Feehily, Rosalind Haslett, Róisín Ingle*, Marian Keyes* and Gavin Kostick
55 degrees and rising readings of Scottish plays by Stephen Greenhorn, Zinnie Harris, David Greig and David Harrower

2004
Pilgrims in the Park by Jim O'Hanlon
Tadhg Stray Wandered In by Michael Collins
Dislocated readings of plays by Marius Von Mayenburg, Benny McDonnell and Leo Butler

2003
Handel's Crossing by Joe O'Connor, *The Medusa* by Gavin Kostick, *Chaste Diana* by Michael West and *Sweet Bitter* by Stella Feehily (a season of radio plays)
Shorts by Dawn Bradfield*, Aino Dubrawsky*, Simon O'Gorman*, Ciara Considine*, Tina Reilly*, Mary Portser, Colm Maher*, James Heaney*, Tara Dairman*, Lorraine McArdle*, Talaya Delaney*, Ger Gleeson*, Stella Feehily* and Bryan Delaney*
The Buddhist of Castleknock by Jim O'Hanlon (revival)

2002
Contact by Jeff Pitcher and Gavin Kostick
The Buddhist of Castleknock by Jim O'Hanlon*
Still by Rosalind Haslett*

2001
The Carnival King by Ian Kilroy*
Wired to the Moon by Maeve Binchy, adapted by Jim Culleton

2000
Y2K Festival: *Consenting Adults* by Dermot Bolger, *Dreamframe* by Deirdre Hines, *Moonlight and Music* by Jennifer Johnston, *The Great Jubilee* by Nicholas Kelly*, *Doom Raider* by Gavin Kostick, *Tea Set* by Gina Moxley

1999
The Plains of Enna by Pat Kinevane
True Believers by Joe O'Connor

1998
The Nun's Wood by Pat Kinevane*

1997
From Both Hips by Mark O'Rowe*

1996
The Flesh Addict by Gavin Kostick

1995
Sardines by Michael West
Red Roses and Petrol by Joe O'Connor*

1994
Jack Ketch's Gallows Jig by Gavin Kostick

1993
Buffalo Bill Has Gone To Alaska by Colin Teevan
The Ash Fire by Gavin Kostick (revival)

1992
The Ash Fire by Gavin Kostick*
The Tender Trap by Michael West

1991
Howling Moons/Silent Sons by Deirdre Hines*
This Love Thing by Marina Carr

1990
Don Juan by Michael West

* denotes first play by a new playwright

Preface

The full-length works in this selection are all roughly contemporary works set in Dublin, and as we all know, in the first few years of this century Dublin changed, changed utterly: a terrible housing bubble was born.

Of course when it comes to saying something more complex than 'we all got rich, built extensions, but lost our souls – and now look likely to go bust again anyway', things get a bit more tricky.

I'm not sure that artists think consciously in such formulations as 'society has changed; I must now reflect upon that change'. Perhaps they uneasily feel they ought to. But if they think about the big thing too much and not enough about letting the characters speak through them, then the work can become a little stiff, a little overt. On the other hand critics, who like to connect an artwork to here-and-now issues, do like to read a 'bigger picture' into plays which may or may not have been intended, or even be there at all. Certainly we, Fishamble, enjoy working on plays that are not only profound works in themselves, but also have something sharp to say about where we are now. In other words, works that might help audiences re-imagine, re-interpret their own way of life. Overall the sense that the play, through the investigation of one dramatic scenario, is standing in for much bigger things is a co-creation of the artist, the production, the audience and the critical response. A play then becomes a sort of synecdoche on a big scale.

In this collection you will hear many individual voices (I worked with all the writers involved and they are *very* individual!) which put together provide a partial, unfinished, mosaic of Dublin from 2002 to 2007. Young – but not that young – people worry about where they will live, what they can earn, if all this will come crashing down (literally in the case of

Noah and the Tower Flower). Relationships seem fluid, contingent and provisional – up for negotiation. Yes, the family is still there and the suburbs too, but these too are not what they were, no longer the centre of things, but a place challenged and provoked. Faiths too are undermined, or indeed simply not there, not relevant. Moral codes, if they exist at all, are generated by the actions of new groupings, new tribes. Politically these plays do not seem to me to truly belong to the much-discussed post-9/11 age; neither though do they seem party-politically traditional. Rather, they take for granted that the old ways are dead. If politics is in some way the discussion of a *polis,* a citizenship, then the plays offer fascinating discussions of the different ways within a small set of relationships that people are fumbling or lunging towards new social networks.

You will also find shorter plays in this collection; these are a riot and I hope you enjoy reading them.

Gavin Kostick
Literary Officer
Fishamble: The New Play Company

Introduction

Fishamble: The New Play Company produces first plays by new playwrights as part of its *Fishamble Firsts* initiative. This anthology, published during the Company's twentieth birthday year in 2008, is intended as a record and celebration of first plays produced by Fishamble since 2002, when the first anthology of such work was published, also by New Island.

The playwrights represented here have created a selection of first plays that are as innovative and imaginative as they are diverse. It was a great pleasure for all at Fishamble, and the creative teams working on each play, to bring these first plays by new voices in theatre to fruition. The anthology includes five full length plays, as well as a small selection of short first plays by new playwrights which were part of Fishamble's multi-writer productions, *Shorts* (2003), *She Was Wearing …* (2005), and *Whereabouts* (2006).

Still by Rosalind Haslett was the winner of a play competition run by Fishamble in association with Temple Bar Cultural Trust, and was staged in Meeting House Square in 2002. As well as engaging with the site-specific nature of the project, it captures the pressures that urban living can create on relationships in a beautifully understated way.

The Buddhist of Castleknock by Jim O'Hanlon was produced in 2002 and revived in 2003. It is about a family at Christmastime that asks some seriously funny questions about how a changing Ireland deals with multi-culturalism and immigration at the start of the twentieth century.

Monged by Gary Duggan was first performed in 2005 and revived in 2006, winning the Stewart Parker Trust Award for that year. It is a very vivid and exciting play about dreams, fear and identity among three twenty-somethings on a drug-fuelled weekend in Dublin.

The Gist of It by Rodney Lee received its premiere in 2006 and is a charming, quirky and very funny view of a dysfunctional relationship between a widower and his film-maker daughter.

Noah and the Tower Flower by Sean McLoughlin was first performed in 2007, and won both the Irish Times Best New Play Award and the Stewart Parker Trust Award. It is a fascinating portrait of the tender relationship between a recovering drug addict and a man who has recently been released from prison.

The short work by new playwrights in this volume are the monologue *Happy Endings* by Róisín Ingle which is inspired by Amnesty International's *Stop Violence Against Women* campaign and five two-hander plays – *Game* by Stella Feehily, *Tara Has Written a Play* by Tara Dairman, *Meeting Venus* by Simon O'Gorman, *Twenty-Two* by John Cronin and *Drapes* by Belinda McKeon – which vary in terms of style and approach, but which each provide fascinating glimpses of dynamic, vivid encounters between couples. The short plays chosen are self contained (even though they were part of a larger project) and, I think, could be produced very successfully in a different context.

This anthology contains credits from the original productions because the success of those first productions is inseparable from the energy and commitment shown by the extremely dedicated theatre artists and practitioners involved.

The nature of theatre is live, immediate and transitory. After a production ends, the play only lives on in the memories of those who shared the experience onstage, backstage and in the audience. This publication provides access to the plays and gives them the potential for further life in new productions that can explore and engage with their creative energy in the future.

Jim Culleton
Artistic Director
Fishamble: The New Play Company

Still

BY ROSALIND HASLETT

Still was first produced by Fishamble: The New Play Company, in association with Temple Bar Cultural Trust, on 14 August 2002 in Meeting House Square, with the following cast and production team:

Grace	Gertrude Montgomery
Wendy	Liz Kuti
Jackson	Stephen Swift
Director	Jim Culleton
Designer	Sinéad O'Hanlon
Lighting Designer	Mark Galione
Sound Designer	Vincent Doherty
Visual Designer	Cashell Horgan
Producer	Jo Mangan
Administrator/PR	Cerstin Gundlach
Production Manager	Lee Davis
Stage Director	Marjolijn Venema
Stage Manager	Lisa Mahony

'The innovative Fishamble company recently held a new play competition won by Rosalind Haslett ... the novice writer is on the right track, knowing that good theatre has more to do with relationships than with complex plots ... the whole is greatly enlivened by Jim Culleton's direction' *The Irish Times*

'The use of multi-media is highly inventive and can be very effective ... an imaginative, oddball play from a writer to look out for' *Sunday Tribune*

'A playful, witty and insightful reflection ... Haslett's writing is very original and daring ... a very remarkable play' *Irish Examiner*

NOTES ON STAGING

Throughout the script I will refer to the topography of Meeting House Square. The 'south wall' is the wall of the building housing the Museum of Photography, and all the others are relative to this.

The stage of the Ark will be used, and the audience will be seated facing this. Projection will cover the two main walls (east, south) with footage appearing on the screen situated on the south wall. A podium will be set up at the SE corner for the purposes of the monologues. Areas DSL and DSR will also be used for these monologues, which are distinct from the dialogue.

The noise of the traffic (always naturally present) is occasionally heightened (with the aid of sound effects) in order to demonstrate its proximity. The characters all remain completely oblivious to it, keeping up the convention that they are inside a house at all times.

The play bears resemblance to a sitting-room drama, or a soap opera. The dialogue is low key and natural, always underplayed; a good reference point would be a television drama like *This Life* or a film in the manner of *The Royal Tenenbaums*. It is so naturalistic it becomes almost surreal. Although the play itself deals with feelings of disappointment, stagnancy, isolation and miscommunication, an atmosphere reflecting these emotions should not pervade the performance spectacle. The music and images must be bright and lively, throwing the understated dialogue into relief.

The early scenes between Wendy and Jackson (the build-up to their meeting, etc.) should be played as a love story. The audience should have the impression that this play could easily have been a light-hearted romantic comedy – but it is not. Without losing the energy of the earlier scenes, the end of the play should seem hollow, the video/sound sequences gaudy and artificial, the characters conservative, stuck in their respective behavioural patterns.

CHARACTERS

Grace – *late twenties, dark and striking. Her features are strong and heavy; she looks almost as though she was outlined in black marker at birth. She is brisk, business-like and bossy, but also extremely impulsive and spontaneous by nature*

Wendy – *late twenties. Her features look slightly smudged; she appears to be in soft focus at all times. Always dressed carelessly. She is dreamy, vague and fluid in her manner, but much more concerned with the practicalities of life than* **Grace**

Jackson – *early–mid twenties. He is restless, enthusiastic and vibrant; constantly seeking distraction, unfocused in life, uncertain of himself and how others see him. Waiting for someone to create him*

Prologue

PRE-SHOW

As the audience enter, the walls are covered in projections of crumbling bricks, which are projected onto the texture of the walls themselves (south and oyster) creating a sense of derelict buildings, rubble, the aftermath of conflict.

The low sound of (what could be) bees humming – summertime sounds – plays over this.
The FIRE ANNOUNCEMENT will be made at this point.

THE SHOW BEGINS

Once the audience are seated, the images on the south wall are replaced by a video sequence of a busy road (Dublin, 2002), shot live on a digital camera situated by Dame Street or one of the other main city centre roads.

Whilst this is occurring, the sounds of the 'bees' begins building into the noise of traffic. The effect should be overwhelming – sounds surrounding the audience on all sides in order to create the atmosphere of a frantic, busy, hurried street scene. Horns are beeping, engines are buzzing, people are shouting and chattering. Once the sounds have reached an almost unbearable level (quicker and louder than expected) they begin to break into the theme tune. This should be bouncy and upbeat in the manner of a theme tune for a Hollywood-style romantic comedy, but with some crunching chords, or perhaps in a minor key, so that something is slightly disconcerting (reference – opening credits of *You've Got Mail,* or the song 'Cigarettes and Chocolate' from Rufus Wainwright's album *Poses*).***This sequence will last for 30 seconds.***

OPENING CREDITS

Wendy, **Grace** *and* **Jackson** *move towards the sofa (which remains on stage throughout). All three look extremely ordinary – dressed casually, plainly. They sit down*: **Wendy** *stage right*, **Grace** *centre stage and* **Jackson** *stage left.*

They sit upright, without moving. All three are poker faced.

Immediately still images of the characters are projected onto the screen (south), which should be divided into three strips, as for the opening sequence of a television drama of the 1970s/80s (e.g. Dynasty). *The images show the characters in 'everyday' poses at a variety of different locations. We get the impression of* **Wendy/Grace/Jackson** *at home/at work/on holiday, etc. – their day-to-day lives compressed into a few stills. Yet the pictures don't look natural – they are highly artificial. The difference between* **Grace** *at home and at work is like the difference between Malibu Barbie and Disco Barbie – a masquerade.* ***This sequence will last 30 seconds.***

SNAP (using reverb).
The music slithers to an abrupt halt. At the same time, a flash of flat white light. This flash could possibly come from backlights so that the effect is transposed – the audience should feel the full effect of the excessively bright flash.
The three are released from their positions immediately after the 'snap' and begin making adjustments to their persons. It is clear that the excessively bright flash was uncomfortable for all of them.

As the music starts up once more, they affect slightly different attitudes, remaining poker faced.
SNAP.
Another flash, music stops.
New images are projected onto the screen, again in a row of three, but this time below the former images. The screen is now divided into six.

They break once more. Adjustments. They are still.
SNAP.
A final flash, music pauses, and a third set of images is projected onto the screen – this time the faces in the photos are angled towards the stage of the Ark. **Grace, Wendy** *and* **Jackson** *on screen are looking at* **Grace, Wendy** *and* **Jackson** *on stage.*

As they leave, the images on the south screen begin spinning vertically, in the manner of a fruit machine. Suitable noises accompany this (pings and whizzes – mechanical sounds). Pictures of other people, as well as images of fruit (double cherry, lemon, apple, tomato) are dotted through the reels of spinning photos. After a while the spinning stops and the pictures are 'nudged' forward, until once again the screen shows **Grace, Wendy,** *and* **Jackson** *in a row. As each of these three images comes to rest, one after the other, the ping of a bell is heard (jackpot noise) and coloured lights flash.* ***5–7 seconds.***

The animated back projection (on stage) shows an outdoor scene viewed from a window. The title Still *appears.*

New images begin to appear: a collage of photographs (bits and bobs, musty furniture, broken bicycle wheels, dress-maker's dummy, books, old radios, etc.). These are animated, and projected on the south screen. ***10 seconds.***

Act One

The following split-second change-overs should mimic the snaps of the opening credits. They should be fast and choppy. When we return to the scenes with **Grace** *and* **Wendy** *it should seem as though they have been on pause for a short while.*

ACT 1 SCENE 1: THE SLUICE

The convention for the scene titles is that they will be projected onto the screen on stage, they will flash up for a few seconds at the beginning of each scene (incorporated into the animated image).

Warm yellow light floods the playing area. The effect is comforting and homey, less garish and frantic than the earlier sequences.

A video plays on the screen on the south wall; a hand-held camera pans a room of a cluttered old house, taking in every nook and cranny. The door is closed; the room appears to be entirely self-contained, until the camera comes to rest on a window. The shot gets closer and closer until it is framing the window alone. Still on this frame, the curtains of the window are pulled (mimicking the curtains of a traditional proscenium arch theatre). The picture gets darker and eventually fades to black; the projected title opposite also fades out. Simultaneously, the back projection shows an animated version of same – pan of room ending on closing curtains. The title 'The Sluice' appears. ***This sequence will last 20 seconds.***

The warm, yellow light on the playing area is all that remains.

The back projection shows a cartoon image of the interior of a house.

Enter **Wendy**, *wearing old clothes, dirty jeans and an oversized shirt. Her hair is tied back and it is obvious she is prepared for work of some description. There are three large boxes in the space. They are clearly labelled:* ***KEEP, THROW AWAY,*** *and* ***ASK GRACE.*** *She picks up each of the boxes, overturning them one after the other, littering the floor around her with the objects that spill out of them. She kneels on the ground in front of this heap and begins to root through, separating it into piles on the ground around her, occasionally tossing something into one of the labelled boxes. This is a time-consuming process, obviously giving her much trouble. She often puts an object in one pile, then reconsiders and moves it to another. Enter* **Grace**, *wearing a coat and carrying her camera and a tripod. She has just returned from work and is clearly not in good form. She sets her stuff down and takes off her coat.*

Grace You're keen. (*She removes her shoes and takes a seat on the sofa, putting her feet up*) Jesus, my head hurts. I'd love a bath.

Wendy Look at this! But you think this is bad? There was almost a landslide when I opened the cupboard in the hall. It was heaving.

Grace (*ignoring her, attending to her own aching limbs*) It's always such a nightmare doing the schools. Wailing kids everywhere, teachers chasing after them with combs … most of the kids were screaming before the brush had even touched their tatty little heads. (*She rubs her temples*) Have we got any painkillers?

Wendy No. We don't keep them.

Grace We don't keep them?

Wendy No.

Grace Why not?

Wendy (*shrugging*) We never need them.

Grace *I* need them. I need them now.

Wendy You're just wound up.

Grace Yes, I am wound up, and that's exactly why I need some fucking painkillers.

Wendy Relax.

She moves behind **Grace** *and begins rubbing her shoulders lightly, affectionately.*

Grace Sorry. (*Pause*) I'd really love a bath.

Wendy Well then, have a bath.

Grace There's no point. I'd have to boil the kettle at least five times. It's impossible to relax in this house. (*She flops back in her chair, lethargic, at a loss*) Let's go away somewhere.

Wendy *rolls her eyes and shrinks away, back to her work. She sits back on her hunkers in front of it with a sigh.*

Wendy I'm getting nowhere. I've decided to separate everything into piles.

She indicates the mounds of rubble (the KEEP pile is already largest by far) then holds up the box labelled ASK GRACE. They both laugh.

Grace Well, you've asked Grace. Chuck it all.

Wendy I'm trying, but it's no good. I feel guilty.

Grace It's hardly a moral dilemma, Wendy.

Wendy It feels almost like drowning kittens.

Grace There's no point in being sentimental. (*Shudders. Looking around her*) We've got to be ruthless if this house is going to look like a display for Habitat.

Wendy Never mind Habitat. Right now I'd settle for the basics like hot water.

Grace That's it then. The sooner you stop being so precious about this rubbish, the sooner I can have a hot bath.

Wendy It'd be much easier if you got up off your arse and gave me a hand.

Lights down. (***This is a split-second change-over.***)

ACT 1 SCENE 2: IN TRANSIT

The sound of a train begins to fill the space. The cartoon house is replaced by a Dart, bearing the scene title. A spot comes up on Jackson: he stands on the podium in front of the south screen. Music accompanies his monologue. The screen shows a giant close-up of an eye.

Jackson The half twelve Dart. Thursday. Grey and moist. At this time the Dart is full of old women, maybe a few students, or people like me. People who don't have much else to do with their days. I'm on my way to view a property – one bedroom. Probably pokey, old and smelly, with only a curtain to pull around the bath. I always thought those kinds of places only really existed in dusty, yellowed paperbacks from second-hand bookshops, but of course I was wrong. When the train stops at Seapoint, I look up to see that a woman has entered. She's tall, dark … I can't make out her face, but she's carrying a lot of equipment and when the train starts again the jolt off-balances her. She drops her tripod. I move to help her, and as we both bend down to pick it up she catches my eye. Her eyes are hard, deep set, dark, but the irises are as bright as mercury. If a man looked straight into the eyes of Medusa, she could turn him to stone. (*The eye on the screen blinks and the image fades to black. Music fades in – a short phrase: slow, languid, high pitched as though being played on a saw, or as though the sound-system is bending. Melodic feedback*) I return to my seat and stare out the window.

The spot fades and lights return to **Grace** *and* **Wendy**. *The cartoon image of the house returns.* ***(This is a split-second change-over.)***

Grace I might buy a car.

Wendy (*paying little attention – still sorting*) Can you afford to?

Grace A cheap one … second hand.

Wendy (*scoffs*) A clapped out, unreliable, old banger?

Grace (*raising her eyebrows at* **Wendy**) I've got one of those already. (*She laughs a little. Pause*) I hate waiting for buses that don't turn up.

Wendy Traffic jams would be worse …

Grace I'd like to see you try and tackle public transport with all my equipment.

Grace *keeps talking, ignoring* **Wendy***'s intervening comments.*

Wendy Tailbacks …

Grace I need to be mobile.

Wendy Bottlenecks …

Grace I could take on more work.

Wendy You'd be a nightmare on the roads.

This comment arrests **Grace***'s flow.*

Grace I'm a good driver.

Wendy It's not about skill. You need to be able to keep calm on the roads, stay watchful.

Grace I can be calm.

Wendy It's not yourself you need to worry about, it's other people.

Grace (*ignoring her*) Imagine all the things we could do if we had a car.

Wendy (*drily*) The grocery shopping?

Grace We could travel. Get away somewhere. (*Excitement building*) I'd never be late again.

Wendy You'll always be late.

Grace I am not always late! You'll always be awkward.

Wendy (*joining in*) You'll always leave dirty towels on the bathroom floor.

A silent film begins playing on the screen: **Wendy** *at the beach on a windy day, relaxed, happy, flirting with the camera a little. Although* **Grace** *does not feature in the images themselves, it is clear that she is also present, and that there is an intimacy and camaraderie between herself and* **Wendy**. **Wendy** *appears to be talking to the camera, laughing, joking. It is a familiar, joyful scene of a blustery day at the beach. Some music plays softly underneath.*

Grace You'll always drink the last drop of milk and then forget to replace it.

Wendy You'll always start arguments for no reason.

Grace I'll always win them.

Wendy Only because I'll always let you.

Pause. They smile.

Grace I developed that last roll of film.

Wendy From Killiney?

Grace There's one where you're laughing and there's something about it, maybe the angle of your head. (*Pause*) Your mother's birthday's coming up. I thought you could frame it for her.

Wendy (*smiling. Suddenly they are much more comfortable with one another*) She'd like that.

Exit **Grace** *and* **Wendy**, *carrying a box each.* **Wendy** *takes the KEEP,* **Grace** *takes the THROW AWAY, and the ASK GRACE remains on stage.*

ACT 1 SCENE 3: FRUITFUL

A cartoon coffee cup is projected onto the screen at the back of the stage along with the title.

Spot on **Jackson** *once more: he is on the podium and holds a hand-held microphone. Raymond Chandler-style music. This time the screen shows an intense close-up of a mouth.*

Jackson I kept my appointment to view the property. It was nice actually. Kind of boxy. But new; almost entirely white. It wouldn't have stayed like that for long of course, and the walls were probably made of cardboard, but still, at least it was clean. And way outside my price range. (*He sighs, resignedly*) I bought a copy of the *Herald* and a biro, and found a nook in a little coffee shop off George's Street. The coffee was dark and thick and tasted bitter and burnt, but it smelled good. Coffee always smells like a revelation. A departure – of sorts. I had just trawled the accommodation section fruitlessly, and was about to pay my bill and go, when something made me stop. It was instinctive. The way animals can smell fear, I could tell. I could sense her.

Grace *has moved to the NE corner of the square. She and* **Jackson** *are divided by the stage although they are involved in conversation. The audience should be unaware of her presence until a spot comes up*; **Grace** *and* **Jackson** *are two stranded pools of light.*

Grace Is there anybody sitting here?

The phrase of melodic feedback is reprised.

Jackson No.

Grace The man from the Dart with the empty eyes. A novel oasis amidst the desert of mewling kids and overbearing parents I'd been struggling through all day. Fascinating. It's very rare that I see someone who really compels me like that. I even went as far as thinking about following him off the train. (*Pause. She smiles ruefully*) But fate's a funny thing. Sometimes you don't have to do anything at all. Sometimes all you need is a little patience.

Jackson Up close she looked strange. Heavy featured, strong. Eyes that gripped you like vices. (*He pauses and considers. The projected mouth smiles slowly*) But then she smiled. And when she smiled she seemed so bewitchingly ordinary.

Grace Right before you get your picture taken, you should whisper to yourself: *petite pomme*. Little apple. It creates a subtle pout. Nothing too explicit; but inviting. (*She savours the word and smiles a little*)

Jackson (*turning towards her*) *Petite pomme*. The projection mouths these words in synchrony then the image begins to crack up.

Grace (*laughing*) I don't believe people who claim to be unphotogenic. Cameras can be very revealing. People often don't like what they see. But the final still can't show anything you haven't willingly displayed to the camera. Photography is an act of mutual consent.

Jackson But isn't it sometimes more fun when you surprise someone? More exciting when you don't have permission?

Pause. She stares at him for a while, considering, then unexpectedly lifts her camera and points it at him. SNAP. (This reverberates, bouncing and echoing around the square.) A bright flash that fills the whole space – enormous contrast to the small pools of light which have been used throughout the scene.

Grace You tell me.

Plunge into darkness and the fruit machine flashes up again. It spins then comes to rest, this time on three apples. The whizz and ping of the bell; flashing lights. ***5 seconds.*** *The images of the junk return to the south screen. A rattling drumbeat begins, building to a harder, faster, frantic beat.* ***10 seconds.***

ACT 1 SCENE 4: THE RENOVATION

Return to back projection of interior of house, bearing the scene title.

Later in the evening – this needs to be signified through costume. Enter **Wendy***, still in her dirty 'work' clothes. She approaches the KEEP and the THROW AWAY boxes and continues sorting through them. She seems to have got no further than the last time. Enter* **Grace***. She has obviously just emerged from the dark room and brandishes recently developed stills.*

Grace (*staring at* **Wendy** *for a little while, considering*) If we could sort out all the larger pieces that we don't want to keep within the next few weeks, we could auction them off.

Wendy There's quite a lot of them.

Grace That's true. Perhaps it would be a good idea to get some help.

Wendy Could we afford it? (*Sitting back to look at* **Grace** *and raising her eyebrows in anticipation*) You do mean professional, of course.

Grace No. (*Pause*) I was thinking we could let the spare room out. To someone who might be able to give us a hand.

Wendy (*laughs*) No Grace. (**Wendy** *turns back to her work for a second, but the idea still niggles. She rounds on* **Grace**) I don't want to be interviewing a load of weirdos as prospective flatmates. We're fine as we are.

Grace Are we?

Pause.

Wendy (*scoffing*) It's a ridiculous idea!

Grace Anyway, it's not a question of weirdos or interviews.

Pause.

Wendy Why not?

Grace And we have a little extra space.

Wendy (*looking at* **Grace** *seriously*) Have you asked someone already?

Grace Yes.

Wendy Who?

Grace Jackson.

Wendy Who?

Grace Jackson.

Wendy Jackson? (*She is both puzzled and suspicious*) Have you known 'Jackson' long?

Grace A while.

Wendy What does that mean?

Grace Not long. (**Wendy** *looks dubious;* **Grace** *attempts reassurance*) But it's an ideal arrangement. I met him when he was flat hunting. That's what gave me the idea.

There is a slight pause.

Wendy You invited him to move in before asking me?

Grace (*shrugs*) Yes.

Long pause.

Wendy (*quiet, subdued*) I suppose you're entitled.

Grace Wendy.

Wendy It's not like we're settling in.

Grace I didn't mean anything.

Wendy This was always only temporary after all.

Grace You're welcome to stay as long as you like. You know that.

Wendy I thought it was temporary for *both* of us, Grace.

Grace Temporary? (*Considers this word*) I know this house better than the back of my own hand. I know where the floorboards creak, where the best hiding places are, how to twiddle the key in the lock so it opens first time. It's so familiar it chokes me. But this is my house. I own it now.

Wendy Half of it. What about your brother?

Grace James is in London. I can hardly see him moving back.

Wendy Given half a chance James would have it demolished.

Grace (*concedes with a wry look*) Or turned into bedsits.

Wendy Stacked-up shoeboxes.

Grace (*falls quiet for a little, sighs*) I love this house. But it's a dump. You saw this place straight after she died. My grandmother always was a hoarder. But I've never seen anything so bizarrely thorough. She barely left a gap. I don't know. (*Shakes her head*) I don't know that I'd live here myself. But I *would* like to know it's still standing. That *someone's* living here.

Wendy Is James still pushing you to sell in a hurry?

Grace (*shrugs*) He wants his share, that's fair enough. But he'll just have to wait till it's ready to be sold. God knows when that will be. It really is an awful dump. (*Briskly back to business*) That's why we need someone to give us a bit of a hand.

Wendy (*sighs and shakes her head*) Temporary or not, Grace, for the meantime, this dump is our home. It's not some kind of hostel for wandering strays.

Grace (*breaking into a smile*) Believe me, Jackson is not a wandering stray. Wait till you meet him. (*She laughs and tosses a photo into* **Wendy***'s box*) I think you'll like him.

Grace *raises her eyebrows at* **Wendy** *and leaves.* **Wendy** *picks up the photograph and looks closely at it, examining it from different angles. After a while, a little smile creeps across her face. She tosses the photo back into the KEEP box and begins fiddling with her hair, releasing it from its bobble, smoothing it down, fluffing it up. She extracts an old object from the box that could serve as a mirror and looks into it, touching her face. Then with a sigh she throws this into the box as well and exits, carrying the box.*

Act Two

ACT 2 SCENE 1: AIR BRUSHING

The title is back projected and animated and remains on screen throughout the speech.

Enter **Grace**, *in darkness, with hand-held microphone; she stands DSR. When she is in place a pool of light discloses her.*

Grace When I was ten years old I found a tattered old envelope in the dresser in our kitchen. It had fallen down the side and lodged in a little nook by the wall. Inside the envelope was a set of old black and white prints. Wedding photos – my grandparents' wedding. It amazed me how those flat little scraps of paper could blossom into full, plump stories. Every night, I would huddle under the covers and read those pictures over and over as though they were my favourite book. (*Pause*) I fell in love with the people in them. My camera carries the most private part of me, so there's nothing satisfying about taking a photo and having someone else develop it. It's an unnecessary, even unpleasant, intervention. Nobody wants a stranger rifling through their knicker drawer. Anyway, I couldn't give up the thrill of manipulating the image. Burning in the sky to make it bruise. Dodging, holding back the image, to cancel out the features on somebody's face. Can you imagine having the power to erase someone like that? (*Slight pause*) But it's important not to let yourself tamper with the image too much. Power's like that – it can be dangerous because it dumbs the senses, makes you blind. It's not easy to find ways of remembering happiness, grief, pain, even love. And it's not fair that even vast, insurmountable emotions can wither, and leave … nothing. But those little slips of paper endure. I need them to be my second set of eyes, a portfolio of my memories. That's why I can believe in eternal love – it exists in a snapshot. And I always fall in love with the people in my photographs. (*Enter* **Jackson**, *on stage.* **Grace** *cannot see him*) Always.

The spot fades. Sounds of the drumbeat again as cracks begin to appear on the south screen. ***10 seconds.*** *The warm, yellow light of the house returns, along with the cartoon back projection. Once more the collage of junk is projected onto the south screen.*

Jackson (*looking somewhat overawed and considering the mounds of bric-à-brac*) Jesus!

Grace *enters behind* **Jackson**, *unseen.*

Grace All this was my grandmother's. The house was like a flea market when she died. Still is, I suppose. You can see why we're trying to do a clear out.

Jackson It must be difficult going through your grandmother's stuff.

Grace It's been an absolute nightmare. There's just so bloody much of it.

Jackson But I meant the sentimental value, the memories. You probably don't want to part with it.

Grace (*shrugs*) I'm dying to get rid of it. It's just junk.

Jackson You never know. Some of these might be antiques.

Grace (*unconvinced*) Well if you find any, you can keep them.

Jackson (*laughs*) I'll hold you to that.

His gaze sweeps around. He catches sight of the THROW AWAY box and moves towards it. He begins gingerly pawing through it.

Grace (*looking at him carefully*) You don't have much stuff, do you?

Jackson I like to travel light.

Grace (*raises her eyebrows sarcastically*) No baggage.

Jackson These are pretty much all my worldly possessions.

Grace That's quite an achievement. But it's not a bad way to be. People try and claim ownership is power, but actually it's just responsibility, believe me. Once you own something, it's like you're chained to it. Imprisoned by your own possessions.

Jackson Are you chained to this house?

Grace No, no. This is just a temporary arrangement. We're sluicing the place. Absolutely gutting it, renovating, and then we'll sell it on. That's the plan.

Jackson And where will you go once it's sold?

Grace Who knows when that'll be?

Jackson So your plan doesn't stretch to the long term?

Grace (*non-committal*) It's temporary. Like most things. I suppose when we're finished, we'll probably rent an apartment somewhere.

Jackson We?

Grace Wendy. Didn't I tell you? She lives here too; you'll meet her soon.

Jackson Is she your sister?

Grace Just a friend.

Jackson But you live together?

Grace At the moment, yes.

Jackson And she'll move with you, when you leave?

Grace Probably.

Jackson So she's not quite so temporary?

Grace I suppose not. (*Cautiously*) If that's how you want to put it.

Jackson I just wondered. (*Pause, change of subject*) I'm surprised. You don't seem like the kind of person who throws things away recklessly. Inheriting a place like this is a stroke of luck. You could probably turn it into a bit of an earner.

Grace I don't throw things away recklessly. No matter what I throw away, I always keep a copy. (*Pause as she suddenly turns to* *look at* **Jackson**) Do you know what struck me most when I first saw you?

Jackson Your tripod?

Grace (*she continues staring, unnervingly*) You looked straight into my eyes. People don't often do that. With strangers, that is. I suppose it involves an element of trust. Do you know what I mean?

Jackson You mean the eyes are the windows of the soul?

Grace Maybe.

Jackson They're not, you know. I'd say they're the windows of the liver. You should see mine after a night at the pub.

She smiles suddenly and disarmingly and wields her camera. SNAP. **Jackson** *rubs his eyes.*

Jackson I think I blinked.

SNAP.

Grace (*raising her eyebrows*) You definitely did that time.

Jackson (*furrowing his brow*) I wasn't ready.

SNAP.

Grace (*snide*) Isn't it more fun when you're not expecting it?

SNAP.

Jackson Jesus, Grace. Not now, OK?

Grace OK.

SNAP.

Jackson *backs away from her, batting at the camera as though it were a fly. He stands up from the sofa and moves away, shaken and disgruntled. He is arrested by the low hum of the traffic, which is building, pervading the air. It sounds as though the air is full of static. As though a thunderstorm were brewing.*

Jackson You're so near to the road here. Listen to that traffic. Can you hear it?

Grace I suppose. I hadn't noticed till you said. This house is somehow very sheltered. After a while you hardly notice the noise from outside.

Jackson Surely you hear it at night?

Grace (*shrugging*) It never bothers me. I can't really explain it. This house is kind of like a bubble. Safe. Still.

Throughout the tail end of this scene, the noise of the traffic has been growing in magnitude. Immediately after **Grace***'s last line it builds into a sequence that echoes the one in the Prologue, but this time the traffic noise is mixed with frantic beats. This is accompanied by the visual.* ***15 seconds.***

ACT 2 SCENE 2: MOVED

The title is animated on the back screen and remains for the length of the speech. **Wendy** *appears at the top SL balcony holding a hand-held microphone. She is lit only by a spot.*

Wendy Lately – or maybe since we moved here – I've been having trouble sleeping. This house is a kaleidoscope of strange reflections that only muffle and dupe, and here I find myself slipping in and out of consciousness. Sinking into vivid, curious dreams. Perhaps because I spend my nights moon-eyed, my days are troubled by dreams. Cloying dreams that stick to me like treacle. Clouded visions I seem to just inhale. (*She pauses. When she begins again it is slowly, trying to piece together a memory*) The other day I was in the supermarket, and while I was queuing at the till, I could feel my flesh begin to sag towards the floor. It was dripping from the frame of my body like thick, viscous liquid. And it was everywhere. It *covered* the floor of the supermarket. Just like when you spill a glass of milk and it suddenly seems to multiply itself, spreading further and wider until there's so much there that you wonder how it ever fitted inside the glass to begin with. My body was gushing, bursting out of itself. I was petrified, and so embarrassed, because all the other shoppers looked horrified. The way people look at a mother who can't control her child, only worse, because they weren't just disapproving, they were actually *disgusted.* They were disgusted that there was so much of me. I was everywhere. All I wanted was to suck myself back inside me, seal the edges, and hop up back to my corner on the shelf.

The spot fades; **Wendy** *exits. The fruit machine images return. This time when they come to rest on the three characters,* **Wendy** *is nudged forward to be replaced by* **Grace**. *We see two* **Graces** *and a* **Jackson**. *5–7 seconds.*

ACT 2 SCENE 3: DODGING THE IMAGE

Grace *stands on the podium, and* **Jackson** *is SR.* **Grace***'s dark room is projected on the back screen along with the scene title.* (*The lights should reflect this, perhaps using some kind of UV lights, or a deep blue gel that picks up both ends of the spectrum, such as Congo blue.*)

Grace These are the shots from the café.

Jackson Let's see.

A photo of Jackson at the café appears on the south screen.

Jackson These are great. Is that really me? (**Grace** *shrugs non-committally, and nods slightly*) These are amazing.

Grace Do you think so?

Jackson Don't you?

Grace I'm disappointed.

Jackson Disappointed? You don't think they're any good?

Grace Not exactly *no good.* (*Shrugs*) Disappointing. I was expecting something different.

Jackson So was I; that's why I think these are great. They're probably the best photos of me I've ever seen.

Grace I think they came out kind of dull. There's not much here that you can't see with a cursory glance. It's flat, vacant.

Jackson I'm not stupid, Grace.

Grace (*arrested, stops and addresses him directly*) No. I'm sorry, Jackson. I didn't mean that you were stupid. If there's nothing in the image it's my fault. (*He seems unconvinced. The projected image begins to fade*) Think of it like a test. I ask questions with the camera and you answer them. Your answers are basically what make it interesting, and you can't really get it *wrong* or anything; any answer is good. The problem here was that I wasn't asking any questions, or maybe just not the right ones … (*Pause.* **Grace** *lifts a new set of stills*) Look at these ones of Wendy. Now these are great shots. She really draws you in, doesn't she?

Jackson Wendy your housemate?

Grace And yours.

Jackson (*takes one of the photos and stares at it intently*) She's very beautiful.

A large projected image of **Wendy** *begins fading in on the south screen – it is a still from the footage at the beach.*

Grace (*takes the photo from him*) She's intriguing. Wendy is the one person who has the ability to constantly surprise me. Her shots are never disappointing.

Jackson A different answer every time?

Grace (*smiling*) Every time.

Jackson Or maybe a different question?

Grace No, I think the question's usually the same. (*They look at each other for a second*) Listen, we can give it another go if you like, maybe come up with something a bit more satisfactory.

Jackson Can I keep one of these anyway?

Grace No. I'm going to chuck those. (*She begins gathering the pictures up, and then something catches her eye*) Actually, you can keep this one if you like. Of Wendy.

Grace *tosses the other pictures into the box marked THROW AWAY and exits.* **Jackson** *is left holding the image of* **Wendy**, *gazing at it. The image on the screen begins moving.*

ACT 2 SCENE 4: PETITE POMME

Cartoon house with appropriate title appears on back screen. Enter **Wendy** *carrying the ASK GRACE box and a shopping bag filled with fruit.* **Jackson** *turns to look at her. They face one another some distance apart. They hold this gaze for a long while, sizing each other up. The footage of* **Wendy** *at the beach playing silently on the screen fades out.*

Jackson (*surreptitiously glancing back at the photo he is holding*) Wendy?

Wendy Yes.

Jackson (*dropping the photo into the KEEP box and extending his arm to introduce himself*) Jackson.

Wendy I guessed.

Pause. They remain locked in one another's gaze.

Jackson I was just looking at some of your photos. They're very beautiful.

Wendy They're Grace's photos.

Pause. She sets down the box, still holding the bag.

Jackson You look different in person.

Wendy (*rifles through the bag a little*) I told you. They're Grace's pictures.

Jackson I'm sorry; I didn't mean to be rude. It's just that you look … different.

Wendy Good. I'd like to think there was a little more to me than one photograph. One expression. (*She smiles, suddenly, brandishing an apple*) Have an apple. I bought them at the market today. They're delicious.

She tosses him one and he catches it. He bites into his apple. She bites into her apple.

Jackson (*nodding at her and indicating the apple*) This is good! (*Smiling to himself*) '*Petite pomme.*'

Wendy *laughs heartily.* **Jackson** *is visibly taken aback by her reaction.*

Wendy *Petite pomme*? Typical Grace. She uses the same lines on everyone.

Jackson *furrows his brow a little, then shrugs it off and contents himself by taking another bite of his apple. They eat their apples happily, noisily.*

Wendy So what do you think of the house?

Jackson I love the house. (*Looking around*)

Wendy The clutter gets to you after a while. It should be diminishing, but it's just too easy to add to it. We seem to add as much as we throw away.

Jackson (*laughs*) It's easy to grow attached to the strangest things, especially when you know you can't keep everything.

Wendy (*moves towards* **Jackson** *and picks up the ASK GRACE box*) I think it's probably easiest just to chuck it all without even looking at it first. Once it's gone you'll never miss it. Never know the difference.

She picks up the KEEP box and hands that to him.

Jackson Because you won't know what you're missing? (*He takes the box from her and looks at her*) I always like to know what I'm missing. I don't like missing opportunities.

They are standing beside one another looking into each other's eyes. Enter **Grace***; she stands in the spot* **Wendy** *has just moved from.*

Grace I see you two have met. (*Her voice breaks the moment between* **Wendy** *and* **Jackson**) Give us a hand with this sofa. I want it moved. I can't bear having it slap bang in the middle of this room any longer.

Wendy What'll we sit on?

Grace Anything. I don't care. Nothing could be worse than this monstrosity.

Wendy Why don't we just leave this where it is till we get something new?

Grace No. You take that end. (**Grace** *and* **Wendy** *stand at either arm.* **Jackson** *stands to the side and watches*) Have you looked at it? It's hideous. 1, 2, 3.

They lift the sofa a little, then drop it again.

Wendy It's heavy.

Jackson (*flopping onto it*) But it's *very* comfortable.

Grace (*looking at Wendy*) Don't bother getting attached. We're not keeping it.

Wendy You make it sound like a stray cat. (*She joins* **Jackson** *on the sofa. She stretches luxuriously*) It's perfect.

Grace (*sits down.* **Jackson** *sits in the middle, between* **Grace** *and* **Wendy***; they talk over him.*)

Grace It's getting dumped this week. We've got to be ruthless.

Jackson It smells so old. Musty.

Wendy (*sniffing the sofa and sneezing*) Dusty.

Grace Old and disgusting, and probably full of mites. (*She shudders*)

Jackson But still, very comfortable.

Wendy You can just sink right into it. (*She does*) This is exactly what I need. I'm wrecked.

Jackson I'm destroyed.

Grace I'm exhausted.

Wendy I feel harangued.

Jackson I feel harassed.

Grace I just want to disappear into oblivion. It could be the rest I need.

Wendy I'll join you. Maybe we could get a package deal?

Grace We could go on a proper holiday. What do you think, Wendy?

Wendy Guess.

Grace No, seriously. Why not? Will you come with us Jackson?

Jackson (*laughing*) You know me. My bags are always packed.

Grace I obviously don't mean right this minute. But soon. Maybe when we finish clearing out the house.

Wendy You better make the booking for five years' time.

They giggle.

Jackson Where will we go?

Grace Spain. Remember that poem about the 'cold sun' and 'The fine, frenzied ivory of potatoes, Wave on wave of tomatoes rolling down to the sea'?

Wendy Very nice … but you know Neruda wasn't Spanish?

Grace He wrote about Spain.

Wendy He was Chilean.

Grace He still spoke Spanish. Anyway that's what we want to see. 'Wave on wave of tomatoes rolling down to the sea'.

Images of heaps of tomatoes are projected onto the oyster and the south wall. They begin fading in gently throughout the remainder of the scene and will remain for ***30 seconds*** *in total.*

Wendy We'd better go to Chile, then.

Grace Whatever. I don't really care.

Wendy It'll be good to get out of this house.

Grace Out of this city.

Wendy I've never been to Spain.

Grace I'll pick up some brochures tomorrow.

Wendy It'll be nice to have a tan.

They begin to stand up.

Jackson What'll we do with the sofa?

Wendy I think my arms would break if I tried to lift it again.

All look to **Grace** *expectantly.*

Grace Let's just leave it here in the meantime. We can sort it out tomorrow. (**Wendy** *and* **Jackson** *exchange looks and smile*) It's probably too grotty to sell on, anyway. (**Wendy** *and* **Jackson** *laugh*) We're *not* keeping it.

The south wall shows the fruit machine again. This time when it settles on the three characters, they are nudged forward to be replaced by images of tomatoes. *5–7* ***seconds.*** *Music, similar to that used for the beach footage, plays throughout this.*

Act Three

ACT 3 SCENE 1: THE SLUICE

The title is animated and back projected for the length of the speech. Enter **Jackson**. *He kneels in front of the three labelled boxes and begins sorting through them, echoing* **Wendy***'s actions in scene one. As he does so, a video of Wendy's face can be seen on the screen of the south wall. She is applying a facemask, looking into the camera as though it were a mirror.* ***30 seconds.*** *When the film finishes,* **Jackson** *remains, lit dimly, and* **Wendy** *enters. She is lit by a spot. She stands at the NE corner of the square, holding a microphone, wearing only a short nightshirt, some slippers, and a facemask.*

Wendy Yesterday I found myself holding an old shoe. I was in the living room. I don't know how long I'd been there, but I must have just … stopped. I don't think it's the first time it's happened. I enjoy these pauses though. I enjoy knowing that I have gaps in my life that I can just dive into, soar out of and feel nothing but bliss. In one fading memory of a family holiday I can picture jellyfish floating along the shore, white and glutinous. I was young at the time, and I didn't know that they could sting, but *instinctively* I was scared of them. Never trust an animal with no spine – it's just not natural. When I got stung, I began flailing about in the water. I wasn't in deep, but I was panicking. It must have been the first time I'd really felt pain, and the weird thing is, now, I really can't *actually* remember what it felt like. Physical pain is always forgotten. It may be recalled as an event, but never a sensation. Once you realise that, it becomes almost thrilling. You can sink into the excruciating moment, knowing that if you bear it out it'll be over forever. That same summer, my brothers buried me in the sand – fully clothed. No matter how many times I washed my trousers, I couldn't get the sand out. Years later I was still carrying that holiday about in my trouser pockets. And the funny thing is, if it wasn't for the sand, I would never have remembered the pain, and that perfect gap would've been filled. Our bodies forget. It's our hearts that remember.

She begins to walk towards **Jackson**. *When he sees her he is shocked. She stops. They stare at one another.*

Jackson I'm sorry. I didn't realise …

Wendy No, I'm sorry. I didn't know you were here. I thought everyone was out. (**Jackson** *begins hurriedly throwing things back into the boxes*) Weren't you working tonight?

She picks her way across to the sofa and sits down on it, covering her knees with her nightshirt.

Jackson Yes, but it was quiet. The manager sent me home. (*He sits beside her on the sofa*) Grace is out, I think.

Wendy Yes.

Embarrassed pause.

Jackson It's a beautiful evening.

Wendy Is it?

Jackson I went walking for a little while, by the canal. There's an amazing sunset, all pinks and oranges bleeding across the skyline. It's really breathtaking.

Wendy Really?

Jackson Just as the sun was disappearing, the light caught in the water and the whole world changed colour for a split second. I've never seen anything like it. You didn't see it?

Wendy No. I've been indoors.

Jackson (*raising his eyebrows*) Of course. (*Pause*) Have you got much done?

Wendy Actually, I've taken the night off. Relaxing a little. I thought I had the house to myself.

Jackson Sorry. I'm obviously disturbing you.

Wendy No, no. It's actually kind of nice to have the company.

Jackson Yeah?

Pause.

Wendy (*indicating her facemask*) I better take this off … it's been much longer than fifteen minutes …

They pull apart, and she begins to wipe the mask off with cotton wool.

Wendy We could open a bottle of wine if you like.

Jackson (*shaking his head*) No thanks. I don't really drink wine. More of a pint man myself. You and Grace know all about that kind of thing though, don't you? What wine to pick for which occasion, all the right places to go for dinner?

Wendy (*shrugging*) I suppose. No. I don't know.

Jackson I'd say you do. You know about it. But you don't really go out very much, do you?

Wendy (*shrugs*) Grace is out tonight.

Jackson You're not.

Wendy Obviously.

Jackson Right. (*After a pause, he looks around the house, then at* **Wendy**) Don't you ever get frustrated? Maybe even a little claustrophobic?

Wendy (*stops short for a second*) I suppose I'm quite tolerant. Of mess, that is.

Jackson Grace won't rest till it's cleared.

Wendy (*laughs*) Grace never rests.

Jackson She's quite a forceful woman. (*He searches for the word*) Driven.

Wendy To distraction most of the time.

Jackson It's good to be passionate, though. Everyone needs some kind of ambition.

Wendy Do they?

Jackson Don't you?

Wendy I'd like to win the lotto.

Jackson Is that all?

Wendy Isn't that enough?

Jackson There must be something you feel passionately about.

Wendy Like what?

Jackson Could be anything, even the smallest thing. A book you read; a person you met? Something you'd like to see or do? There must be somewhere you'd like to go.

Wendy Maybe.

Jackson If you could go anywhere in the world where would it be?

Wendy Athens.

Jackson You like history?

Wendy (*shrugs and shakes her head, smiling*) Prefer mythology.

Jackson Why don't you go? I've never been to Athens. (*She sighs, and he notices a bit of the mask that she's missed. He takes the cotton wool from her and begins wiping her face himself*) Wendy. You're a lovely girl.

Wendy Thanks, Jackson. You're a lovely boy.

Jackson I'm serious.

Wendy Almost tragic, in fact.

He sets down the cotton wool. He is a little hurt.

Jackson I only meant to give you some advice.

Wendy Advice?

Jackson I thought I might be able to help.

Wendy Why do you think I need advice?

Jackson The thing is, I wouldn't have bothered if I didn't like you.

Wendy But there's nothing wrong with me. I'm perfectly fine. I'm healthy. I'm not unhappy.

Jackson You just seem a little bored. There doesn't appear to be very much that you care about.

Wendy You think I'm boring?

Jackson Nothing that makes you really enthusiastic.

Wendy Oh my God. Maybe I am.

Jackson You just don't seem to have any *passion*.

She grabs him impulsively and kisses him. He reels in shock, then pulls away to look at her, before he kisses her.

Jackson That was easier than I expected.

Wendy It was sweet of you to try so hard, though.

They kiss again. Lights down. On the south wall, a video sequence plays. It is a montage of **Wendy** *and* **Jackson***'s body parts (an image of her thigh cuts to one of his elbow. None of the images is explicit.) This is accompanied by the sound of the drums that is usually played along with the spreading cracks.* ***15 seconds.*** *The fruit machine returns. It lands on 2* **Wendys** *and a* **Jackson***, but* **Jackson** *is nudged forward to be replaced by* **Grace**. ***5–7 seconds.***

ACT 3 SCENE 2: BURNING IN THE SKY

Back-projected animation of the house along with title. Enter **Grace***, carrying the THROW AWAY box. There is a huge projection of* **Wendy** *on the south wall (the still – not beach footage).* **Grace** *stops and sets the box down. She extracts a tattered old dog-eared book from it and begins flicking through, a smile on her face. Enter* **Wendy**.
When she reaches the south wall she notices **Grace** *standing over the box. Initially she looks surprised, then she is amused.*

Wendy Growing attached?

Grace (*taken by surprise*) Just sifting through some of this stuff. Checking nothing ended up in here by accident before we actually take the plunge and get rid of it. I found this …

She proffers the book to **Wendy** *timidly.* **Wendy** *accepts it with a smile and begins flicking through it.*

Grace It's one of those books I've always meant to read. I suppose I've always really thought I *ought* to, but I've never actually got round to it.

Wendy It's a classic.

Grace Have you read it?

Wendy (*smiling ruefully*) No.

Grace This copy's got all these notes in the margins.

She moves towards **Wendy** *and they crowd round the book together, peering into it while* **Grace** *indicates different passages.*

Wendy It falls open at some of the pages.

Grace Someone must have loved this book.

Wendy I used to get like that over books when I was young. I'd read them over and over and never grow tired of them. I'd read them so much that the spines would break and all the pages would fall out.

Grace It's too much effort to work up that kind of enthusiasm now.

Wendy I can't remember the last book I read to its conclusion. I usually give up before the end.

Grace I hate not knowing how things end. I get so impatient, I usually end up reading the ending half way through. If I don't like it, I don't waste my time reading the rest of the book.

Wendy Very sensible. That's not like you.

Grace I would have said cynical.

Wendy That is like you.

Grace What do you mean? I'm a romantic.

The projection begins to fade.

Wendy (*sighing and looking around*) We're never going to finish this house, are we?

Grace Of course we are. We're making progress.

Wendy We're progressing in the wrong direction. Things keep making their way from the 'chuck' box to the 'keep' box, and nothing ever actually gets thrown away.

Grace (*frowning*) It's hard work, Wendy. You should have expected that.

Wendy It's not work. It's just this constant movement. Things get organized, then disorganized, then reorganized. It feels as though you're getting something done, but then you take a look and realize nothing's changed.

Grace You expect big changes too quickly. It's time consuming, but it'll be worth it. Imagine how this house could look. Can't you picture it?

Wendy (*pause as she considers*) No. Can you?

Grace (*she is defeated and evades the question*) James is flying over in September.

Wendy To sell straight away?

Grace: If we could just make something of the house by then.

Wendy You'll be loaded.

Grace I don't think I want to sell.

Wendy You'll be able to afford one of those apartments. The ones on Charlotte Quay.

Grace A shoebox? That'd be like living in a dentist's waiting room. This is home. I can feel it purr when I put my key in the lock. Just opening the door is like crawling under a huge duvet.

Wendy I've never been able to sleep in this house.

Grace When I'm here I never feel lonely.

Wendy What about when I'm here?

Grace You're always here.

Pause.

Wendy I'm making a cup of tea.

Grace Wendy. You know this is your home too.

Wendy *looks at* **Grace***, then turns and walks off stage. The walls suggest fire: flickering, raging. Sound accompanies this.*

Wendy I dreamt my teeth were falling out. My mouth was closed, but I could feel them gathering like pebbles inside. If I were to open my mouth, I'd lose them all.

Video footage of **Wendy***'s mouth. This short phrase could be spoken live, or pre-recorded and mixed in with the accompanying sound.* ***30 seconds.*** *Reprise of the traffic on the screen. This time it is even more frantic and jerky, perhaps like time-release film. Again, it is mixed in with the music.* ***10 seconds.***

ACT 3 SCENE 3: HABIT(AT)

Grace *and* **Jackson** *both SR. In* **Grace***'s dark room, once again.*

Jackson How are they?

Grace They're excellent; I'm really pleased with them. I used one fast film and the light was fairly strong, so a whole set of them have this really grainy effect. It looks good. (*She hands him one of the prints*) What do you think?

Jackson I'm not sure.

Grace Hang on a second.

She hands him another one. Projection of **Jackson**'s *photo appears on south screen.*

Grace This one's my favourite.

Jackson Is that me?

Grace Do you like it?

Jackson (*slightly downcast*) I would never have recognised myself.

Grace They say the camera never lies.

Jackson Yes, but I look … different.

Grace (*smiles*) They're beautiful.

Jackson Don't you mean intriguing?

Grace Yes. Intriguing. You're intriguing.

Jackson I don't even remember this one being taken.

Grace They're very natural. I think I really captured something.

Jackson (*pauses and then looks at* **Grace**) I didn't know you were taking these.

Grace Does it matter?

Jackson I thought you said photography was about mutual consent?

Grace (*looking at him squarely*) I didn't force you to do anything. I'll make a copy of one of them for you to keep, if you like.

Jackson No thanks.

Image fades out.

Grace Are you sure? Any of them that you like. I won't ask again.

Jackson (*pauses to consider*) What happened to the very first? The one you took of me in the café the day we met.

Grace (*smiling*) '*Petite pomme*'? Of course. You can have that if you like, but you'll have to get it off Wendy.

Exit **Grace** *and* **Jackson**.

ACT 3 SCENE 4: NEVER TRUST AN ANIMAL WITH NO SPINE

Animated on back screen. **Jackson** *remains SR, and radio mixed. Images of the cracks appear under this monologue.*

Jackson I've only ever been beaten up once in my life. I was sixteen. I was with three of my friends and we were walking through a park late at night. We'd done it before and there were four of us, so we reckoned we'd be fine. This time a couple of guys came up to us and asked for a light. They made us a little edgy, but there were other people around so we reckoned we were safe. They kept walking with us, keeping up this kind of banter. We had no idea how far we'd walked, until all of a sudden we realized we were alone with them. My friends ran, without looking back. All I remember is waking up in intensive care with a drip in my arm. I never was much of a fighter. I got over it eventually. But you'd be surprised how deep that kind of dread lodges in your mind. Sometimes, even still, I lose my nerve outside after dark. But you always find ways of coping. I never even bothered learning self-defence. I reckon that's just something you acquire with experience. If you let things go too far there's no turning back. At the first sign of trouble: run.

The fruit machine is shown on the south screen. This time it is nudged forward to show 2 **Jacksons** *and a* **Wendy**. *Accompanying sound.* ***5–7 seconds.*** *Cartoon image of house returns.* **Wendy** *is seated on the sofa, reading the book. Enter* ***Jackson;*** *he leans over her to see what she is reading.*

Jackson Good book?

Wendy (*shrugs*) It's OK, and surprisingly easy to read.

Jackson (*fingering the last few pages*) You're nearly finished anyway.

Wendy (*nodding*) This is the last chapter.

She sets it in the middle of the sofa, as he moves to sit beside her. They are divided by the book.

Jackson I handed my notice in to work.

Wendy Tonight?

He nods.

Wendy Are you looking for something else?

Jackson There doesn't seem to be much available at the moment.

Pause.

Wendy You will have to find something else though, won't you?

Jackson Maybe. (*Pause*) I was actually thinking that perhaps Dublin isn't the best place to look though.

Wendy Oh?

Jackson (*shrugs*) For me, that is. Things here are becoming routine. I don't like falling into habits.

(*Pause*) I was thinking that I might go somewhere different.

She looks crestfallen.

Wendy (*shrugs*) That's probably for the best. It doesn't look like any of us are going to be here for much longer anyway.

Jackson What do you mean? What about the renovation?

Wendy The renovation? (*Laughs*) Grace and her brother are going to sell sooner than expected.

Jackson (*surprised*) That's a shame. You could have really done something with this house if you'd stuck at it.

Wendy What would you know about sticking at it? Grace's grandmother lived here for over half a century, and we're attempting to clean up her whole life in a few months. It probably took years to accumulate all this, but the truth is we could dispose of it in a day if we wanted to.

Jackson One day? Anyway, I thought you did want to. I thought the whole idea was to just do this job as quickly as possible and then move on, but suddenly it's like everything around me is suspended and I'm caught up with it. I can't spend my time waiting around, Wendy. I don't like making preparations for things that are never going to happen.

Wendy Waiting's never as easy as it looks.

Jackson Why don't you come?

Wendy With you?

Jackson (*shrugs*) We could go to Athens.

Wendy (*shakes her head*) I couldn't leave Grace here. This is so clearly the house of a lonely woman.

Jackson It doesn't have to be. You just said, you can change the house. Or you can leave. She can leave.

Wendy We are leaving. In September.

Jackson So why not now? (*Pause*) Grace's brother will come over and help her sell, won't he?

Wendy They're not what you'd call close. None of the family were. I think Grace feels ... guilty. If you'd only seen the house when we first got here. Newspapers, books, broken furniture, unopened mail, baby clothes; all piled flat against the wall. Piled so high they nearly touched the ceiling. It was like a whole new set of walls. I'm beginning to think that moving into a house like this is like sewing yourself into a dress. The only way to get back out again is to rend all the seams. (*She stops, then looks at him for a little while and shakes her head*) Anyway, I'd rather stay for the meantime. I like habit. Routine is just finding a way of living that works.

Jackson (*pause*) If you ever change your mind. (*He smiles slightly and stands up. He makes to leave, then turns back*) I almost forgot. I was looking for a photo. Of me. Grace said you might know where it was.

Wendy I know the one you're talking about.

Jackson Great. She said I could keep it.

Wendy lifts up the ASK GRACE box, picks the photo out and hands it to him.

Jackson Thanks. Actually, I've got one of yours as well, if you'd like it back ...

She shakes her head. He makes to leave, then on second thoughts, turns back to Wendy and kisses her lightly on the cheek.

Jackson Goodbye.

Exit **Jackson**. *She glances after him, then picks up the book and continues reading. Image of the window closing is replayed in reverse. This occurs simultaneously in animation, accompanied by the title* Still. ***5 seconds.*** *The fruit machine plays once more, with accompanying sound. This time it comes to rest on the three characters, with* **Jackson** *in the middle. It stays like this for a few seconds, and then* **Jackson***'s head is nudged forward to be replaced by a tomato.* ***5–7 seconds.*** *Images of tomatoes are projected on the south wall and oyster. Enter* **Grace**.

Grace I've been thinking about that holiday to Spain. Why not? We've got no other plans and we'll deserve it by September.

Wendy Right. (*Pause*) After James has been.

Grace When we've been dispossessed.

Wendy Expelled.

Grace Evicted. Turfed out of our own house and home.

Wendy He has every right, you know. Maybe it's better this way.

Grace It doesn't really change anything.

Pause.

Wendy Spain sounds good.

Grace (*visibly surprised*) Really?

Wendy Why not?

Grace It's just that I was looking through some brochures. It didn't really look the way I expected it to.

Wendy No tomatoes?

Grace Not a one. More like swimming pools and smiling children with beach balls.

Wendy That could be nice too though.

Grace Hmm.

Wendy Maybe we just shouldn't go then?

Grace Perhaps not.

They look at each other and smile.

Wendy Why did you suggest it?

Grace I was hoping you'd put up an argument. You usually do.

Wendy Do I? I'll try and remember next time.

Grace Glad to hear it.

Lights down, the sound of a train. ***(This is a split-second change-over.)***

ACT 3 SCENE 5: IN TRANSIT

Reprise animation of Dart with title, for shorter length of time.

Jackson *stands at the SE corner of the square. He is holding a hand-held microphone and is lit by a spot.*

Jackson The half seven Dart. Wednesday. It is a still, cool evening. A deep shudder, and abruptly we're stopped. Stuck somewhere between Clontarf and Raheny rupturing the sinews of the track. I'm cushioned by people who seem to spend their lives being ferried from stop to stop on buses or trains. Aimlessly. Without any need for the complications caused by arrivals or destinations. I'm sitting alone, staring out the window. Skilfully evading the blunder of grazing anyone else's face with my eyes. Keeping to myself, I'm learning the art of invisibilty. But when a young girl stands to shuffle her clustered belongings, my own focus is splintered. It's the jolt of the train starting again that sends packages spilling across the aisle. I watch her as she gathers them up, tucking them under her legs. And for a while I think about moving to give her a hand.

Lights down on **Jackson**. *Back to* **Grace** *and* **Wendy**. *(This is a split-second change-over.*

ACT 3 SCENE 6: STILL

Cartoon house back projected, without title.

Wendy Perhaps if we're not going on holiday you could use your profits from the sale to buy that car you were after.

Grace Hmm, I can't drive though, can I? I suppose I might buy that apartment.

Wendy What apartment?

Grace Well, you know, the one on Charlotte Quay.

Wendy The shoebox?

Grace At least it would be clean. And new.

Wendy We can buy all our furniture from Habitat.

Grace Absolutely. I've grown very tired of old curiosities.

Wendy Do you think we should get someone to come in and help us sort out this place?

Grace A professional this time?

Wendy Definitely a professional.

Grace Jackson wasn't much help in the end, was he?

Wendy No help at all.

Grace I saw him leaving a few hours ago. He had his rucksack, all his worldly possessions.

Wendy He's gone?

Grace Didn't you know?

Wendy I suppose I did.

Grace Still. It's a bit of a shock.

Wendy We should have known. Anyone who was planning on staying would have brought more stuff.

Grace Never trust a man with a small rucksack.

They laugh.

Wendy Especially when that's all he's got going for him.

There is a silence.

Grace I'm sorry he left, Wendy.

Wendy So am I, actually. (*Pause*) But not too much. It's easy to get over these things, isn't it? Ask me in a few years who Jackson is; I probably won't remember.

Montage of video projections from throughout the play, beginning on one of **Jackson** *and ending on one of a busy road. This is accompanied by the theme music. Credits scroll on south screen during bow.*

THE END

The Buddhist of Castleknock

BY JIM O'HANLON

The Buddhist of Castleknock was first presented by Fishamble: The New Play Company on 7 November 2002 in Draíocht, with the following cast and production team:

DJ Jules	Johnny Ward
Edie	Ruth Hegarty
Sean	John Olohan
Tara	Mary O'Driscoll
Edward	Conor Delaney
John	Niall Cleary
Rai	Mojisola Adebayo
Uncle Jimmy	Des Nealon
Auntie Kathleen	Anne Brogan
Director	Jim Culleton
Set Designer	Fiona Cunningham
Costume Designer	Léonore McDonagh
Lighting Designer	Debbie Behan
Sound Designer	Paul Brennan
Producer	Jo Mangan
PR/Administration	Cerstin Gundlach
	Breege Brennan
Production Manager	Marie Tierney
Stage Director	Miriam Duffy
Stage Manager	Pamela McQueen
Photography	Colm Hogan
Buddhism Advisor	Michael McLoughlin

The production transferred to Andrews Lane Theatre in 2003 with Stephen Swift in the role of Edward.

'terrifically entertaining … really funny'
Sunday Tribune

'well performed across the board … very funny … marvellous, marvellous'
RTÉ, The View

'hilarious … really funny … I'd recommend it highly … fantastic'
RTÉ Radio One, Rattlebag

'excellent … hilarious, insightful and absolutely true … great ensemble playing … laugh-a-minute success'
Irish Examiner

CHARACTERS
(in order of appearance)

DJ – *real name Julian, aged fifteen*
Edie Sullivan – *early fifties*
Sean – **Edie***'s husband*
Tara – **Edie** *and* **Sean***'s daughter, thirty*
Edward – *their son, late twenties*
John – **Edward***'s younger brother, mid-twenties*
Rai – **John***'s girlfriend, twenty-six*
Uncle Jimmy – *late fifties*
Auntie Kathleen – **Edie***'s older sister, married to* **Uncle Jimmy**

Act One takes place on Christmas Eve
Act Two takes place on Christmas Day
Act Three, Scene 1 takes place on St Stephen's Day
Act Three, Scene 2 takes place a week or so later

Act One

A suburban sitting room in Dublin. This is the 'Good Room', and reflects the comfortably-off surroundings of a well-to-do, middle-class, professional home. Copious – but tastefully arranged – Christmas decorations hang along the upper reaches of the three visible walls of the room. In the back wall, to the right of centre, a door leads out into the hallway, some of which is visible to the audience. In the stage right wall is a large fireplace with mantlepiece. On the mantlepiece, various photographs of the family at salient points in their shared lives – graduations, a wedding photograph, photos of babies. At right angles to the fireplace is a plush sofa, and downstage right of the fireplace is an armchair. There is another armchair centre stage, facing the fireplace. To the left of the door into the hall is a large, beautifully decorated Christmas tree. Elsewhere, boxes of Christmas lights and other decorations are strewn around the room. **DJ** (*short for DJ Jules – real name Julian*) *enters stage left in his boxer shorts.* **DJ** *is fifteen, and sports a trendy fifteen-year-old's haircut. He searches frantically but cursorily among the boxes of decorations then gives up and goes to the door at the back of the stage and calls upstairs.*

DJ Mum!

Edie (*off*) What?

DJ Have you seen my Tommy's?

Edie (*off*) Your what?

DJ My jeans. My Tommy Hilfigers!

Edie (*off*) I put them in the wash.

DJ Mum! What did you do that for?

Edie (*off*) Because they were filthy.

DJ (*under his breath*) For fuck's sake!

At that moment **Edie** *appears in from the hallway.* **Edie** *is in her early fifties, a precise, well-spoken woman dressed in an expensive, if slightly conservative, matching top and skirt.*

Edie What did you say?

DJ Nothing.

Edie Yes, you did.

DJ No, I didn't. I just said where's my Tommy Hilfigers.

Edie I will not tolerate that language in this house, Julian. Have you put the wreath up on the front door yet?

DJ No.

Edie Julian! John and Edward will be here any minute and we still don't have a wreath on the door to greet them.

DJ So?

Edie So, they're coming home for Christmas, and I want the place looking nice for them.

DJ What do they care about a bloody wreath for? They're not twelve, you know.

Edie Just stop complaining and get it out of the basket there.

DJ I hate putting the wreath up. It never stays – it always falls down.

Edie Julian, I'm asking you to do one little job for me. Over the whole of the Christmas. You haven't lifted a finger since you got your holidays.

DJ Right, that's it! If you're going to go round telling total lies and libelling me, I'm out of here!

Edie Julian! Julian, come back here! JULIAN!

But he's gone.

Edie (*under her breath*) For fuck's sake!

Sean *appears and smiles sweetly, but says nothing.* **Sean** *is a couple of years older than* **Edie**, *with a relaxed, easy demeanour.*

Edie I'm telling you, I'm at the end of my tether with him. If he ruins this Christmas with his carry on that's it – he's going to boarding school.

Sean *goes to pick up the paper.*

Edie You're not thinking of sitting down? I asked you to put the wreath on the door an hour ago.

Sean I thought you asked Julian to do it.

Edie Well, now I'm asking you.

Sean Where is it?

Edie In the basket there. And be careful with it. You know how delicate it is.

Sean If it's so delicate, maybe we shouldn't bother putting it up.

Edie Look, are you going to hang the confounded wreath or do I have to do that myself too?

Sean *crosses to the decorations box and takes out a home-made wreath which* **Edie** *has made. He goes to the front door, opens it and starts to hang the wreath on the door knocker.* **Edie**, *meanwhile, crosses to the record player and takes an LP of Christmas songs out of its sleeve. She places the record on the turntable. A crackly recording of 'I'm Dreaming of a White Christmas' begins to play.* **Edie** *stands listening to it for a couple of moments. Then she pulls over a chair and begins hanging the last bits of holly on the walls.*

Edie Thank God for Tara, that's all I can say. I don't know what I would have done without her this Christmas. I don't think she's sat down since she got here. Poor love – she's been that busy helping me she hasn't even had a chance to wrap her presents. No more than I have myself. Quick, Sean – hand me over some of those tags there on the mantlepiece.

Sean Lord God, such commotion and combobulation! You'd swear we were expecting the Pope himself to drop by.

Edie They hate coming home and finding nothing ready, Sean.

Sean Pity about them.

Edie That reminds me – did you manage to fix that leaky tap in the bathroom?

Sean I did a patch-up job. We'll need to get a plumber in to have a look at it after Christmas.

Edie (*looks at her watch*) Do you think it's too late to get a plumber now?

Sean Edie, it's Christmas Eve! Anyway, I told you – I've done a temporary job. You just have to be careful to give it a good hard twist at the end.

Edie I'm sorry, love. I know I'm flapping. I'm just excited is all. I just want everything to be … perfect. (*A beat*) Especially if …

Sean If what?

Edie Especially if it's going to be our last Christmas together. As a family. I'm not saying it is … for definite. But it could be. They're all away now, and they'll start coming back less and less, and … (*She trails off sadly*)

Sean You've done everything you possibly could, love. You've got a fantastic Christmas tree, with … with beautiful decorations and lights and whatnot. (*A beat*) It's down to them now.

A beat

Edie You don't think the tree is lopsided?

Sean (*not even looking at the tree*) Edie, it's fine. Honestly – you're such a worrier. Everything will be grand.

Edie I hope so. I couldn't bear it if this did turn out to be our last Christmas together and it was a disaster. Especially with John's new girlfriend coming.

Sean What's her name again?

Edie Rai.

Sean Rai – Christ, sounds like a fella.

Edie Oh don't, Sean. Can you imagine it?

Sean You'd never know with John.

Edie Get away out of that, you, and stop your messing.

Sean *laughs.*

Sean Anyway, fellow, female or a bit of both – you'd think he'd have given us a bit more notice.

Edie He told me last week … I just … forgot to mention it in all the commotion.

Sean (*shrugs*) It doesn't bother me. (*A beat*) Does it bother you?

Edie No. (*A beat*) Although I was a bit taken aback when he asked if he could bring her. I always think of Christmas as a family time.

Sean Maybe that's what he's bringing her over to tell us.

Edie What?

Sean That she's about to become a part of our family.

Edie We haven't even met her yet!

Sean Or that we can expect another member of the family in nine months' time.

Edie God, Sean, don't say that – even for a joke. My nerves would never stand it.

Sean Brace yourself to inherit two brand new family members, Edie Sullivan – three if it's twins!

Edie Ach, don't be ridiculous, Sean – sure, they only know each other a couple of months. Anyway, the only reason she's coming here is that her family have gone away to Kenya for the Christmas.

Sean Kenya? They must be gone on a safari or something. Jays, they can't be short of a few bob to be going on safari in Kenya. I don't see the attraction myself. What would anyone want to spend Christmas in Kenya for?

Edie I've no idea. They must like the sun, I suppose. Some people do, apparently.

Sean I could never go away for Christmas. I'd miss my turkey and ham sandwiches and my bottle of Guinness with Jimmy and Kathleen on St Stephen's Day.

Edie That'd be you all right. A real homebird.

Sean Sure, why wouldn't I be? Don't I live in the loveliest of homes in the loveliest of countries, as the fella said?

Edie And which fellow would that be when he's at home?

Sean Some French fella – but he must have been living in Ireland at the time.

Edie Mm.

A pause, as **Edie** *gets on with putting up the last of the decorations*

Sean Would you say in Kenya Santy still wears that big red suit? It must get awful warm.

Edie Here, pass me over that holly there and don't mind Santy and his big red suit.

As **Sean** *crosses to get the holly,* **Tara** *appears down the stairs.* **Tara** *is* **Edie** *and* **Sean***'s eldest child. She is about thirty years old. She looks drawn today – her eyes are red from crying, and she looks tired.*

Edie (*gentle*) Did you get through to Paudge?

Tara (*wiping away a tear*) Yes.

Edie And?

Tara Sean Óg's fine. Says to say Happy Christmas.

Edie Ah. Did you hear that, Sean? Sean Óg says to say Happy Christmas to his Granny and Grandad.

Sean Good man himself.

Tara He says he'd much rather be here for Christmas.

Sean I'm sure he would – stuck up there in the back end of Antrim with that jackass of a husband of yours.

Tara I was so looking forward to this Christmas – with the boys back, and John's new girlfriend, and now …

Edie Ssh, Tara, love. We'll still have a wonderful time. I promise you.

She breaks off as there's a ring on the doorbell.

Edie Jesus, Mary and Joseph, that'll be them now. And I haven't a thing ready!

Sean What do you mean, you haven't a thing ready? The bloody place looks like Santa's feckin' grotto!

Edie Sean! There's no need to swear. (*Indicating* **Tara**) Not in front of the children.

Tara Mum, I'm thirty years of age!

Edie That's no reason to stop giving you moral guidance, Tara love. (*A beat*) I'm sorry, I didn't mean that.

A beat.

Edie Sean, run out there and put the kettle on like a good man and I'll get the door.

And she starts to make for the front door.

Tara I'll get it.

Edie Are you sure?

Tara Mum, I'm fine. Honestly. (**Edie** *nods. A beat*) And Mum? (**Edie** *turns*) Thanks. I mean it. You've been great since … well, since the whole thing.

Edie You can stay as long as you like, pet. Can't she, Sean?

Sean Of course you can, love.

Tara Thanks.

Another ring on the doorbell.

Tara Coming!

Edie *crosses to the record player and switches it off as* **Tara** *answers the door to* **Edward. Edward** *is in his late twenties, tall, broad-shouldered and confident. The family trickster,* **Edward** *is sporting a red Santa hat and white beard which almost completely obscures his face.*

Edward Ho Ho Ho! Ho Ho Ho! Are there any good children in this house or is this a job for Santy's sack of coal?

Edward *throws a big bag full of presents into the house ahead of him.*

Edie Ach, would you look at him! Edward!

Edward *takes off his beard.*

Edward You recognised me! What was it – the broad shoulders and the lean torso? How're you, Mammy?

And he gives **Edie** *a kiss.*

Edie Happy Christmas, love.

Edward How're ye, Da? Hey, nice tree.

Edie (*beaming, delighted*) Do you like it? I picked it out myself.

Edward It's great. Little bit lopsided, but apart from that it looks great.

Edie It's not lopsided.

Edward Well, not lopsided exactly … but it definitely leans to the right.

Edie *inclines her head and looks at the tree in an effort to gauge whether or not it is in fact leaning.* **Edward**, *meanwhile, takes off his coat.*

Edward No sign of John and – what's-her-name?

Edie Rai.

Sean If indeed it is a her.

Tara Dad reckons Rai's a fella.

Sean Well, you can count on the thumbs of one hand the number of girlfriends John has brought home …

Edie Ah Sean, stop your messing. Your Dad's such a messer.

Tara So what if Rai is a fella? It's the new Ireland, now don't forget, Dad – liberal, secular and infinitely tolerant.

Sean New Ireland my arse!

Edie Sean!

Sean Well, it seems anything goes, nowadays.

Tara Go away out of that, Daddy. I know you – you're as liberal as the next fella. He just likes to play the part of the gruff Irish Father, don't you, Daddy? Still and all, can you imagine (*adopts a pose, and a camp, lispy voice*) Daddy, this is my extra special friend Rai – Rai, my pater Sean!

They laugh raucously, all except **Edward**, *who smiles politely.*

Edward (*dry*) Ah yes. Welcome to the new Ireland.

The doorbell rings again.

Edie That'll be them now. So quit your messing you two, and don't be disgracing me in front of the poor girl.

Sean *and* **Tara** *cease their joking as* **Edie** *opens the front door to* **John. John** *is* **Edward***'s younger brother – slightly smaller and thinner than his elder brother, he is none the less handsome, despite his somewhat scruffy appearance.*

Edie John!

John Hiya, Mum.

John *moves out of the way to allow* **Rai** *to enter.* **Rai** *is about twenty-six, English, of African extraction.*

John Hiya, Dad. Mum, this is Rai. Rai – this is my Mum, Edie, and my Dad, Sean.

Rai Hiya.

A brief pause, as **Edie** *and* **Sean** *adjust their stride. Any hesitation – if indeed there even is a moment's hesitation – is quickly covered over by the effusiveness of their welcomes.*

Sean How are you, Rai? You're very welcome.

Edie You must be exhausted.

Rai I'm pretty knackered all right. We were delayed nearly three and a half hours at the airport. With the snow, you know?

Edie You poor things. Still, wouldn't it be wonderful if we got a white Christmas here? We haven't had a white Christmas in I don't know how long.

Edward According to the weather forecast it's going the other way. They've forecast rain here for tomorrow.

Edie Have you met John's brother, Rai – our resident Harbinger of Doom?

Rai Hiya. Edward?

Edward That's right. The good-looking one.

Rai John's told me a lot about you.

Edward All good, I hope.

Rai Well, fair to middling, as you might say here in Ireland.

Edward *laughs.*

Edward You're picking up the lingo, anyway.

Rai Is it any wonder, living with John?

Edie We'll have you turned into a nice Irish colleen soon enough, Rai, don't you worry.

John (*quickly*) And this is Tara. Tara – Rai.

Rai Pleased to meet you, Tara.

Tara Likewise.

Edie Will you have a cup of tea? You must be parched after all the travelling.

Rai Well, if you're making one …

Edie Tara, run out there and put the kettle on for John and Rai, like a good girl. (*To* **Rai**) I did ask Sean to do it, but I may as well be talking to the back end of a donkey for all the good it does me.

Rai If it's any trouble …

Edie It's no trouble at all, is it Tara?

Tara No. No trouble.

Rai Do you want a hand? Because I could—

Edie You sit down there and make yourself comfortable, Rai. You've had a long journey.

Rai (*to* **Tara**) Well, if you're sure … ?

Tara I won't be a minute.

Tara *exits right towards the kitchen to make the tea. A brief silence.*

Rai It's great to put a face to the names, you know? John talks about you all the time. It's nice to actually meet you all properly.

Sean Well – are we uglier or better looking than you expected?

Rai (*laughs*) Much better looking.

Sean Been talking us down again, have you, John?

John Would I?

They laugh. A moment's silence. **Rai** *smiles across at* **John**, *who smiles awkardly back.*

Edie Well, all I can say is it's great to have you all here for the Christmas. Isn't it, Sean?

Sean It is, love.

Edie You get a bit older, these are the things that keep you going. Having your family around at times like Christmas.

Rai I hope I'm not intruding. John said—

Edie Not at all, Rai. We're delighted to have you. Aren't we, Sean?

Sean We are of course, love. Thrilled.

Rai That's very kind of you.

Tara What do you think of the tree, Johnny? Edward reckons it leans.

John *inclines his head and looks at it.*

John I suppose it does a bit. But sure, that can easily be rectified.

Tara Apparently not. Apparently it's doomed to lean.

Edward The leaning Christmas tree of Castleknock, wha'?

John Still, it'd be worth shifting the base around anyway to see if there's a bushier side. It's a bit bare towards the bottom.

Tara And the top. Sure, there are hardly any branches up the top.

Edie God, yous are all very pass-remarkable. I spent hours in a wet, muddy garden centre choosing that tree. I bet you don't stand around criticising the Christmas tree your mother chose, do you Rai?

Rai Er … no. No.

Edie Of course you don't. You probably wouldn't dare. But this lot …

Edward It's a lovely tree, Mum. And you have the place looking fabulous. Hasn't she?

John 'Course she does. It looks great. Although I meant to say – the wreath on the door has fallen off.

Edie Ah Sean, did you not put it up properly? (*to* **Rai**) The one job I leave to somebody else …

Sean I was only doing it because Julian was nowhere to be seen!

John That'd be Julian, all right.

Edward (*to* **Rai**) You haven't met DJ Jules yet?

Rai DJ Jules?

John Wait till you see him. You'd swear he'd never left the ghettoes of Los Angeles.

Edward Except for the fact of his being white as the driven snow.

Edie Edward!

Edward What?

Edie *nods discretely in* **Rai***'s direction.*

Edward What's Rai got to do with DJ being white?

Sean (*quickly*) Well if he doesn't get here soon, the great white hope of Irish rap music is going to miss coming to midnight mass.

Edward (*good-humoured*) I'm sure that's the idea.

Edie He always does this. Disappears straight after his dinner and you don't see sight nor sound of him until God knows when. And we still haven't put Mammy's Angel on the top of the tree.

Sean You put another decoration on that tree and it'll collapse!

Edie (*to* **Rai**, *ignoring* **Sean**) It's a family tradition. On Christmas Eve, when everyone's back, the youngest member of the family puts Mammy's Angel on the top of the tree. As a sort of a way of putting the finishing touches to the decorations, and to remind us of the true meaning of Christmas.

Rai That's … lovely.

Edie The whole thing's gone so commercialised these days, I think it's nice to remind ourselves what we're really celebrating.

Rai Absolutely.

Edie We call it Mammy's Angel because it used to belong to my mother and she left it to the kids when she died.

Edward Some people get thousands of pounds when their grandmother dies, or a house, or a car. We got a glass angel from Hector Grey's.

Edie Don't mind him, Rai. It's not glass. It's Waterford Crystal. (*To* **Edward**) Get it out of the drawer there, Edward, till we show it to Rai. It's in the bottom drawer, the one with all the photo albums.

Edward *crosses to get the angel out of the drawer.*

Edie You'll love it, Rai – it's just beautiful. Isn't it, Tara?

Tara It is, Mum. (*To* **Rai**, *regarding the tea*) Milk?

Rai Please.

Edward *comes back with the angel, which is wrapped in a piece of white linen.*

Edward Jays, Mum, it looks like you've got it in a funeral shroud. Is it dead?

Edie (*unwrapping the angel*) He certainly is not. He's alive and well and living in Castleknock.

Edward How do you know if an angel's a 'he' or a 'she'?

Tara Same way as you do for normal people, I suppose.

Edward (*in mock horror*) Ah no, they don't … ? Surely not …? (*Examining the angel*) Where is it …?

Edie (*to* **Rai**, *ignoring* **Edward** *as she holds the angel up for* **Rai***'s approval*) What do you think?

Rai It's … beautiful.

Edie It's an antique. It's nearly a hundred years old.

John And worth an awful lot of money, apparently.

Rai Yeah?

John They had it valued last year. The whole thing is worth over €400.

DJ That yoke?! No way!

The others turn to see **DJ** *who has entered stage left and is tip-toeing in the direction of the hall, hoping to escape unnoticed.*

Edie Where have you been?

DJ Out. (*To* **John**) Is it really worth over over €400?

John That's what the antique dealer said.

DJ Bloody hell!

Edie Julian!

DJ Sorry. But €400 – that's unbelievable.

Sean Well, there you have it. That's what the fella said.

Edie Julian, did you say hello to Rai?

DJ (*grunts*) How're'ye.

Edie Anyway, we'd never sell it. Ever. It gets passed on to the eldest daughter – it's come right down through the maternal line from my great-grandmother.

Rai Like African custom.

Edie Like … ?

Rai In many African countries, it's the maternal line which is important – kids take their mother's names and that. Have done for centuries.

Edie Quite right, too. I'm afraid we haven't quite developed that far in Ireland yet. (*She turns and spots* **DJ** *about to head out the front door again*) Where do you think you're going?

DJ Tommy's.

Edie Oh no you're not. We're all going to do the Angel ceremony, and then we're off to midnight mass.

DJ Mum!

Edie I'm not arguing, Julian. You know the rules. Christmas Eve is family time. Isn't that right, Rai?

Rai Well …

Edie You see? Even Rai agrees with me. Right – everyone – gather round. Julian. As the youngest member of the family—

Edward As far as we know …

Edie Edward, please! (*To* **DJ**) As the youngest member of the family, you get to put Mammy's Angel on the top of the Christmas tree.

DJ (*sarcastic*) Whoopee!

Sean Julian!

Edie Sean – pass me over the Baby Jesus there, please. He's on the mantlepiece beside the matches.

Sean *crosses to the mantlepiece to get the statue of the Baby Jesus. He hands it to* **DJ**, *who sighs and reluctantly stands on the chair* **Edward** *has dragged into position for him by the tree. Suddenly,* **DJ** *lets out a cry and crumples his legs suddenly as if he's dropped the Angel.*

Edie Julian!

DJ Fooled yous!

Edie It's not funny, Julian. That Angel is nearly a hundred years old. Now place him gently on the top of the tree, and no more fooling around.

DJ *leans up and starts to put the angel at the apex of the Christmas tree.*

Edie Sean?

Sean Hm? Oh, yes. Sorry.

Sean *closes his eyes and prepares to pray.*

Edie Gently, Julian! I didn't say fire him on! That's Mammy's Angel you have there!

DJ Sorry!

Edward (*sings*) He's got the whole world …

John *and* **Edward** In his hands!

Edie Edward! Sorry, Sean. On you go.

Sean Lord, we place this statue of Mammy's Angel on the top of our Christmas tree—

Edward Our rather beautiful, non-leaning Christmas tree—

Sean We place this statue on the top of the tree as a reminder of the true meaning of Christmas. In doing so, we ask you to watch over us as Mammy's Angel watches over our living room, and keep us safe over the Christmas period, so that in the midst of all the fun and the merriement—

Edward And the booze—

Edie Edward!

Sean That in the midst of all the celebrations we may not lose sight of the true essence of Christmas – the birth of Jesus Christ our Lord. Amen.

Others Amen.

Edie *opens her eyes.*

Edie Right then. All hold hands.

They do so, with various levels of discomfort and embarrassment.

DJ This is so embarrassing! Nobody else I know has to do stuff like this at Christmas!

Edie They don't know what they're missing out on, then. Isn't that right, Rai?

Rai *smiles politely.*

Sean Besides, it's tradition.

DJ So?

Sean So we do it every year.

DJ Why?

Sean We just do, that's all.

Edie Whose turn is it to choose this year?

John I chose last year.

Edward And I chose the year before that.

Tara No, you didn't. I chose two years ago.

Edward You did not. I remember I chose 'I Saw Mommy Kissing Santa Claus' and it was vetoed because Dad said it wasn't a carol.

Edie Come on, Tara, love, it doesn't matter. You choose.

Tara All right. But I'm telling you, I chose two years ago. So it couldn't possibly be my turn to—

Sean Ara, Tara, pick a feckin' carol, will you, and let's start singing!

Edie Sean, please. (*She nods towards the crib on the dresser*) Not in front of the Baby Jesus.

Sean Look, I'll bloody pick one!

Edie No, it has to be one of the children. That's the tradition.

John DJ, you pick.

Edward And none of your rap numbers.

DJ I don't know any carols.

Edie Of course you do. What about 'Away in a Manger'?

DJ Oh, yeah.

Edie So is that it?

DJ What?

Edie Is that your pick?

DJ Yeah. I suppose.

Sean Right then. At last. 'Away in a Manger', picked by Julian.

DJ *throws his eyes to heaven.*

Edie On the count of three. One, two—

Tara Hang on, what about Rai?

Edie What about her?

Tara (*to* **Rai**) Do you know 'Away in a Manger'?

Rai Don't worry about me.

Edie Are you sure, Rai, love? Because we can always pick another one.

Sean Jesus preserve us – we'll be here till New Year if we've to pick another one!

Rai Honestly, don't worry about me. I don't … I don't really know any Christmas carols, to be honest with you.

Edie Oh. I see.

A pause.

Sean Look, are we going to sing or aren't we?

Tara Right. On the count of three. One, two—

Edward Hold on.

Sean (*losing patience*) What now, Edward?

Edward Shouldn't we pick a key?

Sean What?

Edward Should we not decide on a key we can all sing in?

Edie Edward, we've never had this problem before.

Edward Before was different.

Edie How was it?

Edward Before, DJ's balls hadn't dropped.

DJ Right, I'm out of here!

DJ *lets go of whoever's hand he's holding and heads for the front door.*

Edie Edward!

Edward Ah here, DJ, I was only joking you.

DJ No, I'm not staying around here to be insulted!

Edie He was only joking, Julian. Weren't you, Edward?

Edward 'Course I was. Come on and join in the festivities, DJ.

DJ No! It's bad enough having to stand around holding hands like a whole family of poofs without being insulted as well!

Edward I was only having a laugh. It's Christmas – where's your sense of humour?

Edie He's probably embarrassed to sing now his voice has broken – is that it? Is that why you're a bit touchy?

DJ I'm not touchy! I'm just f—

Sean (*quickly*) Come on, for Jaysus sake, and let's sing the feckin' song! Are you right? Julian?

DJ *reluctantly comes back and rejoins the group.*

DJ One more word out of him and I'm going, I'm telling you!

Edward I promise – I won't say another word.

Sean Right. Anyone else with anything to say before we start? No? Good. On the count of three, in the key of Dad.

DJ Tell him he's not funny.

Sean One, two, three.

They start to sing, uncertainly at first, but with increasing gusto – all except **DJ** *and* **Rai**, *who doesn't know the words.*

All Away in a manger
No crib for a bed … *etc.*

The others keep singing as **Edie** *breaks off.*

Edie Julian!

DJ What?

Edie Sing!

DJ I am singing.

Edie Well, sing louder. I can't hear you. (*sings*) … lay down his sweet head.

DJ (*under his breath before he starts singing*) Fuck's sake.

Edie *shoots* **DJ** *a look but continues singing.*

All The stars in the bright sky

Look down where he lay
The little Lord Jesus
Asleep in the hay

When they reach the end of the first verse, they all stop singing apart from **Edie**, *who continues tunefully, spiritually with the second verse, eyes closed.* **Sean** *joins in as best he can – but he can only remember the odd phrase here and there.*

Edie (*sings*) The cattle are lowing
The baby awake
The little Lord Jesus
No crying he makes
I love you, Lord Jesus
And ask you to stay
Close by me forever
And love me I pray

Edie *and* **Sean** *finish the second verse together.*

Edward Well done, Mum. That was lovely.

Rai You've got a beautiful voice, Mrs Sullivan.

Edie (*delighted*) Thank you, love. Although you should hear Sean singing properly. Now there's a voice. When he knows all the words.

Sean It's just that second verse. I'm never sure of the second verse.

Edie You don't say.

John But he's a great voice when he puts his mind to it, don't you, Da?

Sean Ach, well – it wasn't a bad voice once. Though it isn't a patch on your Uncle Jimmy's. Now there's a voice for singing the ballads.

Edie You'll hear Uncle Jimmy singing on St Stephen's Day. They always come over for a bit of Christmas cake and a sing-song on St Stephen's Day.

John (*to* **Rai**) Boxing Day.

Edie Of course, you don't call it St Stephen's Day, do you? Boxing Day. What an odd name for a day. I wonder where that came from?

Rai Search me. I never knew it was called anything else.

At some point during this next conversation, **DJ** *sneaks up to his bedroom.*

Edie Clearing up the boxes all the Christmas presents came in, maybe. Or putting them back into their boxes.

Edward Internecine boxing matches because twenty-four hours cooped up together has finally driven everyone around the bend?

Tara Why do you always have to be so negative, Edward? We're having a perfectly nice time here.

Edward I do apologise.

Edie (*quickly*) I suppose there must be some reason it's called Boxing Day. Otherwise they'd have just stuck with St Stephen's Day, wouldn't they?

Edward Which came first, eh – the chicken or the egg?

Sean (*quickly*) Listen, we're going to miss midnight mass if we don't get a move on. It's nearly ten past ten.

Edward (*explaining to* **Rai**) Midnight mass starts at half ten around here. A local peculiarity.

Edie It's so the children can come too. They get too tired if it starts later than half ten.

Rai Ah.

Edie You'll just have time to put your stuff up in your rooms, and then we'll have to be off. John, show Rai where she's going to be sleeping.

John Where *is* she going to be sleeping?

Edie I've put her up in Tara's old room. It's the nicest room.

Rai What about … ?

Edie Tara's sleeping in the spare room. She doesn't mind at all, do you, love?

Tara No.

Edie Edward, I've put you in with Julian, and John, you can sleep on the camp bed down here.

Rai I can sleep on the camp bed. I don't mind.

Edie (*almost aggressive*) You most certainly cannot! This is your first visit to Ireland – how could I send you back to your mother telling her you were made to sleep on a camp bed in the living room?

Rai Thank you. Thank you all. You've all been most welcoming.

Sean We need to get a move on or we'll be dead late.

John I'll show you your room.

They head off up the stairs, **John** *helping* **Rai** *to carry her bags.* **Edward** *follows them, also carrying his bags.* **Tara** *exits stage left towards the kitchen to get her coat. A beat. It is as if* **Edie** *is waiting until the others have disappeared upstairs before speaking. When she does speak, she does so very tentatively.*

Edie So. What do you think?

Sean Of what?

Edie Of Rai. Do you like her?

Sean Of course.

Edie There's no 'of course' about it. You don't have to like her.

Sean She's John's girlfriend. So of course I like her. (*A beat*) Why – don't you like her?

Edie I do. She seems like a lovely girl.

Sean There you are then.

A beat.

Sean Still, she's certainly … how can I put it … she's certainly more … well … *tanned* than I expected.

Edie Sean!

Sean I'm not saying there's anything wrong with that. On the contrary, I think it's quite … exciting. But there's no point in pretending we haven't noticed.

Edie It doesn't bother you?

Sean Not in the least. You?

Edie Good Lord, no.

Sean Great. I thought you might be …

Edie Well, I'm not.

Sean Great. That's … great.

A pause. **Sean** *exits to the hall to get his and* **Edie***'s coats. When he comes back, he's laughing gently to himself.*

Edie What?

Sean I'm just thinking – could you imagine Jimmy and

Kathleen if their Carmel brought home … you know … a coloured boyfriend?

Edie I wouldn't have thought they'd bat an eyelid.

Sean Kathleen would. Kathleen's suspicious of anyone who wasn't born in Castleknock village!

Edie (*defensive*) It's different for a girl.

Sean Get away out of that. You're just saying that because Kathleen's your sister.

Edie You think Jimmy would be any better?

Sean I think he'd be worse! I love him dearly, but he's a terrible old bigot, is Jimmy.

Edie I hope it's OK on Stephen's Day.

Sean It'll be fine. They'll be too polite to say anything. Trust me.

A beat. **Sean** *and* **Edie** *look as if they might kiss, but at that moment, the others appear down the stairs.*

Edie (*flapping a little, embarrassed*) Are we right, so? (*Looking around her*) Where's Julian? Julian! (*But* **DJ***'s gone flying out the front door ahead of her*) I don't believe it – he's disappeared again! The minute I take my eyes off him he's gone, the little … !

Sean We'll just have to go without him. There won't be a seat left if we don't get the skids under us.

Tara And believe me, Rai, you do not want to have to stand through one of Father Aidan's Christmas sermons.

Rai (*awkward*) I hope you don't think I'm being rude, but – I think I might give midnight mass a miss.

Edie Oh?

Rai If that's all right. I'm … I'm just exhausted with all the travelling.

Edie Oh. What a pity. Father Aidan does a lovely midnight mass. And the carol singing is beautiful, isn't it, John?

Rai I'm sure it's lovely, Mrs Sullivan, I just …

John Rai isn't Catholic, Mum.

Edie Oh. (*A beat*) Well, that doesn't mean she couldn't come to midnight mass. Father Aidan is a great supporter of ecumenism.

Rai Honestly, I'm really knackered, Mrs Sullivan …

Edie I hate leaving you here alone on your first night with us. It seems so … inhospitable.

Rai I'll be fine. I think I'll just go straight to bed.

Edie Well, if you're sure. There's tea bags in the kitchen, in the press over the dishwasher. Just make yourself completely at home.

Rai Thank you. I will.

A pause.

Edie Right then. Everyone else ready?
Edward (*yawning*) You know, I'm pretty bushed myself …

Edie (*ushering him towards the door*) Out!

Edward *sighs, reluctantly accepting his fate.*

Edward If we're not back in a couple of hours, Rai, send in the troops.

Rai Have fun.

Sean Right then. Eyes front. Forwaaard march!

They all start to file out. **John** *lingers behind.*

John Mum …

Edie What is it now, John? We're going to miss mass altogether if we don't get a move on.

John The thing is, I don't think I'm going to come either.

Edie Why on earth not? We always go to midnight mass on Christmas eve.

John The thing is, Mum … I don't think I'm really going to be celebrating Christmas this year. I mean, not in the way that—

Edie Not celebrate? What are you talking about, John?

Sean *reappears at the door to the living room.*

Sean Are yous right?

John I'm not a Catholic any more, Mum. So I don't … believe in Christmas. (*A beat, as* **Edie** *looks at him uncomprehendingly*) I've become a Buddhist.

Edie Jesus, Mary and Joseph.

Blackout.

Act Two

ACT 2 SCENE 1

It is Christmas Day, in the early afternoon. As the lights come up, **John** *and* **Rai** *enter.* **John** *is carrying two bottles of champagne.* **Rai** *carries a bag full of presents.*

John Well, so much for a white Christmas. Lashing rain and a gale-force wind.

Rai Your mother will be disappointed.

John But not surprised. I don't think there's been a white Christmas in Ireland in living memory.

Rai Doesn't stop people hoping, though, does it? Shall I put the presents under the tree?

John Yeah, just pile them in the back there with the others. I'll put these in the fridge.

Rai *crosses to the Christmas tree and puts her presents under it, along with all the others. When she's finished, she stands looking up at the Angel on the top of the tree. After a couple of seconds,* **John** *reappears from the kitchen, still clutching his bottles of champagne.*

John Fridge is chock-a-block. There isn't room to fit a thimbleful of champagne, let alone two bottles.

He pulls up as he notices **Rai** *looking up at the Angel on top of the tree.*

John Nice, isn't it.

Rai It's beautiful.

John Despite the connotations?

Rai You know, it's a funny thing. I can't stand nearly everything the Catholic Church represents – no offence, like – but somehow, Catholic iconography always … moves me in some way.

John I know what you mean.

They stand looking up at the Angel for a couple of seconds.

Rai Does it make you regret converting to Buddhism? Missing out on the whole Christmas thing?

John It's only the religious side. We can still join in the rest of the celebrations.

Rai I thought that was the whole point of Christmas – the religious side?

John How many people do you know who celebrate Christmas as Jesus' birthday?

Rai Your Mum does. And your Dad.

John Good, so we're up to two. Two out of a world population of several billion. What's that in percentage terms?

Rai Edward and Tara.

John Tara, maybe. Though I suspect with her it's as much for an easy life as out of any real conviction.

Rai And Edward?

John I don't know about Edward – I can't work him out. (*A beat*) So that gives us two definites, a possible and a maybe. And the rest of the world just gets drunk and stuffs its face with turkey.

Rai *laughs. A beat.*

Rai I think she took it quite well. From the way you were talking, I thought we might have been packing our bags by now. Your dad looked a bit taken aback.

John All he'd be worried about is having his rhythm upset. Especially at Christmas. Speaking of which …

Rai What?

John I thought we could maybe nip up to your room for twenty minutes.

Rai (*suggestive*) Oh yeah?

John Get a spot of meditation in before dinner. The calm before the storm.

Rai Bloody hell. The zeal of the convert …

John I'll stick an oul' Christmas record on, drown out the sounds. I think Buddhist chanting on Christmas Day might just be that one little step too far.

John *starts searching among the record collection for an album of Christmas songs.* **Rai** *comes up behind him sexily.*

Rai We don't have to chant, John. We could always—

John Here we are. Perfect. *Sing-alonga-Christmas – All your Favourite Christmas Hits.*

He takes the record from its sleeve, puts it on the turntable, and carefully places the needle down on it. The record crackles, then an old, very scratched recording of 'Rudolph the Red-Nosed Reindeer' starts up.

John There we go. They won't hear a thing now.

John *starts to exit.*

Rai What about the bottles of champagne?

John I thought I'd stick them in a bath of cold water to keep them cool. I'll bring them down after dinner. Come on.

John *exits followed by* **Rai**, *leaving the stage empty as 'Rudolph' continues to play. After a couple of lines, the needle becomes stuck and the line 'You would even say it glows' is repeated over and over again. Eventually,* **Edie** *appears down the stairs laden with presents. She looks harrassed and exasperated.*

Edie Would no one else think of doing something about the record player, no?

Sean *comes hurrying in on stage left in an apron and a comic-looking white chef's hat.*

Sean Sorry, love – I was busy with the gravy.

Edie *pulls up the needle on the record player roughly. The music comes to an abrupt halt with a nasty-sounding scratch.* **Sean** *winces, but says nothing.*

Edie It was only a lot of old noise, anyway. I don't know who put it on. (*She looks up at* **Sean**) Why are you wearing that silly hat?

Sean It's my chef's hat. For doing the gravy.

Edie It looks daft.

Sean It's only a bit of fun, love.

Edie I'm sorry, Sean. Ignore me. It was just the noise of that record blaring in my ears, and the needle getting stuck and …

A beat. **Edie** *crosses to the Christmas tree and starts putting her presents under it.* **Sean** *watches her carefully.*

Sean Are you all right?

Edie I'm fine. Although I must say, I'm very disappointed the way it's turned out. (**Sean** *looks at her*) The weather. I really did think we had a chance of having a white Christmas. Not this … horrible rain.

Sean Maybe we'll get a white New Year.

Edie Maybe.

A pause. **Sean** *watches* **Edie** *intently as she gets up and begins to pull the table into place for Christmas dinner.*

Edie Give us a hand, will you?

Sean *does so. A pause as they manoeuvre the table into place. At length* **Edie** *speaks.*

Edie Do you think he still wants to exchange presents and … you know, join in the celebrations?

Sean I'm sure he does. It wouldn't be like John to make things awkward. I'm sure it's just … well, just the religious side of things he won't be joining in.

Edie (*acid*) Oh, well, that's all right, then. As long as he still believes in the eating and the drinking and the gluttony. And there was me thinking he'd gone to seed altogether.

A silence. **Edie** *continues setting the table.*

Sean (*eventually*) It's not the end of the world, you know. It's only his religion he's changed. He's still the same John.

Edie Yes.

A pause.

Sean And as long as he's not ramming it down our gullets – which he doesn't seem to be. That'd be the thing that'd worry me. If he became some class of a … of a converter or something. Some kind of proselytising whatd'youcallit. Like a Jehovah's Witness or something, always quoting the Buddhist bible at us. That's what'd drive me scatty. (*A beat*) Do Buddhists have a bible, do you know?

Edie I've no idea.

Edward *enters.*

Sean Edward'll know. (*To* **Edward**) Do you know do Buddhists have a bible?

Edie As far as I can tell they have thousands. Buddhist monks spend donkey's years studying the scriptures.

Sean Sure, I suppose all religions have to have some class of a … of a holy book or a book of rules or whatnot.

Edward You make it sound like a particularly complicated version of golf.

Tara (*off*) Dad!

Sean My gravy!

And he darts off stage left. **DJ** *enters from upstairs.*

DJ Cool, yous are up, can we do the presents now?

Edie No, we cannot.

DJ Why not?

Edie Because I'm just about to serve dinner.

DJ But you've only just got up. How can we be just about to have dinner when you've only just got up? Turkeys take forever to cook.

Edie Is that so? Thank you for those words of wisom, Delia. (*A beat*) Tara's done most of it. With Edward.

DJ How come you got up so late, anyway? You've practically missed the whole of Christmas.

Edie I wasn't feeling well.

DJ What's wrong with you?

Sean Nothing you need worry your head about.

DJ Is it because John's become a Buddhist and he hates Christmas?

Sean He doesn't hate Christmas.

DJ Well, is it because he's become a Buddhist then?

Edie What John does is his own business, Julian. He's a big boy now.

DJ What is it, then?

Sean Look, Julian, go in and give Tara a hand like a good man, will you?

This is evidently **Sean***'s final word on the subject, because he sits heavily in an armchair and picks up his newspaper.*

DJ Can we not do the presents before dinner?

Edie No, we cannot.

DJ Why not?

Edward We don't want to rush the presents, DJ. We want to take our time over them. I want to really savour this year's Car Boot Sale Special.

DJ Get lost!

Edie Julian, it's Christmas Day. Everybody just wants to relax. We'll give the presents out later. It'll give you something to look forward to for the rest of the day.

DJ I don't want something to look forward to. I want to do the presents.

Edie Well, you'll just have to wait until this evening.

DJ Why?

Edie You know very well why. Because we always give out our presents in the evening.

DJ For absolutely no reason.

Edie There is a reason.

DJ What is it then?

Edie Sean, you tell him. He won't listen to me.

Sean What's that?

Edie He wants to know why we always give out our presents in the evening and not in the morning.

Sean Oh. (*A beat. Then, to* **Edie**) Why do we always give out our presents in the evening and not in the morning?

Edie Because that's what we've always done. Because it's the tradition.

Sean There you go, Jules. Because it's tradition. That's as good a reason as any other.

DJ (*contemptuous*) Tradition!

Edie Yes, tradition. And if you've any complaints, you can go up there to the graveyard and complain to your dead grandfather, because it was him who invented the tradition.

DJ It's not fair.

Sean What's not fair about it?

DJ I'm the youngest so I never get to make up the traditions. I just get saddled with a whole load of boring ones left over from eight hundred years ago.

Edward Eight hundred years of oppression, hah, DJ?

At that moment **Tara** *comes through from the kitchen with a tray of condiments.*

Tara That's life at the bottom of the evolutionary pile, I'm afraid, Jules.

Edward That's no way to refer to this proud country of ours!

Tara Get up there and give us a hand. That'd be more in your line now than sitting back dispensing witticisms and cynicisms.

And she exits to the kitchen again.

Edward Here, I've an idea. How about Julian gets to invent a tradition this year to be followed every year hence. What do you think of that, DJ?

Edie Edward …

Sean No, hold on a minute, Edie. Traditions have to start somewhere. If Julian can come up with a new tradition, the least we could all do is follow it.

Edward Assuming it's legal and at least reasonably tasteful.

Sean Absolutely. Julian?

DJ OK. I hereby invent the tradition that presents are given out as soon as everybody gets up on Christmas Day.

Sean Uh-uh. Sorry.

DJ What?

Sean It can't be a tradition that conflicts with an existing tradition. Existing traditions take precedence.

DJ But the whole of Christmas is just one boring old tradition after another! There's no room for any new ones!

Sean You'll just have to be creative.

DJ *sighs and shakes his head. He crosses to the Christmas tree and starts to rummage through the presents piled underneath.*

DJ Which one's mine?

Edie Get away – shoo! Never mind which one is yours.

DJ Mum, it's Christmas Day! If I can't open my present until this evening, the least you could do is let me see it.

Edie No – you'll guess what it is.

DJ That's part of the fun!

Edie Ah, Julian, could you not wait until—

DJ (*shaking a parcel*) Is this mine?

Edie Julian!

DJ Is it?

Edie Sean, tell him—

Sean Julian! Put that present down now!

DJ It *is* mine, isn't it?

Edie Julian!

DJ For fuck's sake!

And he throws the present down violently and storms out into the hall and off up the stairs.

Edie Julian!

But he's gone. A silence.

Edie What was that about?

Tara I think he was hoping for a motorised scooter.

Edie Pity about him. Do you know what those things cost?

Tara You should have asked me. I could have chipped in.

Edward We all could have.

Edie It's not a question of money. He needs to learn – you don't just get everything you want the moment you want it. He's getting far too materialistic, that boy.

Edward Steady on there, Mum – you're starting to sound like a Buddhist!

Edie (*cold*) Spirituality and values aren't exclusive to Buddhists, Edward. Whatever your brother might think.

Edward I don't think John would claim—

Edie Ssh! What's that?

Edward What?

Edie Can you hear that?

Tara Hear what?

Edie That. It's like a mooing sound. Listen.

Sean *crosses to the foot of the stairs and listens too. And from upstairs we too hear a very faint moaning sound.*

Edie Do you hear it?

Sean It's coming from Rai's room.

Tara My room.

Edie They're up to something. I'm going up to put a stop to it.

Edward Mum, it's Christmas.

Edie And?

Edward And they've been sleeping in separate rooms.

Edie So?

Edward So I would imagine they're …

Edie What?

Edward Well, you know … what young Buddhist men and women do … together. In a bedroom.

Edie What's that?

Edward You know …

He raises his eyebrows suggestively. The others look at him.

Edward Oh for God's sake – chanting – meditating. It's what Buddhists do, isn't it?

Edie Right, that's it.

Sean Edie …

Edie Sean, it is not natural. This is my house, and I will not have strange religious chanting going on in it.

Edward The rosary excepted.

Edie And if you don't like it, you can convert to being a Buddhist too!

Sean Edie, love, do you not think you're overreacting slightly to this whole thing?

Edie No, Sean, I don't. On the contrary, I think I have been remarkably patient and tolerant. When John told me he wanted to bring some girl he's only just met into our house for Christmas, I welcomed her into the bosom of our family. And when Rai turned out to be … who she was, I didn't bat an eyelid, unlike some I could mention. And I've tolerated John announcing out of the blue that the Catholic faith is a pile of old codswollop. But I will not have him ruin Christmas for everybody by turning my house into a Buddhist temple! I just will not have it, Sean!

Edie *is close to tears now.* **Sean** *looks at* **Edward** *and* **Tara** *and motions for them to leave him and* **Edie** *alone.* **Tara** *and* **Edward** *exit in the direction of the kitchen. A beat.*

Sean Edie, I don't like John becoming a bloody Buddhist any more than you do. But what can we do about it? It's his life.

Edie I think you should talk to him. Find out if anything's wrong. (**Sean** *looks sceptical*) I'm worried about him, Sean. I'm afraid he's unhappy. John wouldn't do something like this unless he was unhappy. Unless he was searching for something.

Sean Aren't we all searching for something?

Edie You don't just cast off your whole background and heritage and … culture like that unless you're missing something … fundamental inside.

Sean Like what?

Edie I don't know. Something he should have had as a child. Something we should have given him.

Sean Everyone has to find their own way, Edie. That's all he's doing. Trying to find his own way.

Edie What's wrong with the way we've given him? It's served us all right, hasn't it?

Sean It's no reflection on us that John's experimenting with other ways.

Edie Maybe you're right. Maybe it's just a phase. I mean, he's only been a Buddhist about five minutes. Sure, he's like someone who hasn't even made his Holy Communion yet.

Sean Exactly. This time next year he'll probably be in here saying the rosary with the best of us.

Edie I think you should talk to him all the same.

Sean What do you want me to say to him?

Edie Find out if he's planning to join in the Christmas celebrations, for a start.

Sean He said he was, didn't he?

Edie He said he wasn't going to let it spoil Christmas for everybody else. That isn't the same thing. I mean, we don't even know if he's still called John, for Heaven's sake!

Sean What else would he be called?

Edie Well, these Buddhists – don't they take strange religious names when they convert? Mustapha or Haseem or …

Sean Mustapha Sullivan. You've got to say, it has a certain ring to it.

Edie It's not funny, Sean.

Sean Look, if John was going to change his name, I'm sure he'd have told us by now.

Edie He's probably a vegetarian too. You can't believe in reincarnation and then go around eating animals. You could end up eating your own grandmother. What am I going to feed him for Christmas dinner if he doesn't eat meat any more?

Sean Can't he just leave the turkey and the ham and eat the rest?

Edie Ah, don't be ridiculous – he can't just eat Brussels sprouts and stuffing for his Christmas dinner!

Sean Edie …

Edie Sean, our son is clearly deeply unhappy! So unhappy that he's joined a different religious faith. If we don't want to lose him altogether, I think one of us needs to talk to him. And you're his father, he'll listen to you.

At that moment, **John** *appears with* **Rai**.

John Mum, you're up – Happy Christmas!

Edie Happy Christmas, love.

Rai Merry Christmas, Mrs Sullivan.

Edie Merry Christmas, Rai, love. (*A beat*) I wasn't sure if you people said that. Buddhists, I mean, not …

Rai When in Rome …

Edie Of course.

John How was midnight mass?

Edie Very nice, thank you.

John Father Aidan's sermon didn't go on too long? (*To* **Rai**) Honest to God, Rai – sometimes you'd swear that man was on a sponsored sermon, getting paid by the minute.

Edie (*a little terser than necessary*) Father Aidan gave a lovely sermon. Didn't he, Sean?

Sean He certainly did. (*To* **Rai**) Though I have to admit, it wasn't the shortest sermon I've heard.

Edie It *is* Christmas, Sean. The centrepiece of the Christian calendar.

Sean I suppose it is …

Edward *appears back from the kitchen.* **Edie** *spots him, and springs into action.*

Edie Rai, love, why don't you come and give Tara and myself a hand finishing off the dinner?

Rai Sure.

Edie And Edward – if you want to get your presents under the tree before dinner, you'd better get wrapping; we'll be eating in less than a quarter of an hour.

Edward Righto. (*To* **Rai**) Daren't risk the wrath of DJ a second time.

Rai *laughs.* **Edward** *exits up the stairs to wrap his presents.*

Edie Come on, Rai, love. Let's get these vegetables on the go.

And she ushers **Rai** *out towards the kitchen. A pause.* **John** *goes to pick up a magazine.*

Sean John?

John *stops and turns to look at* **Sean**.

Sean I just wondered, you know … before dinner … if we could have a little chat. Just the two of us.

John What about?

A pause. **John** *looks at* **Sean**. **Sean** *fiddles with a pipe and a tin of tobacco which he takes from his inside pocket.*

Sean (*uneasy*) It's hard, this, John, you know? For your mother especially.

John You don't approve?

Sean It's not a question of approving or disapproving. It's more a question of trying to understand.

John Is it Rai you don't approve of?

Sean God no, it's not Rai … Lord, your mother would hate you to think …

John So it's the Buddhist thing?

Sean The Buddhist thing ... yes. It's the religion thing that your mother ... that we find ...

John Difficult?

Sean (*nods*) To understand.

John There isn't much to say, Dad. It isn't a big deal.

Sean Ah well, now, it *is* a big deal, John. Otherwise you wouldn't have done it. You'd have stayed a Catholic and just ... you know ... stopped going to mass and that, d'you know?

John Like the others did?

Sean This is it.

A silence.

Sean It isn't every day you come across the fella who tells his parents on Christmas Eve that he's become a Buddhist monk, d'you know.

John Not a monk. Just a Buddhist.

Sean All the same. It'd be a worry. To your mother, especially.

John There's nothing to worry about, Da. It's just a different path. To the same end.

Sean We're all going to die right enough.

John So there's nothing to get worked up about.

A pause.

Sean Still and all, these kinds of strange beliefs, d'you know? They'd be inclined to frighten your mother a bit.

John Afraid I'll come back as a tree?

Sean Ah no, it'd be more—

John Afraid you'll come back as a tree?

Sean (*exasperated*) Ah John, will you stop! Your mother's worried about you. She thinks there's something troubling you. Is it maybe money, like? Because we could help you out if—

John It's not money, Da.

Sean Or Rai, she's not—

John (*with a smile*) Black? Oh she is, Dad. She's definitely black, I'm afraid.

Sean I meant is she … you know …

John She's not pregnant, no. (*A beat*) Not as far as I'm aware, anyway.

Sean *nods. A pause.*

Sean So …

John So what?

Sean Ach, John, you're making this awful hard. I'm trying to talk to you and … and trying to find out a bit about the whole thing that I can tell your mother and you're not making it one bit easy.

John What do you want to know?

Sean Your mother wants to know if you're planning on giving out presents, for a start.

John Of course. It's Christmas, isn't it?

Sean That's what I said.

John Well, there you go then.

Sean And she wants to know … what it is you're looking for. With the Buddhist bit, like.

John I don't know the answer to that, Da. But the fun is in the looking, isn't it?

Sean *nods. A pause. At length,* **Sean** *breaks the silence.*

Sean You know, I remember one Friday night way back in the sixties sitting down there with the mother and the father one night at home in Athlone to watch the *Late Late Show* on the television. I couldn't have been much younger than you are now, and I had a job working in O'Malley's insurance firm in the town. A good job – nice, steady income – but I was getting restless, d'you know? Anxious to see other things, maybe move up to Dublin or what have you, maybe see a bit of the world. Anyways, we sat down that night, your granny, your grandad and me, and they had a young fellow from Trinity College on to talk about drama, or writing or some such. And what did he do, only instead of talking about drama, he started criticising the Church, and he called one of the archbishops a moron. On the telly now, like. A moron. Brazen as you like. And there was uproar. I remember my father saying he should be thrown out of the college for daring to speak of a member of God's holy clergy like that. A young pup, my father called him. An ungrateful young pup. And your granny over in the corner nodding like her head was going to fall off. But inside I was cheering the young pup. Urging him on. And the next week he came back on and apologised, and then what did he do, only straight away he said the archbishop knew what the word 'moron' meant, but did he know the meaning of the word 'Christianity'? Well, it was all over the next day's papers. And I remember reading the whole thing with a horrified sense of … liberation. Like some class of a dam had burst open inside me, inside the whole country. And I resolved to pack in the job in O'Malleys and go off to Paris, or Prague, or Bucharest, and grow a beard and wear sandals, and read Mao and live in a hippie commune and …

Sean *breaks off. A long pause.*

John And then?

Sean And then three weeks later I met your mother. And we got married, and had Tara. And I don't regret a single moment of it. But it's not so easy to sit cross-legged in a tent trying to work out the meaning of life when you've a family to support.

John *nods, and one senses a moment of communion between father and son.*

Sean Still and all, at least we made it up to Dublin eventually, wha'?

John And you grew the beard.

Sean That too.

A beat.

Sean There's no shame in being happy with your lot, John.

John I know.

Sean There'd be some fellows, now, would always be looking for something else. Never taking the time to stand still and enjoy the view from the top of the mountain, or halfway up the mountain, or wherever it is they've got to. They'd always be racing to get to the next corner to see if the view was better from there. D'you know? There's no shame in standing a while to admire the view.

John No.

Sean And sure, isn't that the whole point of being a Buddhist, as I understand it? Accepting your lot with – what's the word? … 'equanimity', and doing your best to enjoy it.

John That's as good a definition of the Four Noble Truths as any, I suppose. (*He looks up at* **Sean**) The Four Noble truths – the core of Buddhist teaching.

Sean Well, there you have it.

A pause.

John I'm not unhappy, Da. I promise you. You can tell Mum – I'm not unhappy.

Sean *nods. A pause.*

John But maybe I am … I don't know … scared of being happy.

Sean Why in the name of God would anyone be scared of being happy?

John Because once you're happy – once you reach the point in your life where you can stop and look around and admire the view and say 'I am truly happy now' – then you stop growing, don't you? You atrophy.

Sean Why do you?

John Because you stop *wanting* to grow. You stop wanting to change. Or learn. Or seek new experiences. You just want everything to stay the way it is. You don't want anything to change ever again, so you can just remain in that intoxicating state of bliss forever. And eventually the brief moment of happiness evaporates. But not before a giant barbed wire fence has been built around your life. Because once you've glimpsed happiness once, you're condemned to spending the rest of your life in the same tiny field of experience, trying to repeat the unrepeatable. To starting back down the hill again, retracing your steps in search of some past contentment you think you had rather than forging ahead and seeking out new experiences.

Sean And that's why you've become a Buddhist?

John I don't know why I've become a Buddhist, Da. I just know that right now, it suits me.

Sean *nods. A pause.*

Sean So … do you think your mother and I have stopped living because we're … content?

John Do you?

Sean I don't know, John. I honestly don't know. But you're right about one thing. The excitement's in the chase all right. The moving and the searching and the seeking out new experiences – that's all well and good. The trick is knowing when to stop. The trick is knowing when you've found what you were looking for.

Before **John** *can reply,* **Edward** *comes down the stairs with an armful of presents.*

Edward Right, that's the presents done – how are we doing for dinner?

And he crosses to put his presents under the tree.

John I'd better go and see if they need a hand in the kitchen.

And he makes to exit stage right.

Sean John? (**John** *turns back*) One other thing.

John What's that?

Sean You're still called John, aren't you? Your mother's worried you'll have changed your name so you're called after some Eastern prophet or the like.

John Now that you mention it, my Buddhist name is Pema Temsin Wang Po – Ocean of the Lotus Teaching. But you can call me Temsin for short.

Sean (*horrified*) No …?!

John (*with a wink*) Don't worry, Da. I'm still John to close friends and family …

At that moment **Edie** *and* **Rai** *enter stage right, carrying dishes of steaming vegetables, plates of turkey already carved, etc. etc.*

Rai No, please – we can manage fine. You lot stay where you are.

Edie (*indulgent, with a faint air of forced jollity*) Awful, aren't they, Rai? I always say, for everything women's lib has achieved, at Christmas, everything somehow always reverts back to type. The women serve the dinner, the men carve the turkey.

Sean I made the stuffing.

Edward And I did most of the vegetables.

Edie (*ignoring them*) Do the men in your house do the same?

Rai They wouldn't dare. Or they'd have me to deal with.

Edie Well, good for you. Though I think maybe it's partly my fault in this house. I think maybe I spoil my men a bit. 'My men' – isn't that a gas way to think of them now, altogether? As if they're were all my husbands?

Rai You want to get them up off their fat backsides to give you a hand, Mrs Sullivan.

Edie Ach, well, I don't mind doing it. Sure, doesn't it keep me off the streets and out of mischief?

Rai I tell you something – I wouldn't stand for it. John!

John*'s away in a world of his own. He looks up, a little startled.*

Rai Come and give your mother a hand.

John Sorry. What do you want me to do?

Edie I think we're nearly there now.

John There must be something I can do.

Edie Honestly, love, you just sit down there and relax. We can manage. (*To* **Rai**) Can't we, love? (*She continues without waiting for an answer*) Sure, it's practically all done. But thanks for offering, love. It's very considerate of you.

At that moment, **Tara** *appears with the final plate of food.*

Tara That's the lot, folks. Come and get it.

Edie Right. You can all come and sit down now. Someone call Julian. (**Edward** *crosses towards the hall to call* **DJ**) Rai, love,

I've put you next to Tara. Keep the girls together where we can do the most mischief!

Edward (*calling upstairs*) DJ! Dinner's ready. So stop pulling your wire and come on down and pull a cracker instead.

Edie Edward!

Edward Sorry.

DJ (*appearing from the hall*) I want to sit at the end where I can see the telly.

Edie You needn't bother, Julian – we're not having the television on during Christmas dinner.

DJ Why not?

Edie Because we're having our Christmas dinner, Julian. Together. As a family. And we don't want the television blaring in the background.

DJ *You* don't, you mean. No one else minds.

Edie Julian, I'm not going to argue with you. Rai, will you have a glass of wine?

Rai No, thank you.

Sean Ah, go on, you'll have one – it's Christmas Day.

Rai Honestly, I'm fine. We … I don't drink.

Tara Not even at Christmas?

Rai No. Thank you. (*Awkward, not wishing to offend*) It's … one of the things about being a Buddhist. You're meant to try and abstain from intoxicants of the mind.

Tara Well, you can make mine a large one, Dad.

Sean *pours* **Tara** *a large glass of wine.*

John It's not written in stone … not like the Ten Commandments. But … well, if you can, like …

By this stage **Sean** *has moved on to where* **John** *is sitting.*

Sean You're not off it too, are you, John?

John Well, I—

Tara Ah, for the love of God, John, it's Christmas Day.

Edward You're not serious?

John 'Fraid so.

Tara Didn't I see you wandering around this morning carrying two enormous bottles of champagne?

John That was for the rest of you. As a gesture.

Tara (*dry*) How considerate of you.

Sean Lord God, thank goodness we've none of that kind of nonsense with Catholicism. Catholicism is founded on intoxication.

Edie It's founded on the body and blood of Christ, Sean. It's not the same.

Sean Either way – thanks be to the Divine Jaysus Ireland isn't a Buddhist country. (*To* **John**) You won't even have a drop, so? For the Christmas?

A beat, as **John** *wavers.*

John Go on, so – I suppose a little drop wouldn't hurt.

Sean Good lad yourself.

John *holds out his glass and* **Sean** *pours him a glass of wine.*

John (*to* **Rai**) It's just a drop. For Christmas.

Rai Don't look at me, mate. You do what you like.

Sean *sits back into his chair and raises his glass in a toast.*

Sean Happy Christmas, everybody!

All Happy Christmas!

And they clink glasses, etc. A pause, as they set about serving themselves, passing vegetables over and back, etc.

John I have to admit – giving up the drink has been the hardest bit of the whole thing for me.

Sean I can imagine.

Edward Gas, isn't it? He doesn't mind the fact that he might come back as a tadpole, but tell him he'll never enjoy another creamy pint of stout …

Tara So does this mean you'll go to Buddhist hell? Because you broke the pledge?

Rai Buddhists don't really have a hell.

John Or a pledge.

Tara What do they have?

Rai The *samsara* – it's like the endless cycle of birth and rebirth.

Tara And that's the Buddhist concept of hell – living forever?

Rai That's right – coming back time and time again to undergo the pain and suffering of life.

Tara Sounds great to me. Doesn't it sound great to you, Mum?

Edie I don't know. I'd be very suspicious of anything like that.

Edie *trails off uncertainly. She's out of her depth here. A beat.*

Sean What's the alternative? To constant reincarnation?

John Nirvana.

Tara Buddhist heaven.

John Except nirvana is more like a state of mind. You can even reach it during this life. You know, through meditation and that.

Sean And that's why those Buddhist monks spend their days up there in their caves in the Himalayas chanting and meditating?

John Trying to cleanse the mind and reach nirvana.

Edward So what's the difference when you die?

Rai When you die you reach paranirvana.

John A kind of permanent state of nirvana. Peace. Enlightenment.

Sean Well, I don't know about anyone else, but I intend to reach an impermanent state of nirvana right now by drinking myself under the table. Edward?

Edward (*holding out his glass*) Fill her up.

Sean *does so, then gets up and goes to get another bottle of wine.*

DJ (*to* **Rai**) Do you mind the telly being on during dinner?

Rai Doesn't bother me, mate – telly's always on in our house.

DJ See?

Edie Julian, I'm not discussing it any further.

DJ But the *Only Fools and Horses Christmas Special* is on!

Edward DJ, they've had the same *Only Fools and Horses Christmas Special* on for the past four years.

DJ (*triumphant*) Exactly! It's a Christmas tradition!

Sean Julian, stop being silly, and pass me over your mother's glass there.

DJ (*ignoring him*) The *Only Fools and Horses Christmas Special* is as much a Christmas tradition as putting Mammy's Angel on the tree and 'Away in Some Bloody Manger'! How come I have to follow all of your traditions, and I don't get to follow any of mine?

Edie Because our traditions aren't rude and anti-social. Our traditions are about community, about doing things together, as a family.

DJ Stupid things.

Edie You might think so. We don't. Isn't that right, Rai?

Rai I have to admit, I'm kind of a fan of *Only Fools and Horses*. So I can see your point, DJ.

Edie (*dry*) Can you indeed? Brussel sprouts?

Rai No thanks. I'm not all that gone on Brussels sprouts.

Tara (*sotto voce – but not sotto voce enough*) Oh, excuse me, Miss-Fan-of-*Only-Fools-and-Horses*-Doesn't-Like-Brussels-Sprouts!

Sean Tara!

Tara Well, I'm sorry, but—

Edie All right, everybody, that'll do. We are not turning on the television, and that's the end of it.

Rai I wasn't suggesting we turn it on. I just, you know, I just enjoy watching it, you know?

An awkward silence as they eat – the only sound the clinking of cutlery. After a long pause, **DJ** *breaks the silence.*

DJ We could watch *Only Fools and Horses* together – (*mimics* **Edie**) 'as a family'.

Edie (*losing her temper*) Julian! That is enough! If there's any more out of you you'll get no Christmas dinner, no *Fools or Horses* and no flipping present, either! Now just stop it!

A silence, as they all look at **Edie** *in amazement.*

Edie (*calming herself*) Rai, love, help yourself to vegetables, before they get cold.

Rai Thank you.

John Pass us over your wine glass there, DJ.

DJ *does so.*

Sean I see you didn't need to be asked twice if you wanted a glass of wine.

John (*pouring* **DJ** *a glass of wine*) Sure, you can always tape *Only Fools and Horses.*

Edie John!

John What?

Edie He's only fifteen.

John *Only Fools and Horses* isn't over fifteens, is it?

Edie I meant …

She nods in the direction of the wine.

John What?

Edie The wine, John. He's too young to drink.

DJ Mum!

Edie Julian, I don't want to hear it. You're only fifteen, you're not having wine. End of story.

Edward He's fifteen, Mum. He's probably been getting blow jobs down the park since he was twelve.

Edie and **Sean** (*together*) Edward!

Tara Edward's right, Mum. Julian's not going to get—

Edie Tara, I really don't think you're in a position to be giving advice on drinking, do you?

A silence.

Edie I'm sorry, I didn't mean …

Tara That's all right.

Edie Tara, love.

Tara Honestly, Mum, it's fine. Pass me over the cranberry sauce there, would you, Edward?

A beat, as **John** *passes her the cranberry sauce.*

Edie Who's for Brussels sprouts? John?

John No thanks.

Edie No?

John I'm not a big fan, either.

Edie You've always eaten them before.

John I know. But only a couple. And only for the sake of tradition.

Edie I always thought you liked Brussels sprouts.

John *shakes his head.*

Tara I never knew you didn't like Brussels sprouts either.

John I'm sorry, I didn't realise you required a personal press release.

Tara Did you know John didn't like Brussels sprouts, Edward?

Edward Yes.

Edie You did? How come you never said?

Edward What difference would it have made?

Edie I wouldn't have made so many, for a start. If I'd known Rai didn't like them, and neither does John.

Tara Is that part of the Buddhist law too? No Brussels sprouts?

Edie Tara!

DJ I hate Brussels sprouts.

Edie Well, I know that. You hate anything that doesn't contain at least seventy E numbers.

DJ No. I just hate Brussels sprouts, that's all.

Edie And cabbage. And carrots. And courgettes, and—

Sean (*quickly*) Well, I love Brussels sprouts. Rai, you'd never pass them over there, would you?

Rai Sure.

Edie What am I going to do with all the leftover Brussels sprouts?

Edward Brussel sprout soup?

Rai Brussels curry?

Edward Brothel Sprouts?

A beat. The others look at him.

Edward A prostitute's baby. A brothel sprout.

Edie Edward!

Tara You might have told us before I spent an hour and a half cleaning two hundred of the bloody things this morning.

John What the fuck business is it of yours whether I eat Brussels fucking sprouts or I don't?

Edie Look, it doesn't matter—

DJ How come he's allowed to swear and I'm not?

Edie John, don't swear at the dinner table, please.

DJ Oh, but he can swear anywhere else?

Sean Julian, put a sock in it.

Tara Don't go taking it out on me, John.

John Taking what out on you? What are you talking about, Tara?

Sean Here, DJ – how about pulling an oul' cracker there?

He proffers a cracker. **Edward** *gets up and heads into the kitchen with a bowl to get more vegetables.*

Tara It isn't my fault you've become so po-faced you can't even enjoy Christmas any more.

Meanwhile, **DJ** *'s pulled the cracker and won.*

Sean Good man yourself. What have you won?

DJ What do you think I've won? A gay hat and a crap joke.

Edie Julian!

DJ Well, why can't I watch—

Edie If I hear another word out of you about the television—

John (*quietly*) Take that back, Tara.

Tara Take what back?

John What you said about me and Rai just now. Take it back.

Tara I never said anything about Rai. I said you were too po-faced—

John I'm warning you, Tara.

Edie Tara, apologise to your brother.

Tara He said so himself, Mum. He's a Buddhist now, so he doesn't want to celebrate Christmas any more. Dad, pass me the wine.

Sean Tara, love …

Tara Do I have to come and get it myself?

Edie Tara, are you sure?

Tara I'm an alcoholic, Mum. Remember? That's what alcoholics do. They drink. Now please, pass me the wine, Dad.

Edward (*returning with his bowl of vegetables*) Tara—

Tara Don't you start as well, Edward! Just because he (**John**) has poisoned the whole atmosphere. Julian, pass me the wine, please.

DJ You're such a lazy cow!

Edie Julian! Don't speak to your sister like that!

DJ She is, though! She's a fat, lazy cow!

Tara I've actually lost weight, I'll have you know!

DJ You mean you were even fatter before? No wonder you became an alcoholic!

Edie Julian!

Tara The one time of the year we can all get together as a family! The one time of the year we get a chance to be happy—

Edward Well, I don't know about anybody else, but I'm having the time of my life – DJ?

DJ I would be if I could watch—

Edie Don't you dare mention that confounded programme!

John (*very quiet, to* **Tara**) Take that back.

Tara No.

John Take it back.

Tara I will not! It was you—

Tara *pulls up abruptly and touches her forehead. She looks up at the ceiling.*

Tara What was that?

Sean What?

Tara I just felt a … there's another.

Edie Another what?

John It felt like a drop of water.

Edward (*facetious*) Probably just storm clouds gathering …

Edie How can it be … ? Who used the bath last?

John I put the champagne into a bath of water to keep it cold. Why?

Edie Jesus, Mary and Joseph – the tap!

Edward I'll go!

Sean Quick, Edward – before the ceiling comes in on top of us!

Edward *and* **Sean** *run up the stairs.*

John What tap?

Edie The tap in the bathroom – it doesn't close properly!

John But I turned it—

Edie You mustn't have done it properly! The bath'll have overflowed!

John *stares at* **Edie** *in a state of paralysed horror.*

Tara (*pouring herself another glass of wine*) Congratulations, John – you've finally managed it!

John How was I to know there was something wrong with the bloody tap? How was I supposed to *divine* that—

Edie John, that is enough! We've just about had our fill of your carry on this Christmas!

John What have I done?

Edie 'What have I done?' 'What have I done?', he says! I'll tell you what you've done. I'll tell you what you're doing! You're ruining Christmas! You're ruining it for everybody!

Edie *shouts and brings her fist down on the table with a tremendous thud, just as* **Edward** *comes running down the stairs. There is a brief, stunned silence, followed by a gentle creaking sound.* **Sean** *turns just as the Christmas tree starts to topple.*

Sean Look out!

The Christmas tree falls over with a crash. Almost at the same moment, there is another creaking sound from above and the ceiling gives way under the weight of the flooding in the bathroom, sending a cascade of plaster and water onto the middle of the dinner table. The whole thing is over in a couple of seconds, leaving them all drenched and covered in plaster from the ceiling. A beat as they all sit in horrified silence.

DJ (*eventually, turning on the television*) I told you that tree was lopsided.

Blackout.

ACT 2 SCENE 2

It is later on Christmas night. The dinner has been cleared away, as has the plaster from the ceiling. As the lights come up, **DJ** *and* **Tara** *are putting the Christmas tree back up.* **Tara** *stands back from the tree issuing instructions. On the other side of the room,* **Sean** *is reading a book on basic Buddhism, watched by* **Rai** *and* **John**.

Tara Right, left a bit. Left!

DJ You said 'right'.

Tara I said 'right' as in 'all right'. It needs to go left.

DJ For fuck's sake!

Tara OK, hold it a bit more towards me now. (*He does so*) That's it. Right, Jules, if you can keep it there now. That's it. Perfect.

DJ *emerges from the branches at the foot of the Christmas tree.*

Tara You know something? Now that I see it like that, I think you're right – it was lopsided before.

Edward It certainly isn't lopsided now.

Rai What do you think, Mr Sullivan? Could you be tempted?

Sean There's an awful lot of numbers and lists. (*reads*) 'The Four Noble Truths, the Noble Eightfold Path, the Three Marks of Conditioned Existence' – give me the Our Father and the Glory Be any day. Much less complicated.

Rai It's not so bad once you get your head around it. A lot of it is self-evident.

John And a lot of it corresponds to what Catholicism teaches if you dig deep enough.

Rai If you could get beyond the layers of hierarchy and social teaching.

Edward You mean if it wasn't Catholicism.

Sean And you really meditate? For real?

John Of course.

Sean Ye weren't just doing it to wind your mother up?

John Of course not.

Sean Well, rather you than me is all I can say.

Rai So we can't seduce you into converting?

Sean Can you imagine what Jimmy and Kathleen would say?

Edward Don't mind Jimmy and Kathleen – imagine what Mum would say!

Tara (*pouring herself a drink*) Quite right, too. Load of old nonsense.

DJ Do you think if I became a Buddhist I could come back as a Premiership striker?

Edward You might. But you wouldn't be allowed to drink.

DJ Oh yeah. (*A beat*) Ah well, fuck that, so.

Sean Julian.

DJ What? Mum's in bed.

Sean It's got nothing to do with Mum. I don't want swearing in the house either.

DJ For God's sake!

Rai She's been asleep for hours. Do you think she's all right?

Sean I'm sure she's grand. She probably just got a bit of a shock.

John Maybe you should go and check on her. Just to be sure.

Sean Ach, I'm sure she's grand.

Tara She's going to miss the whole of Christmas.

Sean Well – maybe I'll see does she feel like coming down for a game of cards or something. Tara, do you want to get the cards, and we'll see if we can get an oul' game going?

Sean *gets up and crosses towards the stairs.* **Tara** *goes to the dresser and rummages in a drawer for a pack of cards.*

Tara Is it any wonder she's in shock when himself comes home and tells her he's a Buddhist on Christmas Eve. You couldn't have picked a more appropriate time to tell her, no?

John I wanted to tell her face to face. This was the first chance I had.

DJ It's not just that. She's been acting really weird for weeks. Always bursting into tears if I do the slightest thing.

Edward DJ, you'd drive a statue to tears. In fact, come to think of it, you weren't knocking around Ballinaspittle sometime in the early eighties, were you?

DJ Ha ha! Right, I'm going out. I'll see yous later.

Sean *reappears down the stairs.*

Sean Jaysus, one day you ask him to spend with his family, one day of the year, and even that's too much for him.

Tara (*glaring at* **John**) Is it any wonder?

Sean Still sleeping like a baby, poor love. She's been under a lot of pressure lately. Getting ready for Christmas and that.

Rai She wants to try some meditation.

Tara (*snorts*) Meditation!

John It's really good, Tara. Really relaxes you.

Tara I've enough to worry about without getting into bloody meditation.

Rai You don't fancy giving it a go, then?

Tara No. Thank you.

Rai Mr Sullivan?

Sean I don't think so, love. It's not really my … cup of tea, you know?

Edward Go on, Da. You look like you could use a bit of relaxation.

Sean Ah no, I'm—

Edward He'd love to try it. And so would I.

Rai Mr Sullivan?

Sean *looks at her – he's had just about enough to drink to give it a go.*

Sean What do I have to do?

Rai Hey, fantastic!

Tara What about our game of cards?

Sean I thought we should wait for your mum to get up. She'd hate to miss out on the cards.

Rai This exercise only takes about ten minutes. You sure you don't want to try it, Tara?

Tara Thank you. I'll stick to vodka. Dad?

Sean No thanks, love. I don't think my body would tolerate any more alcohol.

Edward Besides, we're meditating.

Tara *crosses to the drinks cabinet and pours herself a vodka, then sits at the dining room table upstage right playing Patience with herself. Throughout the following,* **Tara** *alternates between playing Patience and keeping an eye on the proceedings.*

Rai Right. John and Edward and I can sit on these cushions. Mr Sullivan, you stay where you are.

Sean You mean I don't get to sit cross-legged on the floor? What kind of meditation is this?

Rai You can if you want. I just thought ...

Sean A concession to the elder Buddhist, hah? I'm grand here.

John *and* **Rai** *arrange themselves cross-legged on the floor.*

Rai Right then. Edward – see the way John and I are sitting? You need to sit like that. And then you hold your hands on your lap like this, one inside the other, like a cup, thumbs touching. You too, Mr Sullivan. Just get your feet flat on the ground. That's it. Okay, now close your eyes, and just concentrate on your breathing.

Sean *and* **Edward** *do as bid.*

Rai Concentrate first of all on the breath as it goes into and then exits the body. On the sensation of it travelling down your nostrils into your lungs, and then being pushed up and out again. The idea is to focus your attention on your breathing so that you're completely aware of the present moment, completely focused on what's happening to you at this precise moment in time. That's what meditation is – being totally aware of what's happening to you as it's happening, no matter what it is.

Sean So we just concentrate on our breathing?

John That's right. When we do this exercise at the Buddhist centre in London, we say the phrase 'Um Ah Hung' at the end of each cycle of breaths.

Tara (*snorts*) You *are* joking?

Rai It's just a tool to keep you aware of your breathing. Like an anchor – something to fall back on if you lose your bearings. But you can just count, one, two, three – up to ten.

Edward Sure, we may as well say the 'Um Ah Hung' bit. Get the full experience, what do you think, Da?

Sean Sure, why not? As the fella says, we may as well be 'Um Ah Hung' for a sheep as a lamb.

John Well, if it doesn't make you feel uncomfortable …

Tara You mean more uncomfortable than sitting cross-legged on the floor with a gut full of turkey?

Rai Right then. 'Um Ah Hung' it is. After each out breath. Nice and gently.

They start to concentrate on their breathing and to say the phrase

'Um Ah Hung' on each cycle of breaths. This continues for a couple of seconds. **Tara** *watches all the while, vodka in hand.*

Sean I tell you – it isn't as easy as it looks.

Rai Keep concentrating. Just free your mind completely from everything except an awareness of your breathing.

She takes another breath, and on the out-breath, chants the phrase 'Um Ah Hung' as before. The others follow suit. **Sean** *starts to laugh gently.*

Sean I keep wondering what Jimmy would say if he could see me here. (*He opens his eyes and leans across to address* **Rai**) Jimmy's married to Edie's sister, Kathleen. We had a double wedding, like, and Jimmy is—

John Dad!

Sean Sorry.

Sean *closes his eyes again and goes back to concentrating on his breathing. A silence, broken only by the breathing of the four meditators and their chants of 'Um Ah Hung' after each cycle of breaths. At first, they chant the word at different times, but before long, their breathing patterns have synchronised, and they are chanting the phrase as a chorus.*

Sean (*eyes still closed*) Begod, d'you know – I think it's working. I feel great.

Tara That'll be the whiskey.

Sean No, fair's fair, credit where it's due, the breathing is—

John Dad!

Sean Sorry.

Again the sound of the meditators' breathing and intoning the phrase 'Um Ah Hung'. This goes on for some time. **Tara** *begins to look increasingly agitated. She turns away from the circle of meditators and pours herself another vodka, which she drinks in one go. She's about to pour herself another when* **Edie** *appears in her dressing gown.*

Edie Jesus, Mary and Joseph.

Sean *opens his eyes and jumps to his feet.*

Sean Edie, love. Did we wake you? We were just—

Edie Have you gone completely mad, Sean?

Sean It was only a bit of fun, love. John and Rai were just showing me a Buddhist relaxation technique. D'you know … to help me … relax, and that.

Edie I would remind you all that today is Christmas Day. If you can't relax on Christmas Day …

Tara Mum's right. It's the one day of the year you're meant to be able to relax without needing Buddhist meditation techniques.

John It isn't a religious thing, Mum.

Edie I don't care what it is, John. I don't want it in my house. You've done enough damage for today, thank you very much.

John Mum—

Edie Not content with ruining our Christmas dinner, you have to start bringing hokum-pokum chanting and meditating into the house! Well, I won't have it, John! I think I've been very tolerant up to now! But I will not have my house turned into a Buddhist temple on Christmas Day!

Rai It's my fault, Mrs Sullivan. I'm sorry. I didn't mean to ruin your Christmas.

John You haven't ruined anything, Rai.

Tara Yes she has.

Edie Tara!

Tara Well, it's true. She's caused nothing but tension since she got here.

Sean How about that game of cards now that Mammy's up. Edward?

Edward Absolutely. I'm in. John?

Tara What are you asking him for? Sure, you know he doesn't want to join in any of the Christmas festivities.

John I never said that.

Tara You've certainly given that impression. Hasn't he, Mum?

Edie Tara—

Tara She's just too polite to say it. Everyone's just too polite to say it.

Sean Tara!

John To say what?

Tara To say what they're all thinking. That you've ruined Christmas for everybody bringing her here. We've never had any problems before now. We've always spent a perfectly nice, pleasant Christmas together. And suddenly this year, you have to go and ruin it for everybody!

John I'm warning you, Tara—

Edie John! Tara! Stop it! Now!

Rai John, relax.

Tara And you couldn't even have the generosity to pretend to join in because you're afraid of compromising your precious principles in front of your precious woman!

Rai Maybe I'd better leave.

John Don't be silly, Rai. This has nothing to do with you.

Rai No, honestly, I think this was maybe—

Sean Rai, love, please. Sit down. Tara doesn't mean any of that. Do you, Tara?

Tara Yes, I do. If you didn't want to come home for Christmas, you shouldn't have come. No one made you.

John And no one made me bring Rai either?

Tara You said it.

John Ignore her, Rai. She's just bitter because she married a good-for-nothing armchair republican from Belfast and now she's stuck up there with nothing to show for it but a failed marriage and a child who doesn't want to live with her.

Edie John!

Tara Don't you dare talk about Sean Óg like that! You know nothing about my life, John.

John I know enough to know you're jealous of me and Rai. That you're jealous of us having choices, and exercising them. But it isn't my fault you won't move on, Tara. You can't hold me responsible for your lack of courage.

Tara (*close to tears now*) Mum, tell him to shut up!

Edie Daddy's right – why don't we get out the cards and have a nice game of poker.

John What is it about Rai you find so threatening, Tara? Why are you so afraid of her?

Tara Don't you dare patronise me.

Edie Please, John, it's Christmas Day.

Edward Anyone for a chocolate liqueur? Rai?

Rai No, thank you. I think I've upset everybody enough as it is.

Edie Don't be silly, love. You haven't upset anyone. Has she, Sean?

Sean Of course you haven't, love.

Tara (*drunkenly*) Yes, she has! She's upset me! Coming in here with her airs and her graces and her 'I'm not going to mass' and 'I don't like Brussels sprouts!' When she's a bloody visitor in our house, abusing our hospitality!

John How dare you speak about Rai like that!

Rai Maybe she's right, John. Maybe it was a mistake us coming here together. Christmas is a family time, and I'm not family, and ... I think maybe I should go.

John Go where?

Rai I don't know – check into a hotel somewhere.

Edie You'll never find a hotel at this time. Not on Christmas night.

John Besides, there's no reason why you should leave just because Tara's drunk. Again.

Tara I am not drunk!

Rai Honestly. I think it'd be for the best.

John Ignore her, Rai.

Rai I still think—

Edward Mum's right, Rai – you'll never get a hotel open around here at this time on Christmas night.

Rai In that case, maybe I'll just go for a bit of a walk. Give you all a chance to spend some time together – just the family. And in the morning I'll call and see about getting an earlier flight back to London.

John Rai, listen. It's just Tara. She's had too much to drink and—

Rai No, John. It's not just Tara. Open your eyes and look at what's staring you in the face. I'll see you later.

John I'll come with you.

Rai No! I just want some time alone, John. (*A beat*) Please. I won't be long.

John *hesitates. A beat.*

Rai Don't wait up for me. I can let myself in.

Rai *smiles awkwardly and exits through the front door. Silence.*

John Well. Merry Christmas to you too, everybody.

Blackout.

Act Three

ACT 3 SCENE 1

It is the next day – St Stephen's Day. From the radio, a scratchy version of 'Good King Wenceslaus'. **Sean** *sits by the fire doing a crossword.* **John** *paces nervously, edgy. After a couple of seconds, he crosses to the record player and pulls the needle up roughly.* **Sean** *looks up at him, but says nothing. He watches him, concerned, for a couple of seconds, then gets back to his crossword. A pause.* **Edward** *enters stage left.*

Edward Anyone for a turkey and ham sandwich? Da?

Sean I'm grand for the moment.

Edward John?

John No. Thanks.

Sean I'd have another bottle of stout, though. If you're going.

Edward Another bottle of stout. Righto.

Edward *exits in the direction of the kitchen.*

John She must be on that phone now for the best part of an hour. Tara!

Tara (*off*) What?

John How long are you going to be?

Tara (*off*) Not long.

John How long is not long?

Tara (*off*) Oh for Christ's sake – I'll be off in a minute!

John *comes back into the centre of the room.*

Edward Use my mobile.

John It's not about that. What if she's trying to get through?

Sean There's no one she could have stayed with? One of your pals from around here or something?

John She doesn't know anyone in Dublin.

Edward The door wasn't locked by mistake, was it?

John I checked. Christ, if anything's happened to her …

He crosses to the end of the stairs again, increasingly agitated.

John Tara!

Tara (*off*) Two minutes!

Sean Maybe she got on a flight back to London early this morning.

John She'd have called by now. And there's no answer at her flat. Besides, all her stuff's here. Something's happened, I know it has.

Sean Ach, John, sure what can have happened to her around here?

John She's a woman, Da. A black woman. Out on her own on Christmas night. Anything could have happened.

John *crosses to the stairs again.*

John Tara! Get off that fucking phone!

Tara (*appearing*) Jesus, relax – I'm coming!

John About fucking time.

He grabs the cordless phone from **Tara**.

Sean John!

John What?

Sean *makes a 'calm down' motion with his hands.* **John** *shakes his head and crosses to the phone.*

John What number should I ring?

Tara Well it's hardly a 999, is it?

John She's been missing for eighteen hours, Tara.

Tara She's gone off in a huff. Jays, if we went running to the police every time DJ went off in a huff.

Sean (*quickly*) There's a number for the local police station in the front of the book there.

John *takes the book out and finds the number for the local police. He dials the number.*

Tara You don't think you're being a little melodramatic, no?

John No, I don't.

Tara She's a grown woman, John. And a somewhat wilful one at that.

John You don't know anything about her, Tara.

Tara I know she kicked up a big fuss about going to midnight mass when she knew it would mean a lot to—

Sean Tara!

Tara She probably booked into a hotel.

John She'd have rung to let me know.

A beat as **John** *dials. He finishes dialing and looks up at* **Tara.**

John So if the police find her body lying in a ditch somewhere, I hope you'll be pleased with yourself.

Tara (*crossing to pour herself a vodka*) Oh, for God's sake.

There is a ring on the doorbell. **John** *slams the phone down and goes to answer it.*

Tara That's probably her now. With the new boyfriend she picked up on Dun Laoghaire pier.

But it isn't. It's **DJ**, *on a motorised scooter.*

John For fuck's sake, DJ!

DJ What?

John Could you not go round the back, no?

DJ The scooter won't fit past the cars in the garage.

John *shakes his head in irritation as* **DJ** *starts to scoot off stage left.* **John** *goes back to the phone and dials the police again.*

Sean Hold on there a minute – whose scooter is that anyway?

DJ Mine.

Sean Since when?

DJ Since I swapped it with Tommy.

Sean Swapped it? For what?

DJ For a pair of rollerblades.

Sean The rollerblades your mammy and I gave you for Christmas?

DJ Yeah.

And he goes to leave again.

Sean Hold on there now and don't be rushing off anywhere.

(**DJ** *turns wearily to look at* ***Sean***) Tommy gave you his scooter for a pair of rollerblades?

DJ Plus fifty euro cash.

Sean Where did you get fifty euro in cash?

DJ Swapped the book token Auntie Kathleen gave me with Graham Finn. And I had thirty euro of my own.

Edward Thirty euro tucked away in a coffee jar under his bed and he buys his presents from the pound shop.

DJ That shaving foam cost me three fifty!

Edward You were robbed, so. You can get it down on Moore Street for a euro.

DJ No, you can't. (*Then, quickly, seeing that* **Sean** *is about to interrogate him further*) Is Rai back yet?

Edward John's on the phone to the police now.

John What the hell's keeping them?

Tara It's Christmas, John. Even the police take time off over Christmas.

DJ Do you want me to go out and have a look for her on my scooter?

John Can't do any harm, I suppose.

Sean Go on, Julian. Get out there and see what you can find.

DJ Right. I'll give yous a bell on the old mobile if I hear anything.

And he scoots off stage left.

Sean I thought he said he couldn't get out through the back door because of the cars in the garage? I'll tell you, that's one little shite—

Sean *is interrupted by another ring on the doorbell.* **John** *slams the phone down and races to open the door. We don't see who it is, but we hear voices off.*

Voices (*singing, off*)

The wran the wran,
The King of all birds
St Stephen's Day
Was caught in the furze …

John Fuck off!

And he closes the door in their faces.

Tara John! That was the wran boys!

John *ignores her and takes the phone back off* **Edward. Tara** *continues to look at* **John** *for a moment or two, then turns and pours herself another vodka. A beat.*

Sean She'll turn up, John. I promise you. I can feel it in my waters. There'll be some completely innocent explanation.

John I hope you're right. For her sake.

Edward I hope so too. For all our sakes.

And he heads off upstairs.

Tara I don't know why everyone keeps blaming me. All I said was I didn't think Christmas was an appropriate time to bring a stranger into the house. Which it isn't.

Sean You were very hard on her, love. We all were, maybe.

Tara You didn't say anything to her.

Sean No. But I didn't rush in to defend her either.

Tara She doesn't need defending from you, Daddy – she's well able to look after herself, that one.

At that moment, **Edie** *appears dressed in a dressing gown. She looks pale and unwell.*

Sean Hiya, love.

Edie *smiles weakly at him, but says nothing. She crosses to the Christmas tree and plugs the lights out. A beat, as* **Edie** *stands looking up at the top of the tree.*

Edie I wouldn't even have minded if Mammy's Angel had survived.

Sean At least he went quickly, I suppose. Didn't suffer, like.

Edie *throws her husband a look.* **Sean** *looks suitably chastened.* **Edie** *sits wearily in an armchair and stares into the fire.*

Sean Good sleep?

Edie All things considered.

A pause.

Sean Would you like a bit of an oul' turkey sandwich? Edward's done one of his special sauces.

Edie I couldn't stomach anything right now.

Tara Are you all right?

Edie Fine.

Sean *nods. A beat.*

Edie What time of day is it at all?

Sean Just gone two.

Edie Jimmy and Kathleen will be here any minute. (*A beat*) No sign of Rai yet?

Tara Oh for God's sake! Not you as well, Mum!

And with that she disappears up the stairs. A pause.

Sean She's very … angry this weather.

Edie She's missing Sean Óg, that's all.

Sean I hope she's right about Rai.

Edie Sure, what could have happened to her?

Sean Well, you read in the paper about … you know … people being attacked and that. Mugged, or … or … raped. You know – because of …

Edie Because of the colour of their skin?

Sean It happens, you know?

Edie (*shakes head*) That's one cute little madam. She'll have stayed out to teach John a lesson.

Sean You're very hard on her, Edie.

Edie Haven't I a right to be? After she's spoiled our Christmas on us?

Sean Ach now, Edie. It wouldn't be fair to lay all the blame on Rai. We're quite capable of spoiling Christmas on our own.

Edie We always had perfectly peaceful Christmases before she appeared.

Sean Lord God, woman – what planet are you on? I don't think we've ever had a 'perfectly peaceful Christmas' since the day we were married!

Edie We have too!

Sean When? Name one?

Edie We had a lovely Christmas last year.

Sean Edie, we nearly had to call the police on Christmas Eve to separate the two boys when John spilled red wine over Edward's new trousers!

Edie Well, that one incident apart, it was a lovely Christmas.

Sean And you and Julian weren't speaking to one another after he got suspended from school for smoking. And the year before you sulked for the entire Christmas because Edward went skiing in France instead of coming home. And the year before that—

Edie All right! All right! So we've had a few rows! Are you happy now? All families have disagreements – especially at Christmas. That's why I wanted this year to be special! That's why I wanted it to be perfect! That's all I wanted – one perfect Christmas before they're all gone and it's just the two of us again!

She buries her head in her hands, unable to carry on. During the above, **Tara** *has re-entered. She stands watching her parents anxiously. A beat.*

Sean I'm scared for her, Edie, that's all.

Edie It's affected me as well, you know? (*A beat*) But there's nothing we can do except wait and hope and pray that Rai comes back safely.

Sean *crosses to comfort his wife.*

Sean That's the spirit, love. Never say – ah!

Sean *lets out a sudden yelp of pain.*

Tara Dad?

Edie (*rushing over to him, panicky*) Sean? Sean, what's wrong? Have you … ?

Sean (*through gritted teeth*) I think I just stood on a piece of glass!

Edie (*relieved*) Jesus, Sean, you gave me such a fright. I thought you were … here, hold on to me and we'll get you sat down.

Sean *does so, and the two of them hobble awkwardly towards the sofa.* **Tara** *bends and picks up what appears to be a small piece of crystal.*

Tara It's not glass. It's a bit of Mammy's Angel. I must have missed it when I was hoovering up.

Edie *looks up from where she has just deposited* **Sean** *in an armchair.*

Edie Show me? (**Tara** *does so*) That's odd.

Tara What?

Edie Mammy's Angel was made of Waterford Crystal.

Tara So?

Edie Where did you put the remains of the Angel, Tara?

Tara In the bin in the kitchen. Why?

But **Edie***'s gone off stage right, towards the kitchen.*

Tara What's got into her?

Sean Does nobody care about my shredded foot?

Tara Daddy, you're worse than DJ. Sure, it's only an oul' scratch.

Sean An oul' scratch! You wouldn't be calling it an oul' scratch if—

But he gets no further, because **Edie** *is back, carrying several pieces of the broken angel.*

Edie (*cutting across* **Sean**) That wasn't Mammy's Angel on the tree.

Sean What was it, so?

Edie I don't know, but it wasn't Mammy's Angel. Someone's taken Mammy's Angel and replaced it with this … imitation.

Sean Why would anyone want to do that?

Edie I don't know. But they have.

Sean But who … ?

Tara You can't think?

Sean Julian?

Tara Not Julian.

Sean Who then?

Tara Someone we know almost nothing about who came into the house for two days, admired the angel, and then disappeared without trace into the night …

Edie Ah, Tara, don't be ridiculous.

Tara Who's looked down her nose at this family since the moment she walked in, and then took off at the first opportunity?

Edie Tara.

Tara Who coveted everything this family had because she was jealous and her own family were gone off to Kenya for Christmas?

Sean (*incredulous*) Ah, Tara – sure, Rai has better things to be doing than—

At that moment, **John** *appears from upstairs.*

John Than what?

An awkward silence.

John Well?

Sean Nothing, John. It's just Tara being stupid.

Tara How well do you know her, John?

John I beg your pardon?

Edie Tara, please. You're being silly now.

John What's going on?

Sean Don't mind her, John. It's a lot of old nonsense.

Tara This is because she's black, isn't it?

Sean Ach, don't be ridiculous.

Tara It's because she's black no one wants to say what we're all thinking. (*To* **John**) That wasn't the real Mammy's Angel on the top of the tree. Someone switched it for a cheap imitation.

John What's that got to do with … (*He pulls up as it suddenly dawns on him what* **Tara** *is insinuating*) Please tell me you're not suggesting … ?

Edie John, love, no one's suggesting anything.

Tara I'm just asking how well do you know her, John?

John *turns and heads for the stairs.*

Edie John! John, nobody's saying—

But he's gone. A silence. **Sean** *looks at* **Tara**.

Tara (*defiant*) It's not beyond the realms of possibility, you know. She heard how much it was worth. And *someone's* taken it.

Sean And where would she have got a replacement, tell me that, eh? Sure, they only arrived home the night before last. Do you think she had a spare angel tucked away in her suitcase just in case? It's too ridiculous for words, Tara!

Tara Maybe. But I'm only saying ... we know nothing about her. Nothing at all. And who else could have done it?

At that moment, **DJ** *appears.* **Sean** *turns to look at him.*

DJ Still no sign of her.

Sean Julian, look me in the eye and tell me you didn't steal Mammy's Angel.

DJ (*outraged*) I'm not staying to listen to any more of this – I'm out of here!

Edie No you're not. Uncle Jimmy and Auntie Kathleen are due any minute, and you're going to be here to meet them.

DJ No way! I've already arranged to go to Funderland!

Edie Well, you can just un-arrange, because you're not going. You're staying here.

DJ That's not fair! I go every year! It's my Christmas tradition!

Edie Funderland is on all week – you can go some other day.

DJ But all my friends are going today!

Edie I don't care if all your friends are going to the moon and back by dinnertime. You're not. And that's the end of it.

DJ But, Mum—

Edie No buts, Julian. You're staying here to see Uncle Jimmy and Auntie Kathleen and that's it.

DJ For fuck's sake!

Edie Julian!

But **DJ** *has stomped off upstairs.* **Edie** *sighs, agitated.*

Edie I'll murder him one day, I really will.

She breaks off as the phone rings. **Edie** *goes to answer it.*

Edie Hello. (*A beat. Then, frostily*) Ah, Paudge, hello. Happy Christmas to you too. (*A beat*) Ah you know yourself – very quiet. (*A beat*) How's Sean Óg? (*A beat*) Is he? Ah, God love him.

A Beat. **Tara** *enters stage right.*

Edie She is, yes. She's right here beside me, I'll hand her over to you. (*She puts her hand over the phone*) It's Paudge. Is everything all right, love?
Tara *takes the phone from* **Edie**.

Tara (*terse*) Paudge? Put Sean Óg on. I want to talk to him.

A beat as **Tara** *listens to the response. She motions to her mother that she'll take it upstairs. She exits with the portable phone, crossing* **John** *as he enters pulling on his coat.*

John I'm going out to look for Rai.

Edie Would you not leave that to the police? They have the expertise and the resources and …

John And what?

Edie Well, not that this is the most important thing – it isn't, but … well, you know Uncle Jimmy and Auntie Kathleen are on their way over?

John Jesus …

Edie I couldn't say no, John. They've been coming to our house every St Stephen's Day since we got married. I couldn't call it off at this short notice.

John Mum, Rai has disappeared. She could be lying dead in a gutter somewhere for all we know, and you're going to sit around singing 'Rudolph the Red-Nosed Reindeer' with Jimmy and Kathleen?

Edie Ach, John, love – you're being melodramatic now. If there was any way I could have cancelled it, I would have. I promise you. But I just …

John Hadn't the courage?

Edie It's not a question of that, John.

John What is it a question of then, Mum?

Edie (*pleading*) A couple of hours, John. That's all I'm asking. You know how much it means to Jimmy and Kathleen. Especially Jimmy – you're his only godson. Please, love …

John Mum …

John *makes for the door as* **Sean** *appears stage left.*

Edie (*desperate*) If Rai's not back by the time Jimmy and Kathleen have gone, we'll all go out looking for her. How about that? (*A beat.* **John** *is wavering*) Please, John. I'm asking you to do this one little thing for me. Please?

At that second, **Tara** *comes running down the stairs in tears.*

Tara The fucking bastard! That fucking, wanking, vindictive little—

Sean *and* **Edward** *come running on to see what the commotion is.*

Tara I'll fucking kill him, I'm telling you! I'll fucking, fucking …

She begins to weep bitterly.

Sean What's wrong, love? What is it?

Tara Paudge is going off to the Giant's Causeway with his mother and father for the New Year … and they're taking Sean Óg.

Sean I thought he was supposed to be coming here?

Tara That's not all. Paudge says he's going to fight for custody after all. He says I'm not fit to be a mother.

Edie Why on earth would he say that?

Tara Why do you think, Mum?

Edie Because you like a drink? Sure, we all like a drink.

Tara Yes, but we don't all drink ourslves to sleep with half a bottle of vodka every night.

Sean I never liked that little scut.

Sean *takes* **Tara** *in his arms.*

Sean We'll fight it, love. I promise you. We'll fight it.

There is a ring on the doorbell. A brief pause.

Sean Maybe I should tell Jimmy and Kathleen …

Tara No! Paudge has done enough damage to our Christmas already.

Sean Are you sure … ?

Tara I'll let them in.

Tara *gets up and goes to answer the door. A beat.* **Edie** *looks up at* **John**.

John Look, Mum—

Edie Please, John? A couple of hours?

Before **John** *can reply,* **Jimmy** *and* **Kathleen** *can be heard entering off.*

Jimmy (*singing, off*) Jingle bells, Santa smells
Robin flew away
Kojak lost his lollipop
And called the IRA – hey!

Tara (*off*) Uncle Jimmy!

Jimmy (*off*) How's my favourite niece?

Tara (*off*) I'm grand altogether. Come on in. How're you, Auntie Kathleen?

Kathleen (*off*) Hello, Tara love.

Enter **Jimmy** *and* **Kathleen** *with* **Tara. Jimmy** *is a couple of years older than* **Sean** *– jovial, good-humoured, but not inclined to listen.* **Kathleen** *is* **Edie***'s older sister – long suffering, but not without humour and intelligence, she is evidently very much used to playing second fiddle to her husband's tomfoolery. Ad-libbed Christmas greetings.*

Jimmy (*to* **Sean**) Happy Christmas, Sean. Here, have you been singing again?

Sean No, why?

Jimmy You brought the house down!

And he gestures at the hole in the ceiling above the dining room table. He and **Sean** *laugh uproariously.*

Sean The usual?

Jimmy That'd be lovely.

Kathleen (*to* **Edie**) So what happened?

Edie The bath overflowed – you don't want to know. Come on in there and sit down.

Jimmy (*to* **Tara**) Tell us, any word from the young fella?

Tara Yeah, I was talking to him earlier. He's grand. But he's—

Jimmy Did you hear that, Kathleen? I knew that young fella'd be grand. He has his Uncle Jimmy's fighting genes, isn't that right, Tara?

Tara It is indeed, Uncle Jimmy.

Jimmy And how's the man himself? Me favourite godson.

Tara Isn't he your only godson, Uncle Jimmy?

Jimmy He could well be. That doesn't stop him being my favourite, though. You're feeling better, so?

John Sorry?

Jimmy The oul' Arab's belly kept you from midnight mass. Your mother was telling us.

John Was she now?

Jimmy (*winking, conspiratorial*) I blame your father's cheap whiskey. Now if he'd come around to my place for a proper Irish instead of lorrying back that cheap scotch nonsense your father serves …

John Isn't it a pity we didn't.

Jimmy *laughs, delighted.*

Edie (*quickly*) So. How did you get over the Christmas?

Kathleen Ah, you know yourself – very quiet. You?

Edie The same. Very quiet altogether.

Kathleen I must say, Edie, you've the place looking fabulous. Hasn't she, Jimmy?

Jimmy I always say to Kathleen, Edie and Sean always have the most Christmasey house you'll ever see. It makes you feel Christmasey just looking at it.

Edie Well – Tara was a great help.
Kathleen And such a wonderful Christmas tree. Where did you get a tree as solid and as sturdy as that? It looks like it's taken root there in the corner.

Edward That Christmas tree? Sure, that Christmas tree collapsed like a deck of—

Edie (*quickly*) Do you like it? I picked it out myself.

Kathleen Ach, it's gorgeous. We can never get our Christmas tree not to lean. No matter how hard he tries, Jimmy just can't get it to stand up straight.

Jimmy As the actress said about the bishop, wha'? (*To* **John**) Speaking of which where's herself? The oul' girlfriend. Are we not going to meet her, no?

There is an awkward pause.

Jimmy It wasn't a trick question.

John She's—

Edie She's gone out. To visit some relatives of hers in Malahide.

John *stares at* **Edie** *in disbelief. She returns his look, pleading with him silently to say nothing.*

Edie She's due back later. You might meet her.

Jimmy Ah, isn't that a shame? We were dying to meet her, weren't we, Kathleen?

Kathleen We were, of course.

John *makes to exit stage right towards the kitchen.*

Edie Will you have some ice with that, Kathleen? John, get your Auntie Kathleen some ice there like a good man.

John *exits in the direction of the kitchen.* **Jimmy** *waits until he's safely out of earshot before speaking.*

Jimmy So tell us – what's she like? John's fancy woman. Is she a good-looker, she is?

Kathleen Jimmy!

Jimmy I'm only asking. (*To* **Edward**) Eddie – you're a man hasn't lost his appreciation for the fairer sex – what's she like?

Edward Couldn't be nicer. Which is perhaps more than can be said for her hosts.

Jimmy Go on away out of that – she couldn't have come to a more welcoming household, isn't that right, Edie? Tell us, is she blonde? I'd say John's a blonde man now all right.

Edward *turns away from* **Jimmy**. **Jimmy** *barely notices.*

Edie So tell us, Jimmy—

Tara She's black. Of African extraction, I think the correct phrase is these days.

Edie Tara!

Tara I'm not saying there's anything wrong with that. But you can't deny the fact.

Edie I just don't see that it's relevant.

Jimmy You're having me on?

Tara Scout's honour. (*She glances towards the door to make sure* **John** *is still out of earshot, then turns back to* **Jimmy**) And the reason he didn't go to midnight mass is because he's become a Buddhist.

Jimmy No!

Tara Cross my heart and hope to die.

A beat. **Jimmy** *looks around incredulously for confirmation of this revelation.* **Sean** *looks away as* **Edie** *smiles awkwardly.*

Jimmy A bloody Buddhist, wha'? Isn't that a good one!

Kathleen Now, Jimmy—

Sean Well, each to his own, as the fella says.

At that moment, **John** *arrives back with the ice.*

Jimmy There he is – the man himself. The Buddhist of Castleknock, wha'?

Jimmy *laughs raucously at his own wit.* **John** *glares at* **Edie**.

Jimmy Come on in here, Johnny boy, and give us a go on your magic carpet!
And he starts to guffaw again. The others eye **John** *warily, wondering how he will react to* **Jimmy***'s teasing.* **Edie**, *in particular, catches his eye with an imploring look that says 'Please just grin and bear it – for me'. A silence. At length* **Jimmy** *stops laughing.*

Jimmy Ah, here. I'm only joking you, Johnny boy. Sure, each to his own, as your daddy says. Isn't that right, Kathleen?

Kathleen It is. And you'd do well to remember that.

Jimmy Sure, I was only joking. John knows that, don't you, John?

John *just smiles. A pause.*

Edie Edward, fix your Uncle Jimmy another whiskey there like a good lad, will you?

Edward *crosses to the drinks cabinet and starts to pour a whiskey for* **Jimmy**.

Jimmy Good man yourself, Eddie.

There is a slightly awkward pause as **John** *and* **Edward** *fix the drinks and hand them out.*

Tara Speaking of joking, tell us the one about the Pope dying again there, Uncle Jimmy.

Edie Oh yes, I love that story – how does it go again?

Jimmy Ach, ye don't want to be hearing that old story again, do ye?

Tara 'Course we do, Jimmy. Don't we, Da?

Sean I'm not sure we have much choice, do we?

Tara How does it start again, Jimmy?

Jimmy Well, it starts with the two fellas working at the

Vatican – the Irish fella and the English fella, and – ah here, sure I've told ye this story hundreds of times. Doesn't anyone have a Christmas joke?

Tara We can tell Christmas jokes afterwards. After the Vatican story.

Jimmy (*sighs*) Well, the Irish fella and the English fella are working away in the kitchens of the Vatican when word comes through that the Pope is after dyin'. And all the staff are sent home until they can pick a new Pope. Because it's an awful complicated process picking a new Pope, so they have to close the whole of the Vatican down until they can pick one. Is that the right word? 'Pick'? What's the word I'm looking for?

Edward Elect.

Jimmy Good man yourself, Eddie – that's the word. They have to close the Vatican down while they elect a new Pope. Jays, how did I forget that word?

Kathleen God, Jimmy – would you ever get on with it. We'll be here all night.

Jimmy Right so, where was I? Oh yes, the two lads are after being sent home while they elect a new Pope in the Vatican. Only before they go, they're warned not to breathe a word to anyone. They want to have the replacement Pope all lined up, d'you see, before they announce that the old Pope is dead – for the purposes of continuity, and the well-being of the flock and all that kind of thing, d'you know?

Tara I love this story.

Jimmy So now home they go, the Irish fella and the English fella, and on the plane home, the Irish fella, being a betting man, he says to the English fella, 'I'll tell you now, William what we'll do,' says he. 'You go back to London, and I'll go back to Galway, and we'll raise every penny we can lay our hands on and put a bet on the Pope being dead within the next month, and think of the odds we'll get! We'll make a fortune.' And the English fella thinks this is a great idea altogether, and this is what they'll do. And so off they go their separate ways. Anyways, the two lads lose touch, and ten years later, the English fella finds himself in Galway on business – 'cos he's a multi-millionaire now, like, after mortgaging his house, and his mother's house, and his sister's house, and everyone belonging to him's house, and putting the whole lot on the Pope being dead within the month at odds of a thousand to one. But when he eventually finds his old mate Mick from the Vatican and pays him a visit in his top-of-the-range Rolls Royce, isn't Mick living in a tiny hovel, without a penny to his name except what he makes begging in Galway town. And the English fella is amazed, and he says to Mick (*affects English accent*) 'What happened, Mick,' he says – (*normal accent*) he was English, you know? 'What happened Mick,' he says. 'Did you not do the same as me and put every penny you could lay your hands on on the Pope being dead within a month and become a multi-millionaire overnight like I did myself?' And Mick looks at him sadly and says he, 'I did,' he says. 'I raised every penny I could lay me hands on. But do you know,' he says, 'when it came to putting the bet on, I couldn't resist a double with the Archbishop of Canterbury!'

Tara *and* **Edie** *laugh delightedly at the punchline.* **Kathleen** *smiles, obviously proud of her husband's ability to tell a joke and hold an audience. Even* **Edward** *and* **Sean** *can't help smiling. Only* **John***'s smile seems forced, unnatural.*

Jimmy You'll never get the Irish out of Ireland, hah!

Tara The Archbishop of Canterbury! I love that story!

Edward (*dry*) It must be the way he tells them.

Edie God, I love a good laugh at Christmas. Does anyone know any Christmas jokes? Edward, you must have an old Christmas joke for us.

Edward I didn't think they came much older than Uncle Jimmy's joke.

Edie How about you, Tara? Do you know any Christmas jokes, love?

Tara Ach, I'm no good at telling jokes, Mum. Sure, you know that.

John I'll tell you a Christmas joke.

Jimmy Good man yourself, John. (*Winks at* **Tara**) Who said Buddhists have no sense of humour, wha'?
Edie (*quickly*) Go on, John. Give us your Christmas joke.

Jimmy *Ciúnas. Ciúnas.* Whist now for the Buddhist of Castleknock!

Kathleen Jimmy! Be quiet!

John Well there was this family – 'd'you see' – a normal, run-of-the-mill, middle-class family—

Jimmy Like ourselves!

Kathleen Whist now, Jimmy – you've had your chance. Go on, John.

John Well, there was this ordinary middle-class family – from Castleknock, say – and whenever anyone would ask them the question, 'How did you get over the Christmas', they would always reply with the same stock answer: 'Ah, you know yourself – very quiet'.

Jimmy 'Tis true for you. That's what people always say, all right. 'Ah, very quiet.'

Kathleen Jimmy!

John And begob, it didn't matter if the Christmas was, for the sake of argument, very loud; or very raucous; or full of intrigue and surprise and extraordinary occurences which wouldn't look out of place in a murder mystery novel; whenever anyone asked any member of this Castleknock family 'How did you get over the Christmas' – an interesting turn of phrase in itself, incidentally, likening the Yuletide period, as it does, to a particularly virulent bout of yellow fever – but whenever any member of this model family was asked 'How did you get over the Christmas', each and every one of them could be relied upon to trot out the old refrain – Edward?

Edward Ah, you know yourself – very quiet.

John Got it in one. In fact, I think one could safely say that were a murder to be committed in this family on Christmas Day itself—

Edward Not an improbable event, in all fairness.

John Or a rape, say, or any other … atrocity – one suspects that the answer to the question 'How did you get over the Christmas?' would remain mercifully unaltered.

Jimmy (*delighted*) It would too! He's dead right!

John So despite the fact that it was a good ten to fifteen years since this model family from Castleknock had got as far as the second course of their annual Christmas dinner without someone leaving the table in tears, or someone punching someone else—

Edie Please, John—

John Or, as happened on one memorable occasion, the police nearly being called when one member of the family spilled red wine on the new trousers of another member of the family – sorry about that, by the way, Edward—

Edward Please, don't mention it.
John Thereby adding to the kerfuffle before dinner even began when yet another member of the family – who probably should have known better – rather overdid the Christmas cheer and had to have her stomach pumped—

Tara You bastard.

John Still, even on this most unquiet year, the family from Castleknock trotted off to midnight mass together and stood around cheerfully afterwards in the canary yellow earmuffs the youngest member of the family had bought them each as a special Yuletide gift the year before, telling any friends and neighbours who would care to listen that Christmas had indeed been very quiet.

Edward (*tugging his forelock*) You know yourself.

DJ *appears down the stairs to see what's going on.*

John Ah, DJ. The donator of the yellow earmuffs himself. You're just in time to hear the end of my joke.

Jimmy *Is* there an end to this joke? Because I, for one, am getting—

John Oh yes, we're building nicely to the climax now. Because one year, it came to pass that a new element was added to the mix, which was to spoil the carefully balanced cake completely. Think, if you will, of what might happen if you added gelagnite instead of gelatine—

Edward Semtex instead of sugar?

John Armalites in place of armagnac?

Edward Machetes in place of marzipan?

DJ What are they talking about?

John Excellent, DJ. A fine and worthy contribution to the conversation. What indeed?

Sean John—

John Well, the point is that no longer could this family from Castleknock – let's call them the Castles—

Edward The Castles from Castleknock? I like it.

John No longer could the Castles convince themselves—

Edward Or by extension others—

John That their Christmas – or indeed their lives – were very quiet. Because although this new presence wasn't like them – begob, the poor deluded thing didn't even celebrate Christmas –

Edward Shame!

John But worse – she had turned the head of one of the family's favoured sons and brainwashed him into an almost cavalier casting off of God and country—

Edward God bless Ireland!

John Of nationhood and religion, of tradition and customs which so enraged the Castles from Castleknock that they turned on the devil incarnate, and froze her out, and took every opportunity to point out that she was, as she knew herself to be deep down, an outsider, an interloper, a queer and dangerous influence—

Edie John, please – stop it!

John Until finally she could take no more, and the poor woman – herself brought up on fables and stories of a sceptred isle of a hundred thousand welcomes and blessings – the poor woman fled, and the Castles were sad, and mourned dutifully, but not enough to halt the refrain 'Ah, you know yourself, very quiet' or to stop them inviting their favourite uncle who nobody liked because he was a small-minded, racist bigot—

Edward Easy, John …

A beat. **John** *looks at* **Edward**, *then across at* **Jimmy** *with barely disguised contempt.* **Edie** *is in tears now, her head in her hands.*

Jimmy Go on, John.

John That's it. That's the end of the joke.

A pause.

DJ I don't get it. (*A beat*) Where's the punchline?

John You're the punchline, DJ. And thank Christ we've got you, or we'd all have gone mad years ago.

A silence. At length, **Kathleen** *speaks.*

Kathleen I think … I think we should go.

Tara But we haven't had our sing-song!

Kathleen I don't think anyone's really in the mood for a sing-song right now, Tara, love.

Tara Why, because John's turned into a miserable, bitter little misanthrope? You're not going to let that spoil our Christmas sing-song, are you? Uncle Jimmy?

Jimmy (*looking straight at* **John**) I'll give yous a song.

Kathleen Jimmy, please—

Jimmy Tara's right. It'd be shame to allow our good-natured annual sing-song to be … sabotaged. Johnny boy? You wouldn't object to one song now, would you?

John *shrugs.*

Edie Jimmy please, don't—

Jimmy Good man yourself. We can salvage something from our Stephen's Day yet.

Tara Go on, so, Jimmy – give us your song. And I'll fix us all another drink.

Jimmy It's more of a poem, now, though, than a song.

Tara A poem. Sure, we love poetry in this house, don't we, Eddie?

Edward Love it? We live it, Tara. Our lives are just one long Gaelic lament.

Jimmy Fair enough, so.

Jimmy *clears his throat and starts to recite the Luke Kelly poem, 'For What Died the Sons of Róisín'. He begins in an almost gay, jovial manner, a grotesque parody of the gravelly-throated Dublin poet. But as the poem progresses, he becomes more focused, less showy, more intent. He keeps a close eye on* **John** *throughout the* *recitation. But* **John***'s face betrays no emotion. Instead, he continues to look down at the floor throughout.*

Jimmy For what died the sons of Róisín, was it fame?
For what died the sons of Róisín, was it fame?
For what flowed Ireland's blood in rivers,
That began when Brian chased the Dane,
And did not cease nor has not ceased,
With the brave sons of '16,
For what died the sons of Róisín, was it fame?

For what died the sons of Róisín, was it greed?
For what died the sons of Róisín, was it greed?
Was it greed that drove Wolfe Tone
to a pauper's death in a cell of cold wet stone?
Will German, French or Dutch inscribe
the epitaph of Emmet?
When we have sold enough of Ireland
to be but strangers in it.
For what died the sons of Róisín, was it greed?

To whom do we owe our allegiance today?
To whom do we owe our allegiance today?
To those brave men who fought and died
that Róisín live again with pride?
Her sons at home to work and sing,
Her youth to dance and make her valleys ring,
Or the faceless men who for mark and dollar,
Betray her to the highest bidder,
To whom do we owe our allegiance today?

For what suffer our patriots today?
For what suffer our patriots today?
They have a language problem, so they say,

How to write 'No Trespass'
must grieve their heart full sore,
We got rid of one strange language
now we are faced with many, many more,
For what suffer our patriots today?

Sin a bhfuil.

There is a tense pause at the end of **Jimmy***'s recital. Nobody is quite sure how to react.*

John (*quiet*) I'm going out to look for Rai.

He crosses to get his coat. The others watch him go.

Edie Wait!

They all turn to look at her in surprise.

Edie I'm sorry, Kathleen, but I think you and Jimmy should leave.

Jimmy Edie?

Edie We'd like to be left alone now. As a family.

Jimmy Edie, I didn't start it.

Edie I'd like you to leave all the same.

Jimmy *looks at her, then nods slowly.*

Jimmy Fair enough. (*He crosses to get his coat, brushing past*

John *as he does so*) Are you right, Kathleen?

And he disappears out the front door. A pause, as **Kathleen** *puts on her coat.*

Edie I'm sorry, Kathleen.

Kathleen I understand, love.

Edie I'll call over in the next day or two.

Kathleen Do that. (*A beat*) And thanks for your hospitality.

Jimmy (*off*) Kathleen.

Kathleen I'll see you all soon.

And she follows **Jimmy** *off. A silence.*

John I'm sorry, everybody. For ruining your afternoon.

Edie You didn't ruin anything, John. It was Jimmy ruined it.

John Still and all … I'm sorry.

A pause.

Edie We're sorry too, love.

Tara Are we?

Edie For not being more accommodating. Aren't we, Sean?

Sean We are. And for putting you through that.

John Ach …

Another long pause.

John You know, you're not meant to get attached to things as a Buddhist. (*A beat*) Looks like I'm going to make an even worse Buddhist than I did a Catholic.

Edie We'll find her, John. I promise you we'll find her. Come on, everybody. Get your coats.

Tara Where are we going?

Edie We're going out to look for Rai. All of us. Come on. Get your coats and let's go.

Tara *is about to protest, but something in* **Edie***'s voice, and the events of the past couple of minutes, make her think better of it. She hesitates a beat, then crosses and exits.* **Sean** *follows her, as does* **Edward**. **DJ** *heads towards the kitchen.*

Edie Where do you think you're going?

DJ I'm going to tell Tommy I can't go to Funderland! God!

Edie As long as you're not trying to get out of looking for Rai.

DJ I don't want to get out of looking for Rai. I was the one out looking for her while yous were all sitting around talking shite with Uncle Jimmy!

Edie It's true for you. Go on, tell Tommy you can't go to Funderland and let's get cracking.

DJ *and* **Edie** *exit, leaving* **John** *alone on the stage. He sits by the fire, exhausted and dejected, his head in his hands. After a couple of seconds* **Edward** *appears, holding his coat. He stands for a moment watching his brother, wanting desperately to reach out to him, but unsure of how to go about it. Eventually,* **John** *looks up and sees him. He smiles a forced, tired smile at his brother. A pause.*

Edward That snow is coming down heavy now. Looks like it's going to stick. If only it had come yesterday. Mum would have had her dream white Christmas.

John If it had come yesterday, Rai could well have frozen to death by now.

Edward I'm sorry, I didn't …

John 'S all right. (*A beat*) Jesus, Edward – if anything's happened to her …

And he starts to cry silently. **Edward** *crosses and puts his arm around* **John**, *who buries his head in his brother's chest.* **DJ** *appears back into the living room carrying his jacket.*

DJ God, look at yis! Not only is me sister turning into me mother, but I've a pair of fuckin' queers for brothers! No wonder I failed my Junior Cert!

Edie (*appearing back*) Julian!

DJ I don't believe it – she's everywhere!

Edward Omnipresent is the word you're looking for Jules. Like the Buddah.

DJ Not you as well! Jaysus!

Edie Right. Come on, the lot of you, and let's get a move on.

The family starts to make its way towards the front door. But just as **Edie** *is opening the door, the phone rings.* **Sean** *is closest to it and he picks it up. The others watch him intently.*

Sean Just one moment. (*Holds phone out to* **John**) It's the police.

John *glances nervously at his mother, before crossing to take the receiver from* **Edward**.

John Hello? Yes, that's right. (*A beat*) Is she all right? (*A beat*) I'll come straight up. Thank you. (*He puts the phone down and looks up at the others, numb*) They've found Rai. They've taken her up to the hospital.

Edie Jesus, Mary and Joseph. Is she ...?

John They don't know. She's still unconscious.
Edward Come on – I'll run you up to the hospital.

Edward *grabs his coat and follows* **John** *out the front door. A silence.* **Edie** *sinks into the nearest armchair.* **Tara** *crosses to sit on the arm of the chair.* **Sean** *and* **DJ** *stand in silent shock as the lights fade slowly to black.*

Blackout.

ACT 3 SCENE 2

In the blackout, a loud and bracing rendition of 'We Wish You a Merry Christmas'. When the lights eventually come up, it is a week or so later. **Edward** *stands looking out of the window as* **Sean** *reads his paper.* **Tara** *appears stage left. She is clearly tense, agitated.*

Tara Has anybody seen Rai's jacket?

Sean Did John not take it up to the hospital to her?

Tara Would I be looking for it if he had?

A beat.

Sean I wonder what's keeping them?

Tara John rang to say they'd be delayed. The police were still taking statements and that.

Sean They'll miss their flights if they're not careful.

Tara That's why I'm packing Rai's bags for her. Give them a head start.

Sean Poor Rai. Wasn't much of a holiday for her, was it? Beaten to a pulp by a crowd of gurriers, followed by three days above in the hospital.

Tara On her first visit here too. No doubt now she'll leave thinking we're all like those … animals.

Edward No doubt.

Tara How was she when you went up?

Sean I never got in to see her. The nurse said she wasn't really up to having visitors, only John. And sure, could you blame her after what happened?

Tara Well – it's up to us to redress the balance by showing her some honest to goodness Irish hospitality for the few minutes they'll have left. Is the kettle on?

And she exits towards the kitchen, left. A beat.

Edward She's changed her tune.

A pause. **Sean** *sighs deeply and looks at his watch. Suddenly, he looks like an old man.*

Sean I'm telling you, if I ever lay my hands on the bastards attacked her, they'll not get away from me alive. So help me God.

Edward Well, let he who is without sin …

Sean This is it. (*A beat.* **Sean** *looks at his watch*) They won't even have time for a cup of tea in the hand if they don't hurry up. (*Another beat*) I think I'll maybe go and help Tara with the tea. Give myself something to do, d'you know?

Sean *exits towards the kitchen.* **Edward** *lies heavily on the couch and closes his eyes. After a couple of seconds,* **DJ** *appears in from the hallway. He looks around furtively, decides that the room is* *empty, then hurries over to the Christmas tree. He pulls up a chair, takes another look around to satisfy himself that no one is coming, then pulls Mammy's Angel from under his jumper. He quickly puts the Angel on the top of the tree, then disappears out of the room post-haste. After a couple of seconds,* **Edward** *speaks.*

Edward Careful you don't drop that, DJ. It must be worth – ooh, the price of a motorised scooter I'd say?

DJ *stops.*

DJ I swapped it back. Satisfied?

Edward If you'd only waited till the Christmas decorations had been taken down, no one would have been any the wiser till this time next year.

DJ Jaysus, no wonder I'm a juvenile delinquent with an older brother like you!

And he heads off stage left, passing **Sean** *as he goes.*

Sean Where are you … ?

But **DJ** *is gone.* **Sean** *might follow him, but he is distracted by the sound of* **Edie, John** *and* **Rai** *returning.*

Edie (*off*) Mind yourself there now.

Sean *turns to put the biscuits he is carrying down on the sideboard.*

Sean (*to* **Edward**) Return of the war heroine, wha'?

He pulls up as **Rai** *comes into the living room, helped by* **Edie** *and* **John**. **Rai** *walks using a single crutch. Her face and neck are heavily bandaged, and her face is swollen and bruised. Her free arm is in a sling. Her voice, when she speaks, is cracked and weak.*

Sean Good Jesus …

Rai Not even a pretty face any more.

At that moment **Tara** *bursts in. She too pulls up as she sees the extent of the damage.*

Rai It's not as bad as it looks. The crutch is only temporary.

Sean *shakes his head in disbelief. Another silence.*

Sean What did the Guards say?

John They didn't hold out much hope of catching them.

Sean How many of them were there?

Rai Three or four – it's hard to tell when you're curled up in a ball trying to protect yourself from being kicked to death.

Sean All young fellas?

Rai *nods.*

Edie It'd frighten you, wouldn't it? For the future of the country. When the young people are …
She trails off, unable to bring herself to continue.

Edward (*gentle*) It isn't off the ground they licked it, Mum …

Edie No. No, I suppose it isn't.

Sean (*to* **Rai**) Some memories you'll take home of the land of Saints and Scholars. You'll be glad to see the back of it.

Rai It'll pass. One day. One day I might even want to come back. (*To* **John**) Did you book the taxi?

Tara Edward's offered to give us a lift.

Rai Damn police kept haranguing me for every last detail. Where was I going when it happened, what was I doing in the park. Had I provoked them. I told them I didn't see them, and I've no idea where I was going – I've never even been to this damn country before in my life. But they didn't seem to get it. Or if they got it, they weren't that interested.

Sean What did they say? Did they think they'd catch them?

Rai They said they'd investigate. But I ain't holding my breath.

John The Guards said they're dealing with this kind of thing three or four times a week.

Edward (*facetious*) Even in Castleknock?

A pause.

Rai I'd better get a move on or we'll miss the flight.

John I'll give you a hand.

Rai Thank you.

John *crosses and puts his arm around* **Rai***'s shoulder, and they make as if to exit to the hall.*

Tara (*awkward*) Actually, I … took the liberty of packing your bags for you. I hope you don't mind. I just thought with you being in a hurry, and just arriving back from the hospital and … Well – I hope you don't mind.

A beat as **Rai** *looks at her.*

Rai Thanks, Tara. Thank you.

A pause.

Edward Well, if you'll excuse me. In the absence of someone to pack my bags for me, I'd better get a move on.

Edward *disappears into the hall and up the stairs.*

John I'll get our stuff.

He gently manouevres **Rai** *into an armchair by the fire, then turns and exits into the hall.*

Edie Sean, run up there and help John. I'll make us a quick cup of tea in the hand.

And she exits left as **Sean** *disappears up the stairs, leaving* **Rai** *and* **Tara** *alone together. An awwkard silence.*

Tara I meant what I said earlier. I really am sorry.

A beat. **Rai** *acknowledges the apology in silence.*

Rai (*eventually*) I heard about … your ex-husband … wanting to keep your baby and that.

Tara Yes.

Rai I'm very sorry.

Tara Thank you.

Rai If there's anything we can do, me and John … you know?

Tara I'm going up there now. His parents have a mobile home near the Giant's Causeway. If he thinks he's going to take Sean Óg off me without a fight, he's got another thing coming.

Rai Attah girl. You fight your corner. (*A beat*) Good luck, yeah?

Tara Thank you.

Another pause.

Rai Did you know there's a Tara in Tibetan Buddhist mythology? Two, actually. White Tara and Green Tara.

Tara I always thought Tara was an Irish name.

Rai Maybe. But according to the Mahayana scriptures, the Enlightened Being Chenrezi was given the task of rescuing all living beings from *samsara* – the cycle of endless rebirth – and helping them to reach nirvana. But the task was so onerous he became exhausted and depressed, and cried great tears of despair which fell to the ground and grew into lotus flowers. From these lotus flowers were born the enlightened beings Green Tara and White Tara, whose destiny was to assist Chenrezi in his work and become symbols of the Buddha's great compassion towards all people.

Tara The patron saint of compassion, hah? Who'd have thought it?

Rai Sean Óg, for one.

Tara Maybe.

Rai I've heard the way you talk about him. He's a very lucky boy.

Tara Thank you.

At that moment **Edie** *appears with a mug of tea.*

Edie There you go, Rai. Excuse the presentation.

Rai *takes the tea from* **Edie**. **John** *appears in from the hall carrying two large bags.*

John I think that's the lot.

Tara (*to* **Rai**) You don't mind me coming as far as the train station with you?

Rai Of course not.

Rai *smiles at* **Tara**, *who smiles back awkwardly. Nobody is quite sure what to say next.*

Rai Before we go – I got you a little thank you present. For having me. It's nothing big – just a little something for the household.

Edie Ah, Rai – did you hear that, Sean? Rai got us a present.

Rai (*rummaging in the front compartment of her bag*) I wanted to give it to you before I left.

Edie Rai, love, that's very kind of you. (*Reading the tag on the present*) 'A little something no Christian home should be without. Happy New Year. Love, Rai'.

Rai If you don't like it John and I can bring it back.

Edie *pulls open the packaging. An ornamental statue of the Bodhisattva Kuan-Yin falls out into her lap.*

Edie It's absolutely gorgeous. Isn't it gorgeous, Sean?

Sean It certainly is.

Edie Oh Rai, it really is beautiful. (*A beat*) What is it?

Sean Ach, Edie, can you not see what it is? It's a Buddha.

Rai It's a Bodhisattva, actually. That's like the next one down from a Buddha.

John A Bodhisattva is a kind of Buddha who has stayed behind to help the rest of us lesser mortals to reach Nirvana.

Rai This one is a Chinese Boddhisatva called Kuan Yin. (*To* **Tara**) The Chinese version of Chenrezi. (*To the others*) It means literally, 'taking heed of the sound'. Chinese Buddhists believe she watches over the world listening to its cries and saving people from pain and anguish and disease.

Sean A sort of a Buddhist Mary, wha'?

Rai If you like.

Edie It's beautiful, Rai. And a lovely gesture.

Edward And one, I might suggest, of which we are entirely undeserving.

Rai Well – it's just something I … wanted you to have …

A pause.

Edward Right. I hate to break up the party, but it's time we were making a move.

Sean All good things, hah? No getting away from it.

Tara No. See you, Mum.

And she gives **Edie** *a kiss.*

Edie Goodbye, Tara, love.

Tara Shit. I think I'm going to cry.

Edie Go on – don't be getting me started.

Tara Bye, Dad.

Sean Bye, love. And good luck with Paudge.

Edward Are you right? See you, Mum.

Edie (*to* **Edward**, *giving him a hug*) Goodbye, love.

And **Edward** *heads for the front door.*

Tara Thanks for a … lovely Christmas, Mum.

Edward You're going to miss your train, Tara.

Tara Right.

And she turns and follows **Edward** *out into the hall.* **Edie** *sees them out.*

John Take care of yourself, Dad.

Sean You too. And take care of Rai.

John I will.

John *holds out his hand for a handshake. A beat, before* **John** *leans forward and gives* **Sean** *a very tentative, very awkward hug. By now* **Edie** *has returned.* **John** *turns to her.*

John Bye, Mum.

Edie Goodbye, love.

John *hugs her. They hold one another for some time. Meanwhile,* **Sean** *comes up to* **Rai**.

Sean Will you come and see us again sometime?

Rai Who knows? If I'm invited.

Sean You're welcome here anytime, Rai. Isn't she, Edie?

Edie Of course you are, Rai, love.

Rai Goodbye, Mrs Sullivan. And thank you.

Edie No, Rai. Thank you.

A beat. **Rai** *turns and starts to hobble towards the door, helped by* **John**.

Rai Say goodbye to DJ for us.

Sean If we can find him.

Sean *and* **Edie** *stand as we hear the noise of the others getting into the car, etc., off. Ad libbed goodbyes from* **Edie** *and* **Sean** *as we hear the car pulling off.*

Edie Well. That's it. Just the three of us again.

Sean Thanks be, as the fella says, to the Divine Jaysus.

Edie (*with less conviction than usual*) Sean!

Sean Well, they're more trouble than they're worth. I mean, what's the reward for twenty years of hard labour? The prospect of a whole load more of them in their own images getting under your feet every Christmas? Good riddance, I say.

A beat.

Edie (*picking up the Bodhisattva*) Kuan Yin. She who takes heed of the sound.

Sean You've a great memory for names all the same, Edie.

Edie Sure, didn't I spend my youth remembering the names of the saints? One little Chinese saint isn't going to baffle me at this stage of my life. What about putting her here on the mantlepiece? Or how about …

Edie *looks about the room for a suitable resting place for Kuan Yin. She stops short as she notices that the angel her mother gave her is back on the top of the tree.*

Sean What?

Edie Mammy's Angel. He's back on the top of the tree. How did he … ?

Edie *and* **Sean** (*together*) Julian!

Sean The little shite!

A beat.

Sean Better late than never, I suppose.

A pause.

Edie (*eventually*) You know, Sean, maybe Mammy's Angel has had her day.

Sean How do you mean?

Edie Well, maybe its time we gave someone else a go at the top of the tree.

Sean Kuan Yin?

Edie There's no harm in seeing what it looks like …

Sean There is not. No harm at all.

Edie And she *is* sitting, so it might look very …

Sean Appropriate?

Edie You never know. Besides, there's no law says she has to stay there if we don't like it.

Edie *hands him the nearest chair.* **Sean** *positions the chair and carefully takes the angel from the top of the tree, replacing it with the statue of Kuan Yin. He gets back down and the two of them stand for a second or two looking up at the top of the tree.*

Edie What do you think?

Sean Not bad. It's not your mother's angel, but … mm – not bad at all.

Edie I think she looks as if she was born like that.

Sean What, with the tip of a Christmas tree up her arse?

Edie Sean! No … sitting cross-legged and serene on top of her perch, surveying the world and listening to its cries.

Sean (*teasing*) You're not thinking of converting … ?

Edie I'm too old to be thinking of converting to new religions, Sean. I'm only just over what the nuns did to me.

Edie *sits back on the sofa. A pause as they sit looking up at the statue of Kuan Yin on the top of the tree. The lights start to fade very slowly – almost imperceptibly – from now until the end of the play, accentuating the glow of the fairy lights on the Christmas tree, and* **Rai***'s Boddhisatva perched on the top.*

Edie It wasn't a complete disaster, was it, Sean?

Sean No. Not a complete disaster.

Edie I just so desperately wanted it to be nice for them. That's all I cared about. I wanted it to be nice for them. And for you. In case it's our last Christmas …

Sean Edie, it was a lovely Christmas. And please God, we'll have many more just like it. (*A beat*) Well … maybe not just like it.

Edie *laughs gently. A beat.*

Sean It might be hard to believe right at this moment, but who knows – in years to come, maybe we'll look back on this as our best Christmas ever.

Edie *smiles wearily at him.*

Edie Maybe.

They hold one another's gaze for a couple of seconds, then start to kiss, a long passionate kiss one suspects they haven't experienced in some time. After a few seconds, **DJ** *appears in from the hall, unnoticed by either* **Edie** *or* **Sean**.

DJ Oh my God! Youse two are disgusting!

Blackout.

THE END

Monged

BY GARY DUGGAN

Monged was first performed by Fishamble: The New Play Company on 14 April 2005 at Project Arts Centre, Dublin, with the following cast and production team:

Bernard	Paul Reid
Dave	Rory Keenan
Ray	Jonathan Byrne
Director	Jim Culleton
Designer	Sabine Dargent
Lighting Designer	Mark Galione
Sound Designers	Vincent Doherty Ivan Birthistle
Production Manager	Des Kenny
Stage Directors	Breege Brennan Mags Corscadden
PR	Cerstin Mudiwa
Script Development	Gavin Kostick

This production toured Ireland and to the UK in 2006 with Emmet Kirwan in the role of Dave.

Monged was subsequently presented as a staged reading by Fishamble in association with Origin in 2007 at the Glucksman Ireland House in New York. This version was directed by Jim Culleton and produced by George Heslin.

Monged is the winner of the overall Stewart Parker Trust Award 2006

'Duggan writes very well ... Jim Culleton's slickly energetic production ... a cross between *Ulysses* and a buddy movie ... pacy, punchy narratives ... a little gem of a performance' *Fintan O'Toole, The Irish Times*

'fast-paced, blackly-comic tale is directed with a deft hand ... spot-on performance ... Duggan and Fishamble have pretty much got it right' *The Event Guide*

'well written ... well staged ... a lot of laughs ... possible cult hit' *RTÉ 1, The View*

'manic energy ... constant movement ... hilarious' *Irish Independent*

'richly evocative ... wonderful images ... fine, pacy, stylised direction ... Duggan writes beautifully ... (Fishamble) continues to take risks on new writing and new ideas ... smash hit ... climb aboard and enjoy the ride' *Sunday Tribune*

'an excellent play ... perfect' *entertainment.ie*

' ... relentless pace and drugged up momentum ... rich description and a generous fix of wit ... entertaining' *rte.ie*

'a great show ... not without controversy ... a must-see' *Newstalk 106*

'a night at a Fishamble production is rarely (if ever) wasted ... *Monged* is cracking, wicked, *phat* even ... well worth a visit' *Village*

'Duggan's writing is pacy and raw ... thoroughly engaging' *In Dublin*

'hot-shot writer ... imaginative and insightful ... well worth a visit' *Hot Press*

'As ever on the hungry hunt for new voices, Fishamble turned up Gary Duggan, the kind of storyteller that 2005 found in short supply ... one of the top 5 shows of 2005' *Evening Herald*

'director Jim Culleton recognises, like his designers, that *Monged* works best as a trip ... words sweep the characters along with the pace of a fast-cut film montage ... the script and stage provide constant stimulation ... *Monged* hums with authorial insouciance and its limber approach conceals a more ambitious project: to render a city in surfaces, to measure youth in moments' *Irish Theatre Magazine*

CHARACTERS

Bernard – *works for an insurance company, wants to be a writer, twenty-one*
Dave – *works on a building site, wants to be a drug dealer, twenty-four*
Ray – *works in a bar, wants to be a musician, twenty-five*

The play takes place in Dublin City over the course of a weekend in July. The stage is a simple neutral space, which can become many places. At the back of the stage is a booth-style sitting area (which can be sat on or climbed over).

1: A CITY STREET, MORNING – FLASHFORWARD

A dim spotlight fades up on **Bernard**. *He's sitting on the edge of the stage, looking utterly wasted. He talks to himself with his eyes closed.*

Bernard I'm sitting down on the ground. The ground's great like that, the way you can sit on it or lie on it anytime you want. Water's not like that. You can't sit or lie on water whenever you feel like it. You'd sink or drown, or something. But the ground's always there for you to rely on wherever you go. Always there when you feel like sitting down or lying down. I love the ground. (**Bernard** *opens his eyes, he looks about dizzily, holding his head*) What am I doing? My brain's not working. I feel like a half-made jigsaw that's been shook about inside its box. Oh yeah, that's why I'm sitting here. Taking a breath of calm to rearrange myself. Try to put all my pieces back into their proper places. OK, I must know something. I know some things always make sense, even now. My name. I remember that. Bernard.
My age. Twenty-two – no. Twenty-one. So used to lying about my age that I've started to believe myself. When was my last birthday? What did I do? Ah, that doesn't matter now. There's something else more important. What? I was with someone a while ago. Where are they gone? Who was it again?

The light snaps off **Bernard**; *he disappears.*

2: DRIVING, COUNTRYSIDE, AFTERNOON

The light snaps up on **Dave***; he's driving fast. His head bounces to the techno music playing on the radio. He talks to the audience.*

Dave I said Castlebridge Avenue, not Castlebridge Road. Me head is wrecked. And this cunt is gonna think this is my fault. Why can't things be simple? A meeting. A negotiation. A deal. A transaction. And a drink to finish it off. Simple. Right? Of course not, 'cause some spa always fucks it up. And it's not even that hard. At least it shouldn't be. Look at Ken sitting in the pub all day. Not a fucking care in the world. While I clean up his mess. Prick. I said Castlebridge Avenue, not Castlebridge Road. Why the hell couldn't the Cork Fella just give me his number in the first place? Then I could have just called him and told him exactly where to meet me meself. But no. Ken has to make it all covert and clandestine. Turn it into *Goodfellas*. Posin' prick. Big Brother'ud have a conniption if he knew I borrowed his car for this shit. But what other choice do I have? No other way to get out to these badlands.
As if I'd arrange to meet all the fucking way out here. In the middle of nowhere. That new estate is just around the corner from the village, fucking walking distance. There's no-one around there. No-one living there yet. Perfect place to meet. Castlebridge Avenue. Simple.
But no. Fucking Ken couldn't even relay *that* shit correctly. Why am I still with him? (**Dave** *notices someone by the side of the road; he slows down*) There. There he is. Green Honda Civic. 98 C: the Cork Fella. Jesus, he's an ugly fucker. Right culchie red head on him. (**Dave** *mimes stopping the car; he turns the radio off and gets out*) Screech the tyres. Hop out. Walk towards the Civic. Cork Fella leps out quickly. (**Dave** *acts out the Cork Fella with an exaggerated Cork accent and swagger*)

'What the fuck is the story?' (*To audience*) Ragin' red neck on him. Heavy-looking Londis bag in his paw. (*Talking to Cork Fella*) Not my fault man. A fuck-up. I told Ken Castlebridge Avenue, not Castlebridge Road. I was waiting up at the estate for twenty minutes. I was fucked around as much—(*As Cork Fella*) 'Me bollocks!' (*To audience*) Cork Fella cuts me off, pulling out a gun from his Levis. What the fuck? I think. This guy for real? That a real gun? (*As Cork Fella*) 'We arranged here, half three, and you're fuckin' me about boy.' (*To audience*) Don't move. Barely breathe. Gun pointing at me. Real gun. Can read the numbers on the side. Smell the oil off it. Smells like parts from Big Brother's bike in the shed. Stay cool. (*Talking to Cork Fella*) You arranged with Ken. I said Castlebridge Avenue. Line of communication got fucked. A mistake. Human error, you know? Not fucking with you man. (*As Cork Fella*) 'Me bollocks! Are you setting me up?' (*To audience*) Cork Fella's watched too many films. Where'd he get a gun? Why didn't Ken get me one? Then we'd have a bit of a *Matrix* moment here in the country. On Castlebridge Road. (*Talking to Cork Fella*) Man, listen to me. No-one's setting you up. I have some money here for you and everything. Sorry you had to wait around for a while. (*As Cork Fella*) 'Wait around? I been sitting here on my arse with this for half an hour. And you don't show.' (*To audience*)

Cork Fella lowers gun and opens Londis bag. Full of yokes. Fucking hundreds of them. Like more than there's supposed to be. Maybe a thousand. Maybe more. Fuck sake. (*Talking to Cork Fella*) How much is that? (*As Cork Fella*) 'That's what you're getting; that's what you're taking.' (*Talking to Cork Fella*) Yeah but, Ken told me seven fifty. Looks like more than that there. Looks like twice that. (*To audience*) Cork Fella looks at me with round eyes, points the gun at me again. Mad culchie cunt. (*As Cork Fella*) 'Don't fuck me about boy. You're takin' this off me. All of it. After fuckin' me about this afternoon, lucky I don't shoot your arse. What money have you got?' (*To audience*) Give him the money from before. Doesn't even look at it. He's sweating like a pig. A roast pig. On holiday in Ibiza. On a few yokes. He's sweating a lot. The Londis bag is soggy when he presses it into me hands and puts his gun back in his Levis. He looks at me, opens his mouth to say something. Doesn't say anything. Blinks his round, fat eyes, wipes sweat from his upper lip and says: (*as Cork Fella*) 'Don't fuck me about again boy, 'cause I'll ...' (*To audience*) He trails off, shakes his head, sniffs, walks back to his car. Green Honda Civic. 98 C: Cork Fella. Gets in, revs engine, rips off. Too fast, gravel flies. Round corner and over hill. Gone. Mad culchie cunt just pulled a gun on me. Coulda got shot. I'm gonna kill Ken. Posin' prick poncin' about in the pub while I nearly get blown away in the countryside. And I fucking said Castlebridge Avenue, not Castlebridge Road.

The light snaps off on **Dave***; he disappears.*

3. A TRENDY BAR, NIGHT

The warm, coloured glow of a modern bar fades up on **Ray***. Cool lounge music plays in the background. He talks to the audience.*

Ray I get a call on Thursday afternoon. An old friend from college, Annette. She and her boyfriend are going away to Australia for six months on Friday morning and they're having going-away drinks tonight in The Dedalus Lounge. Now I'm broke as usual, but Dave said he might stay with me for a few days and he probably has loads of stuff and I haven't seen Annette in ages, so I say yeah. It's about ten when I walk in. There's a guy spinning at the bar and Annette and the others are sitting in one of the booths. They have Erdinger on tap here. Nice. Order a pint and sit down with the rest. (**Ray** *walks over to a booth where* **Bernard** *and* **Dave** *are now sitting. He joins them, but continues to talk to the audience*) Samantha's out with Dave tonight and fuck me she looks good. Try not to stare … Start talking with Bernard. He asks me where Linda is. I tell him she's over in Galway for her ma's fiftieth. He asks me about the band. I laugh it off and ask him if he saw *Corrie*. It's not long before Annette and her boyfriend – whose name always escapes me – make their excuses. They can't keep their hands off each other for more than half an hour. Ah, young love. We all kiss and hug and wish them well and they leave. I find myself looking at Samantha's cleavage without even noticing. (*We hear the sound of a mobile phone ringing.* **Ray** *stands up, patting his jacket pocket. He mimes taking out his phone*) As if on cue my mobile rings and it's Linda. I swear she's got fucking radar for this sort of thing.

Ray *walks away from the booth into darkness to answer his phone.* **Bernard** *takes over talking to the audience from the booth. The lounge music continues.*

Bernard Ray goes to the jacks and I realise I'm sitting next to Samantha. Dave's gone up to the bar and she's sitting silently, staring into space. Nobody's talking to her. Maybe they're afraid. Maybe they're intimidated. But I'm not. She's only human. Sure she looks like a Greek goddess. Sure she gives every man at the bar a boner each time she gets up to take a piss. But she's still human. She was just a baby once. And she'll get old and die eventually.
Anyway, she's probably just a nurse or a travel agent or

something, so I slide over in the booth beside her and we start to chat. As it turns out Samantha's a lap-dancer. She works in a club called Sirens on Leeson Street. I pretend not to be surprised by this and ask her does it pay well. She says she makes about five hundred and fifty quid a night. That's more than I make in a week. Should have guessed that by the way she dresses. She looks like she knows Brown Thomas like the back of her hand. Dave comes back from the bar with a stack of drinks. He gives me a kinda funny look when he sees me sitting next to Samantha. (*Towards* **Dave**, *but actually internal*) What's that for? For fuck's sake I'm not trying to chat up your girlfriend.

Dave (*towards* **Bernard**, *but actually internal*) Look mate. Just because she's a stripper it don't give you a licence to drool over her when she's out with me. She's my fucking bird, loser. Not some sex object, right? (*To audience*) Fucking spas doing me head in. Every one of them staring at her. Give it up spas. Jesus, need to calm down. Sip my Erdinger. Squeeze Sam's thigh. Sip my JD chaser. OK, that's better. He was just talking to her. Making conversation. Bernard's alright. He's just a geek. Sam barely even acknowledged him anyway. Nothing to be losing the head over, man. Still a little tense from earlier. Gun-toting culchies will do that to you. I've spent the rest of the day trying to chill. Dropped Big Brother's car back to the gaff. Dozy cunt none the wiser that his little Punto has just played an integral part in the trafficking of mucho illegal substances. Got the Luas into town and dumped the gear in Ray's gaff on Mountjoy Square. Had a nice bong with Ray while watching *The Simpsons*. Then across to Sam's place in the Liberties for a little afternoon shag. Lovely. What the fuck is the DJ playing? Sounds like the fucking Eagles or something. (*We hear* **Dave**'s *mobile ringing; his ring tone is the theme from* The Godfather) Shit, there goes me moby. Got

that *Godfather* ring tone yesterday from a fella off the site. Sounds pretty cool.
Squeeze past Samantha. (*To Samantha, standing up*) Sorry babe, back in a sec.

Dave *mimes squeezing past people in the bar.*

Dave Excuse me, excuse me, sorry, could you get the fuck outta me way please?

Dave *gets outside the bar, the music fades and the light changes. He mimes answering the phone and talks to the audience.*

Dave Outside. Answer. Culchie accent. Oh fuck … (*Cork Fella accent*) 'Got your number off Ken.' (*To audience*) Cork Fella. Jesus, what now? (*Talking to Cork Fella*) Yeah? (*Cork Fella accent*) 'Yeah, I wanted to talk to ya again.' (*Talking to Cork Fella*) Right … (*To audience*) What the fuck does this guy want now? I'm gonna kill Ken for giving this psycho me number … (*Cork Fella accent*) 'What happened earlier, was … well, was a bit mad.' (*Talking to Cork Fella*)
Sorry? (*Cork Fella accent*) 'Yeah. I am.' (*Talking to Cork Fella*) What? (*Cork Fella accent*) 'I'm callin' te apologise. That was a bit mad now. The gun, and all. Shouldn't a pulled that. That was a lotta stuff I had on me, and I was well freaked. Paranoid, ya know?' (*Talking to Cork Fella*) Oh yeah, man. I got that alright. Me being late and all. That misunderstanding. Got to ye … (*Cork Fella accent*) 'Exactly. But I realised after that that was all it was, a misunderstanding. And there was no need for me to flip and go all cowboy like I did. Musta scared the shit outta ya.' (*Talking to Cork Fella*) Well … (*Cork Fella accent*) 'There wasn't any bullets in the gun, ya know? So I apologise.' (*Talking to Cork Fella*) Right. Nice one. No hard feelings man. (*Cork Fella accent*) 'Thanks, talk to ya later.' (*Talking to Cork*

Fella) Yeah, cool. See ya. (*To audience*) Hang up. What the fuck? A gun-toting, culchie drug dealer with a conscience? What is the world coming to? Back into the bar.

Dave *mimes squeezing past people back in the bar, the music gets louder and the lighting changes.*

Dave Excuse me, excuse me, sorry, could you get the fuck outta the way please? (*To audience as he sits back down in the booth*) Squeeze past Samantha again. Tell her the whole episode with the Cork Fella. Big grin on me face. Pause now and again to sip on me Erdinger and JD chaser. When I finish, Sam's not amused. In fact she's quite pissed off. You see, she's not too keen on me and the whole dealing thing. Bollocks. (*To Samantha*) Chill out babe. Always had a handle on it. Knew yer man was bullshittin', knew he had no bullets. And he apologised and all. (*To audience*) But she's having none of it. Sips on her G and T. Fiddles with her silver bracelet. I go to hug her and kiss her cheek. She pulls away from me and turns to talk to Bernard. Now, this pisses me off.

Dave *glares over to* **Bernard** *who sits down from him; he's miming having a conversation with Samantha. The light fades down on them and they disappear.*

4. ANOTHER PART OF THE TRENDY BAR, NIGHT

The light fades up on another part of the stage to reveal **Ray** *still on the phone. He looks bored.*

Ray (*to audience*) I'm on the phone to Linda. How long has it been now? I don't know. I'm standing at the back of the bar looking at the brightly coloured fish swimming about in the fish-tank in the wall by the jacks. Wouldn't it be great to be like them? Lose your memory every thirty seconds. You'd never have any problems. You'd never get bored with your little world. And all the other fish around you would always be new and interesting. The DJ is on a bit of a nostalgia trip, playing 'Jump Around' by the House of Pain. That must sound like a kicking soundtrack to Linda in her parents' quiet house in Galway on the other end of the phone. She's crying now. I've tuned out of this phone call so much that I've forgotten what she's upset about. Her da? Her ma? Me? Her cat? I tell her to stop crying, that it'll all work out. She sniffles loudly on the other end. (*As Linda*) 'Do you think so?' (*To audience*) Yeah, of course, I say. It'll be alright. It's not her problem, or something like that. I can barely hear myself not thinking. (*As Linda*) 'Are you staying out much longer?' (*to audience*) she asks, wiping her nose, I suppose. I say I don't think so. I say I'll call her back later. I say when I leave the bar. I say in an hour. I say stop crying. I say you're OK. I say bye. I hang up. I realise that I have been reading a sign about the importance of safe sex for the last five minutes. And it's all gone in. STDs are in my head and not my girlfriend. That's fucked up. I need another drink.

Ray *walks out of the light and disappears. The light fades and another part of the stage is lit up to reveal* **Bernard**. *He stands and addresses the audience, gesturing back occasionally to* **Dave**, *who sits in the booth behind him in the shadows.*

Bernard Dave and Samantha always seem to be fighting. That's all they seem to do together. Fight and fuck. I bet they just like to argue so they can make up and ride the hole off each other. I don't really understand that. It's kind of embarrassing to be sitting beside them while they're shouting their heads off at each other but it's kind of funny too. Eventually Samantha stands up and screams something like, 'posin' cunt,' but the theme to *Shaft* is playing so loud that it's hard to be sure. Then she storms off towards the exit with her white Gucci handbag. She passes Ray on the way, who stares at her arse very obviously as she disappears out the door. He's lucky Dave doesn't notice.

Bernard *rejoins* **Ray** *and* **Dave** *sitting in the booth.*

Ray Where's she off to?

Dave Aw, back to the flat, I don't know. Think she's coming up on her period or something … Fucking women …

Ray Tell me about it.

Bernard Yeah …

Ray *and* **Dave** *give* **Bernard** *a look that says: What would you know? He sips on his drink quietly.*

Ray Do you wanna get outta here? Get a few cans, go back to my place?

Dave Yeah, why not?

Bernard What about Samantha?

Dave Ah, fuck her. I'll give her a call later, when she's calmed down.

Bernard So, drinks down, arses up, coats on and out the door.

The three of them rise up out of their chairs in unison and walk to a different part of the stage. The music fades out and the lighting changes: brighter, less glamorous.

5. RAY'S APARTMENT, NIGHT

Bernard (*to audience*) We get a few cans in Whelan's and walk back across town to Ray's apartment on Mountjoy Square.

The lads mime popping open cans and sit down on the sofa.

Dave How do you guys know each other?

Ray Bernard was in the same class as Linda in college. Met him through her.

Dave You're a business geek as well?

Bernard *nods; the sound of a television set fades up and* **Bernard** *turns to watch it in a trance.*

Bernard (*to audience*) Ray has the orgy scene from *Eyes Wide Shut* playing on the telly for some reason. He's rolling a big joint, not even looking at it. There's so many perfect naked women on the TV that it gets boring after a while. No, really, I'm serious.

Ray Dave, look, she has tits like Samantha.

Dave What? Fuck off. How would you know, loser? Where's your guitar gone?

Bernard Yeah man, haven't seen ya playing it in ages.

Ray It's not that long … The strings were just fucked. Put it away somewhere.

Dave Probably for the best. Was cluttering up the room, man.

Ray Yeah.

Bernard How do you know each other?

Dave Went to school with this spa. Wanna do an E?

Bernard What?

Dave I've a load of yokes inside. Will we do one?

Bernard Now? It's nearly three in the morning.

Ray (*laughs*) Yeah, fuck it. I've nothing on in the morning. You?

Ray *turns to* **Bernard, Bernard** *gives a confused shrug.* **Dave** *gets up and leaves for a moment.*

Bernard (*to audience*) Dave disappears into the bathroom. I sip on my can of Bulmers. Trying to suss things out. Are they

serious? They wanna do E now? Is that not a bit mad? I've never done a yoke before. I'm a little … I don't know. Worried? No, I don't know.
Dave must be a drug dealer. Actually, that really makes sense. He always has a lot more money than you'd think a builder would have. (**Dave** *returns*) He comes back from the jacks with three fat white pills and passes them out. Ray and Dave swallow theirs down quickly with a big gulp of beer. I look at the pill between my finger and thumb for a moment. Sorta dusty. Little flecks of something in it. Shape of a dolphin pressed into one side.

Dave Flippers. They're nice yokes.

Bernard I've never done one.

Ray Nah, don't worry, these are grand ones. Dave had them before. Don't worry.

Bernard Well, I'm not … (*To audience*) Fuck it. Put the yoke in me mouth. Tastes real chalky. Minging. Take a big gulp of Bulmers. The pill gets caught at the back of my throat. Gag it down awkwardly. Cough a little. Sharp shiver. Swallow big gulps of Bulmers. Well, that's that then. What happens next?

Ray Is that what you got today?

Dave No, they're the last few from before. Got a load of new ones today. They've got little *South Park* faces on them. What you call your man with the hood?

Ray What?

Dave You know the fella that always dies. With the hood.

Bernard Kenny.

Dave Yeah. Kenny. Oh my God, they killed Kenny! That's your man, yeah. They got his face on them. Real clear and everything. You can see his eyes and all. I'd love to see how they do that. Get the little pictures on them.

Ray Some craftsmanship man, yeah?

Dave Yeah. There's supposed to be a load of speed in them. Get ye on a mad adrenaline buzz.

Bernard (*to audience*) I don't really feel anything. I finish off my can of Bulmers. Open another one. The other two are chatting away, having a real laugh, talking about school. Lotsa people I don't know. Ginger Whelan. Deco with the pigeon tits. That mad cunt Henno. I don't really say anything for ages. I'm thinking about what this E is doing to me.
My hands feel a bit funny. Tingly. I wriggle my fingers a little and slurp on my can. I notice the cider going further down my throat than usual. I can feel it cool all the way down deep into my chest. That feels …

Dave You're coming up, aren't you?

Bernard (*to audience*) I look at Dave and laugh for no reason. When I do I can feel real shivery surges through me head. Like I can feel my brain working. The blood pumping around inside all fast and warm. Then I get the same feeling in my arms. Then my knees. I laugh again. Totally entranced by this weirdness. (*To* **Dave**) Yeah, I think I am.

Dave Nice yokes, aren't they? They take a while to kick in, but when they do … Wham! Put a bit a music on there, Ray. (*To audience*) I don't think Bernard's done E at all before. He's got that mad first-timer look on his face. Little deranged kid on Christmas morning sorta look. Wide-eyed grin. Head darting about, staring at everything like it's suddenly the most interesting thing in the world. That's a deadly feeling. (*To* **Ray** *and* **Bernard**) Let's go mental.

Ray Let's go to the park.

Bernard Oh yeah, let's do that.

Ray (*to audience*) Bernard told me before that he never did yokes. The ecstasy has opened up the floodgates now. He won't shut up. Mad cunt, look at him. Talking about his job. Talking about his childhood. Talking about his holiday to Prague.

Bernard (*to audience*) All of a sudden I pull back the curtain and the sky's not black anymore. I look at my watch. Half seven. Half seven? Where did all that time go?
Jesus, this is crazy. My whole body is jumping inside itself with a mad excited feeling. I can feel every part of me moving and working, like a machine. Blood pumping. Organs swelling and contracting. Brain ticking. Skin tingling. Aw, wonder what the air's gonna feel like.
The wind all fresh and cool against you. Mad. (*To* **Ray** *and* **Dave**) Ah, can we go outside? Will we go outside? Come on …

The lads stand up and prepare to leave the apartment.

Dave (*to audience*) We all put the last of our cans into our jacket pockets. Let's take this madness onto the road. Duck into the jacks, take a quick piss. Open the top of the cistern, take out my stash that I have hidden there. Take out another three yokes. Rethink it through. Nah. Open up the stash again. Take out six yokes. Will that be enough?

The lads leave the apartment, heading out onto the early morning streets. The lighting changes.

6. MOUNTJOY SQUARE PARK, MORNING

Ray (*to audience*) I lock the door after us and we step out into the cool morning air. That does feel good. I stand on the step outside the apartment building for a moment with my eyes closed. I take a deep breath and open my arms out wide. I feel the cool air inside my throat and nostrils. Nice. I open my eyes. Him and Dave are already across the road, heading into Mountjoy Square.

The lights fade up at the back of the stage to reveal the set of swings.

Bernard (*to* **Ray** *and* **Dave**) Ah, look. They've got swings here. I wanna go on the swings.

Dave (*to audience*) Bernard legs it across the grass and starts to climb over a spiked railing that surrounds a little playground. I follow after him, laughing to meself. Feeling all lost and OK with the world. I climb over the fence after Bernard. It's a little awkward. I have no desire to slice off me balls on these spikes. But there's only two swings and Bernard's just grabbed one. I have to get to that swing before Ray.

Ray (*to audience*) Muppets don't realise that there's a gate open on the other side of the playground. I stroll around casually while Dave struggles over the fence trying not to skewer his bollocks.

Dave (*to audience*) Aw, there's a gate? Fuck. (*Shouting at* **Ray**) That's my swing, loser, don't even think about it! Hop down off fence, leg it over, hop on the last swing. Nice one.

Dave *and* **Bernard** *sit down on the swings like excited children;* **Ray** *saunters over to them.*

Ray (*to audience*) I let Dave have the swing.

Dave (*to* **Ray**) Give us a push, loser.

Ray *starts to push* **Bernard** *and* **Dave** *on the swings.*

Bernard (*to audience*) Aw man. I'm flying. Look at me. I am flying. Jesus. Haven't been on a swing since I was a kid. Missing out man, this is deadly. Back and forth. The world spins up and around in front of my eyes. A big, beautiful blur. Swooping into the grey-blue sky. Sweeping back into the tarmac sea. I must be out of my head now. This is what it's like. I feel real dizzy. I should slow down a little.

Bernard *and* **Dave** *jump off the swings into a pool of light near the front of the stage.* **Ray** *joins them and they all sit down on the edge of the stage.*

Ray (*to audience*) Eventually Dave and Bernard get bored with the swings and sit down in a circle in the centre of the tarmac football pitch. Two pigeons spiral above us. I follow them with my eyes for a while. (*The lads mime the following*) When I look

back at the others Dave is offering Bernard another yoke. He takes one himself, then gives me one. I hold it for a while. The streets outside the playground are getting busier now. People going to work.
It's Friday now, isn't it? I really should call Linda, but instead I swallow the yoke with the last of my Heineken. I think we should join the Rat Race. Let's walk.

The lads jump to their feet, energized. Morning street sounds become audible.

7. CITY STREETS, MORNING

The three lads walk on the spot, glancing about at all around them. They describe what they see to the audience.

Bernard Onto O'Connell Street. Past the Savoy. The movies this week:

Ray Something with Tom Cruise.

Dave Something with a dog.

Ray Something with a monkey.

Dave Something with Julia Roberts.

Ray Something with a fish.

Dave Remake of something with an alien.

Bernard Something with a super hero looks kinda good.

Ray Cross the road, pass the GPO. Cuchullain's looking down through the window at two smiling bums smoking Sweet Afton cigarettes.

Dave There's ugly Scottish people.

Bernard There's ugly Orientals.

Dave There's ugly junkies.

Ray Why is everybody on O'Connell Street so ugly? If I'm walking here, does that make me ugly too?

Bernard I notice that somebody's walked dog shit into Leopold Bloom's head on the *Ulysses* plaque at O'Connell Bridge.

Dave Turn onto Bachelor's Walk. Onto the boardwalk. Clippity-clop. Love this sound.

Bernard Usually I'm sitting here watching the grey-faced zombies trudge past. But now we're the grey-faced zombies. Funny that. So this is what it feels like to be utterly fucked off your head in the daytime. It's not so bad.

Dave (*to* **Ray** *and* **Bernard**) Maybe we should get some beer and go shout abuse at the pigeons and office-workers having lunch in the park.

Ray (*to* **Dave**) Capital idea, my dear man.

Bernard (*to audience*) So we go into Dunnes Stores on George's Street and buy eight bottles of Grolsch.

The street sounds fade; the atmosphere becomes more peaceful.

8. CITY PARK, DAY

The lads continue to describe their surroundings directly to the audience.

Dave We walk through Stephen's Green, but we don't sit down because for some strange reason there seems to a park warden standing behind every bush today. Bernard takes us to a place called the Iveagh Gardens instead.

Bernard It's just off Harcourt Street, near Tripod.

Ray It's really empty and peaceful because it's got a big high wall all around it.

Dave It reminds me of a place out of *Pride and Sensibility* or *Sense and Prejudice* by Emma What's-her-head off BBC on a Sunday.

Bernard We lie down on a little sloping hill under a row of big, dark trees.

They sit down on one side of the stage; the light fades slightly.

Ray Bernard is really wired now; he's laughing and fidgeting and telling us how deadly it is to be young, free and single.

Bernard *stands up again quickly. He seems hyper. The others watch him distantly.*

Dave So far this week he's been out with four chicks, but he hasn't shagged any of them, he's just drank a lot of …

The lighting changes dramatically. **Ray** *and* **Dave** *disappear, leaving* **Bernard** *centre stage, staring out at the audience with wide eyes.*

8. CAFÉ, DAY – FLASHBACK

Bernard (*hyper, to audience*) Coffee, coffee, coffee. Too much coffee. I've drank too much coffee. I'm confused. What's this one's name? I'm afraid to say her name in case I get it wrong. It's escaping me and I don't want to piss her off, 'cause I like her. Fuck. Don't use her name in conversation. Hope she doesn't notice. But I bet she will. Women are perceptive that way. They know when something's not right. No, stop thinking bullshit, she's talking, you should be listening to what she's saying. And she's looking at your eyes, which might mean she likes you or it might mean that she knows a bit about body language. Fuck, what's her name? I have to drink less coffee. You drink coffee so you won't drink alcohol and get drunk, but if you drink too much coffee you get hyper like this and can't concentrate. OK, this is messed up because I met her by chance. I wasn't ready to meet her. If I knew I was going to meet her I wouldn't have drunk so much coffee earlier and I would have remembered to remember her fucking name. Jesus, still talking. Does she ever shut up? At least if she's talking she's not noticing that I'm not following a word she's saying.

Oh fuck, she's stopped. Quick. Smile.

(*Earnestly talking to the girl he's drinking coffee with*) 'Yeah, yeah, I know exactly what you mean. I've been there.' (*To audience*) Phew. That seems to have done it, she's off again. What the fuck is she talking about? Oh shit, I'm supposed to be meeting that northern one for coffee at four. It's nearly 3.45. How do I get rid of this one without hurting her feelings? Wait a minute, do I care what she feels? She seems a bit self-obsessed actually. Maybe I was wrong about her. This always happens. Every girl I meet. It all starts out easy and cool, but then somewhere along the way the conversation becomes a long one-sided monologue about *her* life or *her* problems or *her* dreams. I'm a good listener, they say. Talking to me makes them feel good about themselves, they say. And then they go off and shag some other guy. Fuck that. I mean look at this one. She never shuts up, won't let me speak. She obviously doesn't think I have an opinion worth expressing. Enough of this. Time to go. Quick, smile. (*Earnestly talking to the girl*) 'I'm really sorry, but I've got to go. I'll text you later.' (*To audience*) Good. Smile. Walk. OK, what's this northern one's name?

The light snaps back to the park set-up and **Ray** *and* **Dave** *reappear.* **Bernard** *rejoins them.*

9. CITY PARK, AFTERNOON

They describe their surroundings to the audience; they are fairly spaced out now.

Ray My face feels wet and I realise my eyes are closed. I'm not sure if I've been asleep or if I'm just in the middle of a blink. I open my eyes and realise that it's starting to rain. Big drops of it are falling down from between the branches of the tree above us.

Dave The rain gets heavier and the trees offer no shelter. Bernard does a few spins on the grass, laughing up at the sky. A park warden appears out of nowhere and starts to walk towards us suspiciously. I put the beer back into the Dunnes bag and get up awkwardly.

They get up and move to the booth again. The lighting changes to:

10. COCKTAIL BAR, HAPPY HOUR

The lads sit down in a booth of the dimly lit cocktail bar and mime sipping their drinks.

Bernard (*to audience*) We go to the Odeon and Dave buys us all a cocktail. Mine is thick and creamy and tastes of vanilla. Something Heaven – didn't hear what the skinny guy behind the bar said. Dave has something sweet and crimson. Ray has something to do with a frog. He sips it and smiles broadly and starts to tell us about the last time he was in here when he met a …

The light changes to a spotlight which singles out **Ray***; he stands up.*

11. RAY AND SASHA – FLASHBACK

Ray (*to audience*) Fucking beautiful-looking business chick. Excuse me, fucking beautiful-looking business woman. Sitting on her own at the bar. Oh man. This is when I'm still in college. Some evening, drinking with the lads from the band. Talking about … football? Playstation? *Big Brother*? Some fucking shit … Linda studying for some exam. Not around. Out of sight. Well out of mind. Cross hairs focused on Fucking Beautiful Business Woman at the bar. Why is she sitting on her own? Waiting for someone? Doesn't look like it. Sipping her cocktail, fairly … contently. She surveys the room. Mad eyes on her. Real green. Oh man. Her gaze meets mine. Hold eye contact. Got a good feeling. Little smirk. Fucking suave bastard. Subtle. Other blokes don't even notice. Left side of her lips creep up a little. Nice. Onto something here. Get up, dead smooth, pat me shirt a little. Slide past guys, head sorta towards bar. She turns, scratches her neck, watching me approach on the sly. Catch her eye. Smirk. Nod. She smiles back. Suave bastard. Don't drop the pace, move past her. I'm just going to the jacks, me, this is just reconnaissance. Can smell her perfume. Smells expensive. Oh man. Moment later, back in seat. Completely blanked her on the way back from the jacks. Subtle. Bet she checked me out in the mirror at the bar. Definitely onto something good here. Older chick – sorry, woman. Well on for that. Reckon about thirty, maybe thirty-two. Experienced I'd say. Well, well on for that. She slowly drains the last of her pink cocktail. Time for action. Fast but smooth, at the bar in a silken second. Order a White Russian – very sophis – make sure to catch copious eye contact with her in the mirror when the bar guy turns away to mix. Turn. Smile. Lay some groundwork. Introduce. Nice to meet you. Sasha. Oh man. She's into it. Get her a drink. Sit on stool

beside her. Get comfortable. Forget the lads in corner in a flash. Lose meself in her eyes, lips, hem of her skirt. Sasha. Business Woman. Harcourt Street. Originally from Longford. Living in Dublin three years. No culchie accent. Great fucking tan. Comment on it. Smiles broadly, touches me thigh. Just been on holiday. Turkey. Great sun. Yeah, I say. Best tan ever, she says, look.
Leans toward me. Opens her blouse. Black lacy Wonderbra. Pulls it down a bit. She's showing me her tits on the sly. Oh man. Love sunbathing topless, she says. It's mad the way your nipples go real brown. She smiles broadly. I smile too. Yeah it is, I say. Trying to keep it cool. But not really sure if I am anymore. Sip more Russian. She buttons up her blouse again. Subtle. Sexy bitch. This is definitely on. Foreplay is starting in the bar. Your place or mine only question to be asked. In taxi after second drink. Too busy sucking tongues to notice colour of car or size of driver. No talk from anybody. Only sound of Westlife on radio and kissing in back. Fucking Beautiful Business Woman—Saaasshha—has got a gaff on Capel Street. Brand spanking new apartment, emphasis on the spanking. Can't keep hands off her arse as she leads me up stairs. Both of our tops off before the front door closes. Oh man. This is one kinky, sexy, beautiful, older, experienced, tanned, horny bitch and I'm one smooth, suave, subtle, young bastard to bag her this quick. I put the right shoes on this morning, I tell ya. Kick those shoes off, fall onto bed with Sasha. Her sugary tongue now feels like a part of my own mouth. Sits on me hips, kisses my ear, whispers into it, slowly: 'Can I tie you up?'

Dave I think I know this. I seen this episode.

Bernard What?

Dave On the telly. I seen this before.

Bernard No. This really happened.

Dave Really?

Bernard Yeah. To Ray. Right Ray?

Ray Oh yeah, man. No bullshit. She wants to get all *Basic Instinct* on me. Fire away, I say and let her do her shit. Arms tied to headboard, chews on me lip, wants to blindfold me. Well, well experienced. Not really sure if I can handle all this anymore, but on for it none the less. Blindfolds me. Licks me. Bites me. Rides me. Generally shags the shit outta me. Then, slowly takes the blindfold off me. Except when I look up it's not Sasha that looks down at me. It's some bloke. Some naked bloke. Oh man. Hear a little laugh. Turn and see Sasha sitting naked on a chair by the bed. Holding a little video camera. A little video camera with a flashing red light. Jesus H. fucking lord Christ, what's going on? Let me outta here! Naked Bloke unties me and I lep off the bed, grabbing me clothes and nearly cryin' in shock. Head for the door. You perverted fuckers, I scream, pull on me kaks and fall out of the apartment. I feel all violated and shit. I get dressed awkwardly and stumble down Capel Street. Waiting for my phone to ring. But for some reason Linda never calls that night. Oh man.

The spotlight dissolves back to the cocktail bar set-up as **Ray** *sits back down with the other pair in the booth.*

12. COCKTAIL BAR, HAPPY HOUR

Bernard *and* **Dave** *stare blankly at* **Ray**, *reacting to the story he's just told.* **Ray** *stares down at his lap, drained.*

Dave (*to audience*) Ray doesn't say anything else for a long time. Bernard slurps on the last of his Baileys Heaven and smacks his lips. (**Bernard** *turns to* **Dave** *and throws him a glance that says: What now?)* I look down at wet grass stuck to my runners. When did it rain? (**Bernard** *and* **Ray** *mime the following*) Ray's holding his moby. He turns it on. It beeps. He turns it off again. It stops beeping. He keeps staring at it. Bernard looks around a little jumpily. He's starting to irritate me. The doors of the bar swish open and several suits and skirts walk in, chattering and laughing. The sort of cunts my da would drink with. Don't feel so good here anymore. (*Checking watch*) Seiko tells me it's four in the p.m.

Ray Will we go?

Bernard Where will we go?

Dave (*to audience*) They both turn to me as if I'm their daddy. I don't feel like their daddy. I don't feel like anything at the moment.

Ray Can we go?

Bernard Should we go?

Dave (*to audience*) I shrug and keep shrugging as I slowly get up out of my chair. (*The lighting changes to daylight. The lads' eyes squint, but they remain seated.*) Next thing I know we're in

a taxi and the sky is bright but the windows are wet. Soon we're back in Ray's little apartment.
The room stinks of hash. (**Dave** *mimes the following*) Spend a few minutes trying to open a bottle of beer with me front door key. Finally realise the bottle's a screw top. Ray zaps randomly at the telly. I sip on my beer. I can't really taste it but it feels nice and wet on my cardboard tongue. Bernard is talking to someone but the words don't make any sense to my ears. He wanders off in the general direction of the jacks. (**Bernard** *gets up and moves to another part of the stage*) The TV is now a rapidly moving blur of light, static and noise. I can't keep up anymore. The bottle of beer begins to feel like a giant sponge in my hand and the room gets darker. Soon it'll all be velvety black and I'll be gone …

The light fades down on **Ray** *and* **Dave** *slowly; they disappear.*

13. BERNARD GOES TO WORK, EARLY EVENING

A light fades up quickly to reveal **Bernard** *taking a piss at one side of the stage.*

Bernard (*to audience*) This piss is taking forever. Every bit of water seems to be coming out of me. Getting rid of all the poison outta me, I suppose. Fuck, Ray's apartment really stinks. I can't stay here. My nerves are still jumping. Every little atom of me is still shivering weirdly. I'm not staying here. (**Bernard** *mimes putting his lad away and turning to a mirror*) Finally. Piss finished, turn to wash me hands. See someone in the mirror. Me, I suppose. Jesus, I actually don't look that bad. Fuck, that's mad. I feel like a junkie, but I look OK. (*He looks at his watch*) Four forty-five. Hhmmmm … Do you know what? I think I'll go to work … I don't feel so bad and I look respectable enough. Fuck it, yeah. I will. I need the money. The guys aren't goin' to do anything now, they'll be asleep for ages. Yeah, why not?

Make some final adjustments, spray some of Ray's deodorant and leave the apartment. (*Mimes walking; the lighting changes*) Across Mountjoy Square. Down Gardiner Street. Turn onto Abbey Street. Feeling quite good by the time I walk through the foyer and nod to the security guard. Give him a smile that he's not expecting. He says 'evening' to me in a sort of surprised way as he buzzes me through. Working five to nine doing data entry for this insurance company to cover their overspill from some government savings thing. Don't really understand what this job is about. They pay me to type things into a computer. That's all that matters to me. And they give you biscuits on your coffee break. Handy really. Take my seat at the row of computers beside the chick who does graphic design in college. She smiles at me out of habit, then looks at me in a funny sort of way.

(*Design Chick's voice*) 'Are you alright?' (*Talking to Design Chick*) 'Eh, yeah. Why?' (*Design Chick's voice*) 'Your face is a bit red.' (*Talking to Design Chick*) 'It is?' (*To audience*) I touch my face, it's warm. (*Talking to Design Chick*) 'Nah, I'm fine. I was rushing a bit to get in, ya know? Late as usual …' (*To audience*) The design chick has put some thoughts in me head. Shit. I go to the jacks. When I look at myself in the mirror my face is red as fuck. Like a bleeding tomato. Aw, what the fuck? I splash a shit load of water onto me face and pat meself down carefully with paper towels. I'm still really red. Fuck. And now the skin is pretty sensitive as well. I'm getting all paranoid.

What the fuck is wrong with me? Am I seriously fucked now or what? I wish I was still with the other lads. They'd know if something is wrong with me. And maybe their faces are red too and we'd all have a laugh about it or something. I mean, if we're fucked, at least we'd be fucked together. I think I'll give them a call when I finish here and see what they're up to. Don't want to go home on me own after work. Not like this. Fuck, I better get back inside.

The light snaps off **Bernard** *and fades back up on* **Ray** *and* **Dave** *asleep back in* **Ray's** *living room.*

14. RAY'S APARTMENT, EARLY EVENING

We hear the sound of mobile phone ringing; the ring tone is the Godfather *theme.* **Dave** *awakes awkwardly and sits up.*

Dave (*to audience*) Aaawwww … Where am I? Bollocks, Ray's. Jesus. Stop the music.
Turn that off. *The Godfather*? Oh yeah, that's me … fucking phone. Jaysis, what am I like? (*Mimes answering phone*) Hello? (*To audience*) It's Samantha. She wants to know what happened to me last night, why I didn't go back to her place. I tell her I'm sorry and quickly ask if she's eaten yet. She hasn't, so I tell her I'll meet her for grub and explain all then. She doesn't make a fuss. Sound. Me legs are fucked. Get up you bastards. Splash of water on me mush. Glass a water down me gob. Right as rain. Hit the streets.

Dave *gets up; the light changes;* **Ray***'s sleeping form disappears in the shadows.*

15. DAVE AND SAMANTHA, EARLY EVENING

Dave (*stands in his own spotlight and talks to the audience. He seems happy, confident*) Meet Samantha and we grab an early bird special at Milano's on Dawson Street. I turn my phone off so that we can have some quality time together without some spa buttin' in. Thanks to some wine and cheesecake, Samantha's in a surprisingly forgiving mood. This long day has turned into a beautiful evening. The late sun's cookin'. We go for a walk. When it's sunny there's always lots of spas in Stephen's Green. Laughing spas. Chatting spas. Spas with cameras. Spas with radios. Spas with cans of cider. Spas with suits from Baggot Street and Leeson Street. Little spas with bread for the ducks. I don't like it when there's so many spas, so I take her to Trinity instead. We lie on the edge of the cricket green. There's spas here too. But not as many as in Stephen's Green. I'm really fucking relaxed now. I take off my top and put my hat over my face. She's lying beside me. I can smell her Ralph Lauren wafting over me on the tiny breeze. Even with my eyes closed I can tell that all the spas are staring at her. Fuck you all, she's mine. I've been saying that to myself more and more often. I said it when I seen her this evening. She was waiting for me outside the Central Bank and I seen her before I even crossed the street. She's wearing all white and the silver Gucci sunglasses I bought her last week. At that moment I thought to myself that she looked like something out of another world. Like an angel. Or a supermodel. Or something. Before I got across the road two builders whistled and drooled something at her. She ignored them. Fuck you spas, she's mine. She's tickling or scratching at my nipple with her long nails. The tips of them are real white and shiny. She gets them done at some place in Brown Thomas. A guy I know from the site told me they do men's nails as well. A manicure. For a man. He gets it done once a month to get all the paint and dust and dirt and shit out of his … cuticles, he called them. You wouldn't think he was gay to look at him. I push her hand away from my nipple. It's irritating. I don't like long nails on women. She likes them though. She likes every part of her to be perfect. Everything waxed, plucked, polished, conditioned, cleansed, exfoliated. Sometimes I don't think she's real. She's like a mannequin or a doll or something. That freaks me out sometimes, usually when I'm off my head though. So that doesn't count, does it? The sun is reflecting off her white clothes. She's just a blinding glare of whiteness on the vivid green grass. It hurts to look at her. But I don't need to look at her anymore. I know what she looks like. She looks perfect. As usual. After an hour or so the sun begins to dip quickly behind the buildings. She rolls over and whispers to me. (*Samantha's voice*) 'I have to go.' (*Talking to Samantha*) Why? (*Samantha's voice*) 'Work. Have to go to the club.' (*Talking to Samantha*) Don't go. Stay here. (*Samantha's voice*) 'I can't.' (*Talking to Samantha*) You can. Stay here with me. (*Samantha's voice*) 'No. Come on.' (*To audience*) She tugs me up off the ground and I open my eyes. My hands are on her hips and we're standing facing each other. (*Samantha's voice*) 'What?' (*To audience*) I can't see her eyes through the silver Gucci sunglasses that I bought her last week. I just see myself in the mirrored lenses. I look like a muppet. My mouth's open like I'm going to say something. Maybe I am. Maybe I should say, 'You look beautiful,' or 'I love you', but I don't say anything (I never say anything) and she smiles. (*Samantha's voice*) 'Come on, I'll be late.' (*To audience*) I walk her over to the club where the dickie-bowed gorillas are just setting up shop at the door. I ask Samantha if she wants me to meet her when she's finished. She says she'd like that, so I say I'll be right here at three. (*To audience*)

When I kiss her goodbye I notice the two gorillas saying something and sniggering. Samantha doesn't notice. But I do. She says 'hi boys' to them and they give her a little peck on either cheek as she disappears into the club. Fucking spas. Hate leaving her here. I turn around and get the fuck away from there, back towards Stephen's Green. As soon as I turn my phone back on, it's ringing. (*Ballymun Fella voice*) 'Do you want this or not?' (*To audience*) Aww shite. The Ballymun Fella. Forgot all about him. And all that sneachta … (*Talking to Ballymun Fella*) Yeah, yeah man. Of course. Have the money. Meet you at the canal at Drumcondra in half an hour.

The light snaps off **Dave** *and fades up again on* **Bernard** *at work.*

16. BERNARD AT WORK, EVENING

Bernard (*to audience*) Back at my work station and Design Chick is still looking at my red face funny. (*Talking to Design Chick*) I think I got a bit sunburned or something. (*Design Chick voice*) 'But it wasn't sunny yesterday or today.' (*Talking to Design Chick*) Ah, it was. Wasn't it? In the morning? (*Design Chick voice, shaking head*) 'No. Sure it was raining earlier.' (*Talking to Design Chick*) Oh yeah. (*To audience*) I don't give her any more explanations.
I shouldn't really talk to anyone anymore. You wouldn't know what suspicious shit would come out of my mouth right now. Best to keep to myself. Keep me tomato mush in me computer monitor. Stick a CD and me headphones in the computer. Listening to music helps me type faster. Also gives me an

excuse not to talk to anyone. My fingers are dancing across the keyboard. Look at them cunts go. Daragh McNulty from Blackwater. Heather O'Neill from Roscommon. Deirdre Morrison from Cabinteely. Your money is hopping into the computer. Save your lives away, ye saps. See if I care … The music is starting to lift me again. I can feel me veins pumping. This is mad. Fuck. I'm still wired. I'm in work and I'm still wired. Ha! This is deadly. None of these gobshites knows I'm whacked off me head on a shit load of E and I'm responsible for thousands of euros … My feet are bopping under the desk. My fingers are a blur. Derek Reilly. Edward Cassidy. Niamh Cotter. Jack Gray. Maeve Whelan. Doctor. Builder. Housewife. Journalist. Baker. Gobshite. Spa. Prick. Bitch. Faggot. David Ryan. I went to school with him. David Ryan. You're a plumber now? Jesus. Didn't you always want to be a footballer? I think my head is bopping now as well with the music and typing. Design Chick is looking at me. She says something. I take one headphone out of me ear. (*Talking to Design Chick*) What? (*Design Chick voice*) 'Tea break.' (*To audience*) Seven. Fuck me. (*Talking to Design Chick*) Already? (*Design Chick voice*) 'Yeah.' (*To audience*) She goes to get her black coffee and custard creams. Jesus. Flying along here. I should come in whacked off my head more often.

The light fades down on **Bernard** *as he bops away happily.*

17. PHONECALL FROM LINDA, RAY'S APARTMENT, EVENING

A spot light fades up on **Ray***; he mimes drying his hair with a towel, talking to the audience.*

Ray Post shower. Cleaner. Slicker. Feeling more human. Outwardly at least. Inwardly, all fucked and entangled. (*We hear the sound of* **Ray's** *phone ringing*) And mobile rings now. This ain't gonna help. Here comes the pain. (*Mimes answering phone*) Hey babe. (*To audience*) All she has to say is 'don't' and I know this isn't gonna be pleasant. Poor old brain doesn't want to deal with this now. Try to decipher. Plan a strategy. Work an angle. No excuses present themselves. Listen to the onslaught for a while. Let her fence with the silence I provide on this end. Eventually, I come up with … (*Talking to Linda on phone*) Calm down. (*To audience*) And then … (**Ray** *paces back and forth, talking to Linda on the phone*) Ran outta credit babe. Sorry if you were worried. Just spent the night with the lads. Acting the bollocks a little. Nah, we didn't do any yokes. Just came back to the flat and smoked a joint or two. Watched a vid. *Eyes Wide Shut*. Yeah, again. I know it's crap. The boys like the sex bits. Nah, I think they're boring. Ah, you know. Boys will be boys. What's not to believe? You can ask Bernard the next time you see him. They fell asleep on the couch, had some cornflakes in the morning and we watched some more vids in the afternoon. *Terminator 2* and *Face Off*. I know they're crap. The boys like the gun bits. No, only smoked a joint or two. Why the fuck would we do yokes in the afternoon? Why don't you believe me? Look, I'm sorry, I wasn't thinking. I didn't turn my phone on because I had no credit. I stayed in, I was wrecked. I know I should've turned it on to see if you were calling but … No. Look. I was tired. I wasn't thinking. I went back to sleep after the lads left and I was totally gone. Real deep black sleep like. I didn't dream. How can I dream about you if I didn't dream? That doesn't mean anything. For fuck's sake Linda. What do you want from me? Jesus … Aw, look. Don't cry, will you? Linda … Linda. This is stupid. Why won't you relax? You're not relaxed. You're fucking crying. Over nothing. Yes, nothing. I'm fed up with this shit.

With having to answer to you for everything. No, it didn't used to be like this. What does that mean? You know what I mean. Will you stop fucking crying? I was not out with anyone else. I was not doing E. I was here, in the fucking flat watching *Aliens* with the lads and smoking the odd joint. Well *Terminator 2*, whatever. What fucking difference does it make? Why don't you believe me? I am not lying. I'm getting pissed off because I'm fed up been interrogated over every fucking detail. No, you are. Yes, you fucking are. What? Yes. Yes. Why? OK, I still … do.
That's what I said. There. I just said it. Oh, for fuck's sake. Look I'm hanging up now. Call me back when you're stable enough to make sense. Yeah, yeah, same to you. Goodbye. Whatever. (*Mimes hanging up, turns to audience*) Hang the fuck up. Look. What the fuck can I say? I don't know. I just can't do this anymore. (*We hear the phone ringing again*) I don't fucking believe it. If this is her again (*He mimes answering, continues to talk to audience*) It's not. It's work. Want me in tonight. Extra staff. Big party. Launch show for some magazine. Time and a half. They're opening the Gravity Bar and all. Will I do it? Fuck it. Yeah. Take me mind off this shit.

The light fades down on **Ray***; he disappears.*

18. ROYAL CANAL BANK, EVENING

A very dim light fades up to reveal **Dave**. *He turns to the audience.*

Dave Which way is quicker, Dorset Street or the canal? Jaysis, that half hour is nearly up.

Canal it is. Fuck, thought they were gonna put lights along here. The fucking state of the place. Junkies' playground. Something creeps into me head like a filthy shadow. Remember something on the news a while ago. What was it? Do I want to be bringing it up while I'm walking along here? Too late. That's it, there it is. Suitcase wedged against one of the gates or locks or whatever they call them. (*Sinister internal voice*) A suitcase with a mutilated body. Cut in half to fit in the case. Head and hands chopped … (*His own worried voice*) Shut up brain, don't want to know this now. Keep walking. (*Sinister internal voice*) The head and hands were never found. (*His own worried voice*) You fucker, I told you not to think it. Hate this fucking canal. Should have taken Dorset Street. It's quicker and not so dark … Keep walking. There's the Drumcondra Bridge now. And there's the Ballymun Fella there. Smoking a joint. Nice tracksuit, you classy bastard. (*Talking to Ballymun Fella*) How's it going? (*Ballymun Fella voice*) 'Alright. Jaysis, you look like shite. Why's your face so red?' (*To audience*) What? I touch me face. It's warm. Blood vessels swollen up from too much yokes. (*Talking to Ballymun Fella*) Sunburn. (*To audience*) I tell the Ballymun Fella and give him his money. He shrugs and gives me the coke, then offers me a puff on his joint. I decline. Open up the coke. Ballymun Fella looks at me a little curiously. (*Ballymun Fella voice*) 'It's alright man. Same as before. Peruvian.' (*Talking to Ballymun Fella*) Aw I know, I say. Just want some now. Pick me up a bit. (*Ballymun Fella voice*) 'Oh right. Goin' partyin' tonight are ye?' (*To audience*) I say I don't think so, reminding myself about picking up Samantha later, but when I snort a bit of sneachta, it's pretty good and persuasive. Fuck it. (*Talking to Ballymun Fella*) Yeah, maybe. Cheers man. I owe ye one. (*To audience*) Give him a little nod and smile as he heads back to his red Golf GT. 00 D. Ballymun Fella. I take out my moby as he drives off back to the 'burbs. There's a text from Ray: 'Wanna hit the Storehouse?' I call Bernard. (*Mimes taking out his phone and talks to* **Bernard**) Where the fuck did you go? Fucking work? Are you off your tits? I know you are. What time are you finished? Are you gonna come back out again? Ah go on, I have a surprise for you. Nice one. See you then. (*To audience*) That coke's hit the spot. Think I'll grab a quick pint before I meet Bernard. I head back into town. But this time I take Dorset Street. I hate that fucking canal.

The light changes, illuminating more of the stage. **Dave** *stays where he is, checking his watch.*

19. GUINNESS STOREHOUSE, NIGHT

Bernard *walks towards* **Dave** *from the other side of the stage. He describes his surroundings directly to the audience.*

Bernard The sky's a deep purple blue, still hints of sun, like rainbow petrol streaks on a wet road. Air is humid. Warm. Still. The smell of hops hangs in the air like a thick, invisible fog. I meet up with Dave.

Dave Do you wanna do some coke?

Bernard OK. (*To audience*) He takes out a little plastic bag and opens it up. He takes a twisted, blue biro cap and dips it into the coke, scooping up a tiny amount. It's not as powdery as I imagined; it looks kinda sticky.

Dave Just snort it up hard, hold your nose and keep sniffing.

Bernard OK. (*To audience*) I'm thinking Al Pacino in *Scarface*. I'm thinking Ray Liotta in *Goodfellas*. I'm thinking Liam Gallagher. I'm thinking will this shit go up my nose properly?
I'm thinking this is expensive. I'm thinking I'm not paying for it. I'm thinking fuck it. So then I snort and I'm not thinking anymore. (*They mime snorting cocaine and both of them narrate to the audience from here on, pointing out the things they see*) I'm sniffing.

Dave I'm laughing.

Bernard I'm tasting dispriny phlegm at the back of my throat.

Dave We're walking around the corner. Passing another warehouse. Big blue sign for the storehouse. Group of people heading same direction as us. The Hip, the Cool, the Happening.

Bernard I'm trying to keep a straight face.

Dave I'm licking my lips. This is gonna be a good night. I can feel it.

Bernard Queue.

Dave Long queue.

Bernard Wait. Stand.

Dave Stand. Wait.

Bernard Queue moves. Not so long waiting.

Dave Not so bad.

Bernard Through metal door in blank warehouse front and enter neon wonderland.

The light changes as they enter the brightly coloured interior.

Dave Chick in black, with headset, clipboard, airbrushed face.

Bernard Hope Ray got us on the list OK … Give her our names.

Dave She takes 'em, checks 'em, salutes 'em.

Bernard Points us towards an escalator.

Pulsating dance music becomes audible and continues to grow throughout the following:

Dave Moving on. Top of escalator. Much more open, wide, bright. Hearing music from above. Way above.

Bernard A desk. More cool people queuing. Something weird about that.

Dave Two more chicks in black, no headsets or clipboards but still with identical airbrushed faces. They give us some blue plastic drink vouchers and point us toward a lift.

Bernard Wait a minute … The Lift. The coolest fucking lift on Earth. Like something out of *Aliens* or *Star Wars* or … Fuck me.

Dave Doors close, motors hum excitingly and the lift rockets upwards. Through floors, ceilings, cables, pipes, air-conditioning vents.

Bernard Moving through the building like a multicoloured X-ray. Feel like I'm going to up to get into a space shuttle or something.

Dave Floor Four. Floor Five. Fuck me, this place is huge. Music's getting louder. Boom, boom, boom. Get ready.

Bernard Bing! Floor Six. Suuwwhish!

Dave A new track starts as the doors open and we step out of the lift. This is the shit and we are the men.

The music is now at its top volume; the lads have to shout to be heard over it.

Dave *and* **Bernard** *bop away to the music as another part of the stage lights up to reveal* **Ray**. **Ray** *is working behind a very busy bar. He talks directly to the audience.*

Ray Jesus. I think every fucking trendy is in here tonight. It's three deep at the bar. A platoon of Toni & Guy haircuts sway in front of me. And that prick of a supervisor Dermot is hovering around checking everyone's angle of pour. Got to keep an eye out for him.
Alright, s'pose I better serve some of these retards. (*To various customers*) No, sorry this is a Guinness-only bar. Cocktails are downstairs. Sorry, with you in a sec. Coming up right now … . Yes, it's free. No, all night. (*To audience*) All fucking night. Christ, what time is it? Where's me phone? (*To various*

customers) Coming now. No, Guinness only I'm afraid. (*To audience*) Fuck, it's only half eleven. Four missed calls. Surprise, surprise, fucking Linda. You have one new whinging message on your voice mail. (*To various customers*) Yeah, it's free.
No, the blue vouchers. The yellow ones are from last week. No, sorry. (*To audience*) Fuck, here's this cunt Dermot. (*To his supervisor, Dermot*) No, he had the wrong vouchers. I wasn't being cheeky. I was shouting over the music, man. Yeah, right. (*To audience*) Prick. Think he saw me messing with me phone. (*To customer*) Yeah, it's only Guinness. Twelve pints? OK, that's gonna take a while.

The light fades down on **Ray** *as he mimes pulling a pint. Our attention is focused back on* **Dave** *and* **Bernard** *left on the other side of the stage; they narrate directly to the audience.*

Bernard Jesus ... This place is fucking mad. Feel like I'm in some ad or music video. One of those really colourful ones. Where everyone is a model or an android or something. Wish I was paying more attention when I was getting dressed. Don't think me socks match. Keep pushing my jeans down, hoping no-one will notice.

Dave Everyone here is drinking Guinness. I suppose you have to or something. But I don't drink Guinness. I tried it once when I was fifteen but to me it tasted like a milkshake made of cabbage or broccoli. Minging. Pity I don't like it. 'Cause it's free here tonight.

Bernard Ray is working behind one of the three bars in here. It's too busy to stay at his bar and talk to him so we walk around the club. We join a table with some people we apparently know.

Dave I'm talking about the war in Iraq.

Bernard I'm drinking.

Dave I'm talking about the new bar on the quays I haven't been to yet.

Bernard I'm looking at some chick's tanned tits.

Dave I'm talking about *Top Cat.*

Bernard I'm talking about *Top Gun.*

Dave I'm talking about Top Shop.

Bernard I'm staring at some guy's Hawaiian shirt.

Dave I'm walking downstairs. I'm passing some chick on a mobile phone. I'm noticing her g-string through her white trousers. I'm opening the door. I'm pissing. I'm checking that I look cool in the mirror. I'm checking the chick-with-phone's ass again.

Bernard I'm ordering a drink. I'm listening to a fat guy's joke. I'm getting Tequila Sunrise spilled on me by some hippy chick. I'm listening to another fat guy tell another joke. I'm watching Dave chat up some redhead. I'm finishing another Guinness.

Dave I'm on the phone to someone. I'm knocking back a shot of Aftershock. I'm outside bumming a cigarette off a chick with a fat ass. I'm ignoring her telling me how her mother might have breast cancer.

Bernard I'm asking Dave for more coke. I'm looking at the redhead whose thigh Dave is squeezing. I'm locking a cubicle door. I'm doing more coke.

Dave I'm eating crisps. I'm bumping into someone. I'm pissing.

Bernard I'm talking to the girl who spilled Tequila Sunrise on me. She's foreign. She's wearing a tiny, red boob tube and a long purple skirt that looks like it's been mauled to ribbons by a tiger. A large magnet is pulling my feet toward her. I'm looking at her lips.
I'm learning how to pronounce her name. I'm talking about Italy. I'm talking about Spain.
I'm talking about Prague. I'm talking about Finglas.

The light fades up again on **Ray** *at the bar; he's on the phone.*

Ray Linda, what is it? Did something happen? That message you just left. Fuck sake, I thought something happened to you. Well, I can't talk to you now. I'm working. And if I get caught on the phone to you I'll get a bollocking. I *am* working. I know what day it is. They called me in. Overtime. (*Realising he's being watched*) Oh fuck … (*Calling to his supervisor*) Yeah Dermot, I'll be off in a sec. I know man, yeah. (*Back to Linda on the phone*) I am not fucking out. I'm behind the fucking bar and I can't fucking talk. (*Calling to his supervisor*) Yeah, right. (*To customer*) Just coming there sir. With you in a sec. (*Back to Linda on the phone*) It's fucking mad here Linda. I'll be finished about three. Call me back then. (*Calling to his supervisor*) Look, man, would you have some patience? I'm doing my best. (*Back to Linda on the phone*) I can't, I still haven't got credit. I just forgot. (*Calling to his supervisor*) I know Dermot, I know. I'm hanging up now. (*Back to Linda on* *the phone*) I finish at three, call then. Well, it'll have to do. That's when I'm done. Look it's mad here. I'm going. Bye. (*Calling to his supervisor*) Sorry, Dermot, sorry. (*To customer*) What can I get you? OK, coming up. (*To his supervisor, who has come over to him*) What, man? Can you not talk to me here? I had to take that call. OK, OK, I'll be with you now Dermot. Right, I'm fucking coming.

Bernard *bops away to the music. He's been chatting with the Foreign Girl.* **Dave** *is no longer with him.*

Bernard (*to audience*) I'm laughing. I'm chewing chewing-gum. I'm drinking Red Bull and vodka. I'm squeezing the Foreign Girl's shoulder. (*Talking to Foreign Girl*) Yeah. Well … Do you know someone here? Oh right. What do they do? What? Oh, web designers … sorry. Yeah. Just your accent … No, no, I really like it. It's different. Sure mine probably sounds weird as fuck to you. Really? You over here for long? A year? Oh, I thought you might be on holiday or something. Where do you work? Oh yeah? No, I know it. Really nice sandwiches. Me? No. Well, I've got sort of a part-time thing. Officey work. Trying to write a bit though. Ah, short stories, some poetry. Yeah? Really? Yeah, it's fun. Gives you a good feeling when you finish something and see all the words there on the page. I think … Ah sorry, I'm waffling. Ah, I am. Really, you think so? Thanks … I, eh, I like your skirt. Yeah, it's really cool …

Dave *reappears in the light. He's very coked up now, deranged in fact. He narrates to the audience aggressively.*

Dave I'm doing more coke. I'm pissing. I'm laughing. I'm looking at a painting on the wall. I'm listening to some guy talking about his da's funeral. I'm drinking. I'm singing.

I'm texting someone. I'm puking. I'm laughing. I'm tripping over a stool. I'm sitting on some girl's lap. I'm pissing. I'm looking at how white my dick is. I'm eating more crisps. I'm looking at some chick's fishnet stockings. I'm puking. I'm singing. I'm feeling a knee. I'm on the phone. I'm crying. I'm laughing. I'm talking to the bouncers. I'm having a laugh with the bouncers. I'm slagging the bouncers. I'm getting pushed by the bouncers. I'm outside. I'm outta coke. I'm dialling my phone.

Bernard (*to audience*) Me and this Foreign Girl are really talking a *lot*. About all sorts of stuff. Writing. Families. Art. All kinds of intense shit, you know? But what's funny is, this girl is *listening* to me. This is class. Really fucking class. It's like I'm … *we're* … making a genuine … She leans in real close to me now and she's talking right into my ear and I'm thinking it's not just because the music is so loud … I can see Ray having a bit of a shouting match with some bald guy with a tie. I think it might be his manager or something. The Foreign Girl puts her hand on my chest and without even thinking I lean forward and kiss her. And everything disappears. The heat. The other people. The music. Everything. Except her lips. And her hands on my chest. (**Ray** *crosses the stage to* **Bernard***; he looks angry*) Then she breaks away from me and the world reappears. She's smiling awkwardly and I realise Ray is standing beside us. (*To Foreign Girl*) Sorry. (*To Ray*) Nice fucking timing, man. What's up?

Ray Sorry to intrude, but I just quit my job and Dave's after getting kicked out. He's waiting outside. I think we should leave.

Bernard What? What about—

Ray Are you coming or what?

Bernard Ah fuck man, I don't know. I'm just after meetin'—

Ray Well, I'm fucking outta here.

Bernard Shit. (*To audience*) I tell the Foreign Girl I want to see her again. She says she'd like to see me too. I give her my phone number and another quick kiss. Then I'm following Ray towards the glass lift. I look back but a crowd of people has swallowed her up.

The lights and music fade; **Ray** *and* **Bernard** *disappear.*

20. VARIOUS CITY-CENTRE STREETS, NIGHT

Light fades up on **Dave***, leaning against the edge of the stage.*

Dave (*to audience*) I'm leaning against the wall opposite the entrance of the Storehouse. Staring across at the two gorillas who fucked me out. One of them looks a bit like Steven Seagal. Prick. I take my silver pipe out of my jacket pocket and spark up a little bit of the Dutch weed Meehall brought me back from Amsterdam. I hold in a lungful for about thirty seconds, then let it all out with a big, wide toothy grin for the gorillas. (**Ray** *and* **Bernard** *join* **Dave** *in the light*) Ray and Bernard come out at last. I reach into the front of me jeans and pull me bag of Es from outta me jocks. I make sure the gorillas see me doing this. One of them talks into his walkie-talkie. Bernard looks a bit

nervous. I give him one of the Kennys. Ray snaps his out of me hand and swallows it down without a word. We start to walk away.
I shout back at the gorillas: Sorry cunts, no yokes for youse.

Bernard What do you think of your one?

Ray What?

Bernard What do you think of that girl I was with back there?

Ray She's not bad.

Dave Where's she from?

Bernard I, eh … I don't know. She's, eh … foreign.

Dave Oh right.

Bernard She's not bad, is she?

Ray She's a bit old for you.

Dave Where are we going?

Ray Any fucking where.

Bernard (*to audience*) Dave was right about those Kennys.

Dave Get you on a mad adrenaline buzz.

Bernard (*to audience*) They kick in and the night goes into fast forward.

Ray (*to audience*) My brain starts to stutter all over the fuckin'—

Bernard Apache Pizza!

Dave Three slices of pepperoni and three large Cokes.

Bernard (*to audience*) I only eat the pepperoni and leave the bread.

Dave Another slice of pepperoni and a pint in—

Ray Turk's fuckin' Head?

Bernard Heineken? Fuck Heineken! Er-ding-er!

Dave They've no Erdinger.

Ray Then what the fuck are we doin' here?

Bernard We should be in—

Dave Dakota won't let us in.

Bernard But I was there last week.

Dave Exactly, and you acted like a spare tit with gorillas at the end of the night.

Bernard I did? Oh, I did …

Ray Give me another E.

Dave Here, take two and run six miles before you call me in the morning.

Ray There's a big queue of people queuing to get into Q Bar.

Dave Do you know how fucking stupid that is?

The lads look around in horror, describing what they see to the audience.

Bernard Oh no, here comes the apocalypse.

Ray It's *Night of the Living Dead* on O'Connell Street.

Dave A river of puke and piss runs down the overflowing gutter.

Ray Streaky-faced girls stagger around blindly, carrying their new sandals and scratching their fat thighs through torn tights.

Bernard Three crew-cut lads throw up their Happy Meals outside McDonalds.

Dave Some English cunts in Ben Sherman shirts are playing chicken with the Luas in a shopping trolley.

Bernard An armada of ambulances and police cars roar past Clery's on their way to some unseen mill up.

Dave An ugly couple are screwing on a bench beside a homeless guy with a scarred face.

Ray A tornado of large seagulls swirls around a pile of half-eaten Supermacs, Burger King and Abrakebabra crap, fighting like vultures.

Bernard 'Elaine, come back!!!' screams some junkie and we cross the road towards the Ambassador.

Bernard *wanders off out of the light, disappearing for a moment.*

Dave (*to audience*) Ray stops at a set of traffic lights at, I think, Parnell Square.

Ray Wait.

Dave What?

Ray Where's Bernard?

Dave (*to audience*) It takes us a second or two to notice Bernard struggling to climb over a gate into some park or something. (*To Bernard*) What are you doing man?

Bernard I wanna get in here. Give us a push.

Dave (*to audience*) I hoist Bernard's second foot over the gate and he plonks down on the other side.

Bernard Are yez coming in or wha'?

Dave (*to audience*) Ray looks around a little. I get up onto the gate and hop over. Bernard runs down some steps that lead to a sort of fountain thing. I'm starting to recognise this place a little. Ray sighs loudly and looks at us through the gate.

Ray What if someone sees us? The cops always go past here.

Dave (*checking watch*) Seiko tells me it's … three a.m. Not at this hour?

Ray Especially at this hour.

Dave Ah you're a loser. (*To audience*) I follow Bernard down the steps. Ray follows after.
(*To the others*) What do you call this place again?

Bernard The Garden of Remembrance.

Dave What does it Rememberate?

Bernard I don't remember.

Dave (*to audience*) Bernard is taking off his shoes. I start to open the laces of me runners. I wonder why we're taking off our shoes.

Ray I think it's for 1916 or something. That's the Children of Lir.

Dave (*to audience*) Ray points down at a big statue at the other end of the water. It looks like a few people being attacked by some giant birds. It's pretty freaky. Bernard steps into the water and I climb in after him. Ah, now I get it. We're paddling. Deadly.

Ray *climbs in after them and they shiver and laugh together.*

Ray (*to audience*) The water is fucking freezing. But it feels mad. Like standing in electricity. It shoots up our legs, through our balls, zigzagging through our guts, opening up our lungs and reawakening the ecstasy in our heads.

Dave (*to audience*) It's all very crazy and the sky seems a weird purple colour and I wonder if I'm wired enough to be imagining this.

Bernard (*to audience*) When we get out of the water I can't feel the ground beneath my feet. The electricity zaps back down my legs and my feet feel like they're going to explode like a big sparkly firework.

Dave (*to audience*) I look down at my feet and then my hands. I'm all glowing, my skin is flashing and pulsing. I wiggle my fingers and toes and get these mad trails like car lights in a photograph.

Ray, Dave and Bernard together Off. Our. Tits.

Bernard I am King of Lir!

Dave (*to audience*) I turn and see Bernard waving down to me. He's about twenty-five feet in the air. He looks like he's flying in the purple sky. His bare feet wrapped around the neck of the big bronze bird at the top of the statue. (*The lads climb up onto the back of the booth, clinging to each other, arranging themselves in the shape of the statue. The light narrows to a single spotlight, highlighting them dramatically*) I see Ray climbing onto the shoulders of one of the figures. He's lighting up the joint he rolled earlier. Fucking nice one. One of the giant hands of the statue seems to reach out to me across the water and I step out onto it without fear. I think the statue bends and twists for me or something because suddenly without even noticing, I'm at the top. Sitting with the boys between the hard wings of the top bird. We smoke Ray's joint and look across at the back of the Rotunda and I wonder if any babies are popping out of their ma right now.

Bernard *turns and looks at him with mad, wide, cartoon eyes.*

Bernard This is deadly, isn't it?

Dave (*to audience*) I say yeah and look at Dublin. Taking it all in. Sucking the city up in a big breath of air.

Bernard We are legends.

Ray We are kings.

Dave We are wired out of our skulls. How are we going to get down?

Ray (*to audience*) Well, after a while we figure it out.

The lighting changes and the lads jump down, arranging themselves around the booth as it becomes Ray's living room again.

21. RAY'S APARTMENT, NIGHT

The lads move about doing various things as described. They're fairly wired; the pace is fast and manic.

Bernard (*to audience*) Then it's Ray's gaff. Next stop.

Ray Pit stop.

Dave Piss stop, more like. I'm first in the jacks.

Ray Then me.

Bernard Finally me. Why am I always last?

Dave 'Cause you're a loser. Any drink?

Ray Half a bottle of Smirnoff on the shelf.

Dave Class. Any music?

Ray Leftfield. Rhythm and Stealth in the machine.

Dave Nice one. Any joints?

Ray Under construction. First, due for completion presently.

Dave Glug-glug.

Bernard Boom-boom.

Ray Puff-puff.

Dave Primary needs taken care of?

Ray Uh, maybe.

Bernard Well, not really. Feet still itching.

Dave Mine too. Un momento, s'il vous plaît.

Dave *heads out of the light for a moment.*

Bernard (*to audience*) Dave goes into the jacks again. (*To* **Ray**) What will we do next?

Ray Eh? Dunno.

Bernard Will we go walking again?

Ray Uh, dunno.

Bernard Sun'll be up soon. Can't sleep now. Don't wanna sleep now. Lets walk.

Ray Wait a while.

Dave *returns.*

Dave Nah, fuck that.

Bernard (*to audience*) Dave comes back from the jacks. Holding three tiny, bright white Es.

Dave Dutch Angels. Been saving them. Drop of acid in each pill. S'posed to blow your nut off.

Ray Ah, no. Not now. A waste.

Bernard What ye call them?

Dave Angels. Come on loser. Fuck it. End it with a bang. Die on a high.

Bernard Yeah.

Liz Kuti in *Still*
Photograph © Colm Hogan

Mojisola Adebayo and John Olohan in *The Buddhist of Castleknock*
Paul Reid, Rory Keenan and Jonathan Byrne in *Monged*
Photographs © Colm Hogan

Philip O'Sullivan and Amy Conroy in *The Gist of It*
Photograph © Colm Hogan

Darren Healy and Mary Murray in *Noah and the Tower Flower*
Photograph © Suzan O'Toole

Right: Fiona Condon in *Happy Endings*
Photograph © Hugh McIlveen

Charlie Bonner and Jasmine Russell in *Game*
Des Cave and Geraldine Plunkett in *Tara has Written a Play*
Photographs © Colm Hogan

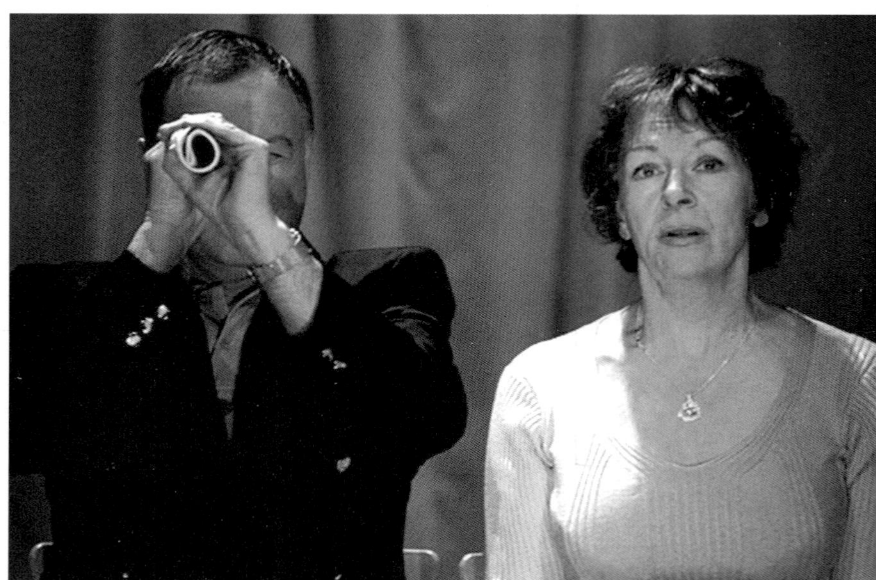

Charlie Bonner and Eamonn Hunt in *Meeting Venus*
Photograph © Colm Hogan

Jose Miguel Jimenez and Dylan Tighe in *Twenty-Two*
Photograph © Elena Benedettini

Olga Wehrly in *Drapes*
Photograph © Elena Benedettini

Ray Oh … Alright. Fuck it.

Dave There you go.

Bernard Down you go.

Dave Here we go.

Bernard Shall we go?

Dave Can we go?

Bernard Will we go?

Dave and Bernard Yeah.

Ray Supplies?

Dave More drink?

Ray Three cans of Heineken in the fridge.

Dave More joints?

Ray Three for the road.

Dave Dandy Randy. Let's go.

The lads are super charged now; they jump into the next lighting set-up.

22. VARIOUS DUBLIN STREETS, PRE-DAWN

The lads mime walking; they describe their surroundings to the audience.

Bernard And off we go. Out the door. Down the hall. Across the road. Through the park.

Ray Gardiner Street. The Diamond. Sean McDermot Street.

Bernard Purple sky showing hints of pink.

Dave Dutch yokes beginning to dissolve. Legs surging harder. Bullshit starting to flow.

Bernard That time I stole CDs from HMV.

Dave That time I shagged a French chick.

Bernard That time a bird flew down our chimney.

Dave That time me da hit me ma.

Bernard That time me granda died.

Dave That time I pissed in someone's hall.

Bernard How did that happen?

Dave Where was this?

Bernard When was that?

The lighting changes to a tight spotlight, singling out **Ray**; *the others disappear in the shadows.*

23. RAY AND LINDA – FLASHBACK

Ray (*to audience*) Her ma and da are gone away somewhere. She has a free gaff for the weekend. Her brother is having a party. They're all mods. They're listening to The Who and smoking joints and strumming their guitars. This is when Linda's seventeen. She's a goth. She hates her brother and his friends. She fucking hates The Who. But she loves me. She invites me over. We go up to her room. A vampire's bedroom. Very black. Red curtains and bed. We talk. We kiss. She puts on a Nine Inch Nails CD and plays it really loud to annoy the mods downstairs. We talk a little more. We kiss a little more. The mods play something by The Jam downstairs. I quite like The Jam but I don't tell her, 'cause she fucking hates them. She gets really mad and leaps off me, turning Trent Reznor all the way up to full volume. Paul Weller roars back up from downstairs even louder. Her brother has a better sound system. She's really pissed off; she wants to leave. I ask her where she wants to go. She says anywhere. Anywhere away from here. Not much near her house. It's sort of out in the country. I say, what about down to the sea? She smiles at me, a little surprised, and kisses me. She presses the repeat button on her CD player and leaves Nine Inch Nails playing full volume in her dark bedroom. She locks the bedroom door after her and takes the key with her. She ducks into the kitchen. The mods have left some of their drink on the table. She nicks a full bottle of Huzzar vodka and gives the finger to the sitting-room door. Paul Weller sings back unaware. She slams the front door so hard after us that the windows shake in their frames. This is when she still surprises me. This is when she still catches me staring at her. This is when she still smiles that way. She laughs all the way to the sea, dragging me down the dark, twisting, dirt path. A pebble beach. A starry sky. A full moon. 'All perfect,' she says, sipping on the Huzzar from the bottle. I look at her. This is when I don't really say much. She smiles, leans toward me, kisses me. I can taste the vodka off her tongue. Her small hands run over my crotch and I'm a little surprised. She pulls me on top of her, tugging up her long black skirt and I can feel the heat between her legs through her tights.

'Tear them,' she says and smiles. Her leather coat rustles the pebbles as she lies down. This is when I've stopped asking her if we could do it. This is when I've stopped bein' frustrated with her. This is when she wants me to have her virginity. I feel like I'm burning up. We melt together, awkward at first, then … just right. I ask her if she's OK. 'All perfect,' she says. And smiles, but her eyes are wet. I kiss her over and over and we wrap ourselves in her leather coat. She falls asleep on me. Her face against my chest. One of her hands in mine.

Her breathing presses against my ribs. Her eyelashes flutter on my skin. Her fingers twitch on my palm. I can feel her dreaming. This is when I know. This is when I still love her. But this is years ago.

The lighting changes and **Bernard** *and* **Dave** *are alongside* **Ray** *again. They continue to walk.*

24. STREETS AROUND EAST WALL, PRE-DAWN

Dave *begins to drift away from the other pair a little; he describes his surroundings directly to the audience.*

Dave Ray's shitin' on about his girlfriend again. I've never met such a boring, dried-up bitch in my life. I don't know why he stays with her. We've passed The Five Lamps and are heading into East Wall. We might be lost, but no-one's really sure who's leading and who's following, so we don't question where we're going. I think some relative of mine used to live around here. I vaguely remember me da driving me around these streets. I think I'm twelve.

I'm wearing a little brown leather jacket, tweed trousers and my big brother's suede tie. It must have been my confirmation. I do remember that whatever relative it was that lived around here, they gave me twenty quid and I bought a class pair of runners. The first Nike Airs. Everyone in me class was jealous. I said fuck you spas, they're mine. Jesus, do you hear me? What am I talking about? These are good yokes. My brain feels like it's giving itself a blowjob. Wow. Walking with my eyes closed. The E's giving me sixth sense. I'm not going to bump into anything. I'm making the world up as I go along. This walking's deadly. Left, right. Left, right. Up and down. Up and down. Forward. Forward. Forward. But … stall it a second. Are we missing someone? Who's here? Bernard and Ray. Was there someone else?

No, no. No. Just us. Who am I thinking of? Just a feeling. Someone behind us. Nah man, there's no one else with us. Just a feeling. Weird. Someone in the corner of my eye. Was it a little kid? Every time I turn around. They're gone. Hiding behind that car. That wall. That gate. Ah, man, cop on to yourself. Keep walking. Another feeling. Think I did see a little kid that time. With white runners, flashing. Then gone. Nike Airs.

Bernard (*to audience*) The sky is definitely brighter now. We're heading somewhere. I think.
Aren't we? We're the last men on Earth. The three of us. Survivors of something. Survivors of something bad. What wiped out everyone else? A war? Some plague? An earthquake? Or just some shitty party ... Where are they all gone? Which one of us gets to be Charlton Heston? I'd say he was deadly in his day. Better than Tom Cruise. Better than Harrison Ford. He was the Omega Man. He was on the Planet of the Apes. He was Moses. He was Spartacus. Or wait, no that was the other fella ... But Charlton was the main man in his day. The last man. (*To* **Ray** *and* **Dave**) That'd be mad, wouldn't it? Are you listening to me? Are you hearing me? (*To audience*) But they're not. Ray's face looks like stone. Grey granite. When his features move, his skin doesn't wrinkle. It cracks. Forming dark, black, straight lines around his eyes and mouth. My eyeballs are break-dancing in their sockets all of a sudden. But I'm not scared because after a while I get used to it and turn back toward the sun, which is just visible now, pulsating between a crane and a warehouse up ahead. (*To* **Ray** *and* **Dave**) If we keep walking we might get to it. (*To audience*) Dave looks even more crazy than Ray.
He's muttering something real fast. Something he did. Something he's going to do. Something he was. Something he's going to be. It's all very confusing. So I turn back to the sun. I wonder how long it's going to take before we get there.

The light changes suddenly. A cold spotlight singles out **Dave***; the others disappear completely.*

25. DAVE'S NIGHTMARE

Dave *stares into the blackness surrounding him; he's confused and scared.*

Dave (*to audience*) What's this? Where am I? I don't know. Look around. Figure it out. Outside. Street. Night time. Another street. Moving. Crossroads. Corner shop. Some big sign. Ad maybe. Can't really make sense of it. Where is this? Oh, here we go. Street signs. Fitzgibbon Street. No … Russell Street. Eh, kinda … North Circular Road. Sounds familiar …
I've been here before. When? North Circular Road, that goes somewhere … Must know something around here. Something ahead. Something big. Really big … Oh! Stadium. Sports stadium. Croke Park. That's Croke Park. Still building. Still building Croke Park. Still building? When is this? I know where I am. I'm at the ca— canal. Stopped. I've stopped. Not moving. Looking into the canal. Water still, no ripples, not moving. Dark. Black. Like tinted glass. Eyes search harder. Reeds. Weeds. Grass. Something glinting … Silver bracelet. Silver bracelet on a hand. A hand with manicured nails. A body. A body under the water. More visible now. Not moving. Eyes get sickeningly better each moment. Another … Another body. No. Another … Body. Body. Body. Everybody. Bodies. Bodies under the water. Filling the canal. As far as … Stop! Stop looking. Light. Another street light. Another street light to my side on. Figure. Figure standing in light. Only one left. Only one here. Can't move. Can he see me? Will he kill me? I make out his face. I see me. *I'm me.* I'm looking at me. Me looking back. Can't move. I know where I am. But I don't know when I'm here. What is this?

Ray *appears out of nowhere and catches* **Dave's** *arm;* **Dave** *jumps. The lighting becomes brighter and we see* **Bernard** *again. They're back on the streets together.*

26. QUAYS, MORNING.

Dave *looks around, confused;* **Ray** *is a little worried.* **Bernard** *is in a world of his own.*

Ray Are you alright man?

Dave Huh? What? I don't know …

Ray (*to audience*) Jesus. This is madness. Dave's been staring at his reflection in a puddle for the last five minutes. Him and Bernard are totally skaggin'. Scarily gone. What are those yokes doing to them? I wonder are they going to be alright. I'm glad I didn't take one. Dave was too busy finishing off my Smirnoff back at the flat to notice me putting the E in my pocket. I've had enough of them. No more. I mean, look at these guys. I don't need that. Take the pill out. Fuck it away from me. Dutch Es at five in the morning. Fuck that. Sorry, I'm not as messed up as you guys. Do I still have a joint left? One? Oh, thank you. There is a god. Somewhere. I'm gradually trying to turn the boys back towards town. Not telling them. Just guiding them. And it's working. We're on the quays, walking back in the direction of the Custom House. I can't believe I walked that far. I'm so fucking tired. The others haven't a notion where they are. Just wandering along. Muttering. I've stopped listening to them. Just walking is taking up every

ounce of reserve energy. Half fucking eight. Linda never called. Not once. Not even a text message. I hope she's alright. I hope nothing happened to her.
I want to hear her voice for some reason. Never thought I'd say that again. (**Bernard** *pulls at* **Ray's** *jacket limply and he turns to him.* **Bernard** *smiles at* **Ray**) Bernard's big, warm stupid grin makes me smile back somehow. His pupils are wide black tunnels into his drug-muddled brain.

Bernard Look at the birds man. Man, look at the birds. The speed of them.

Ray (*to audience*) His eyes zip about following two seagulls spiralling above Jury's Hotel.
I offer him my joint.

Bernard Thanks man, don't know what I'd do without ya.

Ray (*to audience*) I feel guilty now. I don't know what for. Just guilty. For everything.
For taking drugs? For cheating on Linda? For introducing Bernard to Dave? For just being … I don't know. I need sleep. I need me bed. I need to get away from these two.
They're so wired they might go on for longer. I know Dave has more yokes back at my place. Maybe on him right now. I have to stop this. (*To* **Dave**) This is pretty fucked, man.

Dave (*not comprehending*) What?

Ray We've got to get away from each other.

Dave Why? We're nearly there.

Ray (*to audience*) Jesus … Nearly there? Nearly *where*? Bernard's looking into the Liffey. (*Calling to* **Bernard**) Man, be careful.

Bernard If I fall in, would you jump after me?

Ray I don't know. I don't know. I don't think so. (**Bernard** *laughs*) I can't look at him anymore. (*Turns to* **Dave**) Dave looks fucked up. Like a junkie. Like … (*To* **Dave**) You should go home, man.

Dave No, I … There's something I forgot …

Ray Why don't you go back to Samantha's? I'm sure she's worried about you.

Dave Sam … Samantha? Yeah …

Ray Yeah, we'll get you in the next taxi. Right?

Dave Yeah, fuck … That's … Yeah.

Ray *smacks* **Dave** *across the back of the head.* **Dave** *looks at him, confused.*

Ray You're gonna have to get your head together, man. (**Dave** *nods, then suddenly spins to look behind, paranoid again*)

Ray (*to audience*) I give him the joint. He takes it and continues to walk toward the Custom House.

Bernard All the fish are dead.

Ray Come on man. There's no fish in there.

Bernard Yeah, they're all dead.

Ray (*to audience*) Bernard jogs back across the road and we cut through the IFSC, coming out by Busáras. I hail a passing taxi. And spend two minutes trying to get Dave into the front seat. (*To taxi driver as he struggles with* **Dave**, *who is barely conscious at this stage*) Really sorry about this, man. Appreciate it …

Dave (*to taxi driver*) Yeah, I'm really sorry, da.

Ray It's not your da, Dave. It's a taxi driver.

Dave Oh … Sorry, bud.

Ray Dave listen, that stuff you have in my place. I'm getting rid of it.

Dave The stuff?

Ray Yeah. I'm dumping it man, alright?

Dave Aw yeah, that's probably for the best.

Ray Glad you agree, man.

Dave Wholeheartedly.

Ray (*to audience*) Fucker doesn't know what's going on. I pay the driver with a tenner from Dave's pocket and give him directions to Samantha's flat in the Liberties. (**Bernard** *wanders off out of the light and disappears as* **Ray** *watches* **Dave** *heading off out of the light in the opposite direction*) I watch the taxi pull off. But when I turn around to the wall where Bernard was sitting, Bernard's not sitting there anymore. He's gone. Really gone. I look around in each direction for five minutes. No sign of him. I ring his mobile. But it's turned off. Fuck this. Why should I care? This is not my problem anymore. I did my best. And I need my bed.

Ray *wanders off out of the light, leaving the stage empty for a moment.*

27. BERNARD'S BAD TRIP, VARIOUS STREETS, MORNING

Bernard *staggers into the light, very lost. He's very 'monged': chewing his lips, blinking his eyes, swaying dizzily. He mutters to the audience maniacally.*

Bernard I walk down a road. Past a Centra that's open. By a chipper that's closed. I walk under a bridge. I see a dead dog. And a pigeon with only one foot. Then I'm in a church. And there's mass. And I'm sure no-one's looking at me. Jesus doesn't look very happy. He looks the way I feel. Like he needs a big fry for breakfast. Then my eyelids get heavy and the brain TV comes on. Rebecca De Mornay's left arm is ripped apart from a load of needles. And she's crying. Then her body is dissolving in a pool of acid on the kitchen floor. Then I'm performing oral sex on an ugly nun. And loads of ugly, old people are looking at me and laughing horribly. And I can hear metal on metal. Ringing. Tingling. Clanging. Crashing. Bashing. It's all a bit disturbing, so I hold my eyes

open. And the world is just as crazy. But at least it's real, and it's not my fault. And I'm not at mass anymore. My legs are attempting to walk. And my hands are attempting to turn on my phone. It's very grey and a homeless man is sitting against an unused newsstand. He looks like an old statue that's been smashed in the face with a sledgehammer. I give him a fiver and he offers me a cigarette. But I don't smoke. He's telling me about his son who moved to England and his wife who left him for a man from Africa. He makes me feel sad. (**Bernard** *slowly sinks down until he's sitting, slumped on the edge of the stage*) And he keeps talking and his voice becomes music. I can't hear the difference between the words. Just sounds. And I realise, I'm sitting on the ground. I love the ground. The ground's always there for you to rely on wherever you go. Always there when you feel like sitting down or lying down. What am I doing? My brain's not working.
I was with someone a while ago. Where are they gone? Who was it again? So many questions. Annoying me. Where am I? How did I get here? (*We hear the sound of* **Bernard's** *mobile phone ringing*) My phone is ringing. Why is my phone ringing? Who is it? Can they give me some answers? Can they help me? (**Bernard** *mimes answering the phone*) Hello? Oh, hi. How's it going? Yeah, yeah. Three o'clock. Yeah, I can do that. Do you know where Sufi's is?

Bernard *mimes hanging up. He looks happy as he drags himself up off the edge of the stage. The light fades and he disappears.*

28. COMING DOWN IN RAY'S APARTMENT, MORNING

A light fades up on **Ray***; he looks destroyed. He describes his surroundings to the audience wearily.*

Ray I am so fucking sick of this dump. Get my joint ingredients from the *Apocalypse Now* video box by the fireplace and retreat into the bedroom. I stick my phone in the charger. Wish I could just switch off. Plug myself into the wall and recharge. Roll a joint without any brain activity. Just like those soldiers can assemble their rifles blindfolded and … underwater, or something. There's a half-empty bottle of Grolsch by the bed. I almost vomit but I'm too tired to gag, so I take a sup instead. And it's not so bad. I flame up the joint with a packet of semi-soggy matches. Lie on bed, take the first long sumptuous drag of my Rizla masterpiece. Lovely numbness. Smokey coma. Cool, empty Tupperware head. But, ah … big fucking fat syringe into the side of my brain. It says, 'Why hasn't she called?' Try to pull the syringe out, throw it away. Burn it away. Sixth drag … seventh. What's in the CD player? Hit play, doesn't matter. (*We hear a track by New Order begin in the background.* **Ray** *smiles*) You'll do nicely. Ninth drag. Lovely synthy euphoria. Swirly, twangy, soft, soothing, electronic beat.

What track is this? Haven't heard it in ages. I drag my guitar out from under the bed. It's dusty as fuck. But then, what isn't in this room? Present company included. The strings are not that fucked. I attempt to play along with the New Order lads. But I'm slow and off tune. Guitar slides off the bed. Don't even hear it hit the floor. All poxed up now. The room seems to tilt completely and I go from lying on my back to crawling on my hands and knees towards my phone. I push the button

for Linda … It rings for a long, long, long time. Then she answers quietly. She says she can't really talk now. She says it's not a good time. She says I should call back later. She says she doesn't want to talk to me now. She says I'm too pushy.
She says I'm pissing her off. She says I should listen to myself.
She says I sound like a whingey teenager. She says fuck off Ray. She says I'm fucking stoned. She says I'm always fucked. She says she doesn't know who I am anymore. She says … Just forget everything.
She hangs up. And me? What do I say? What can I say? Me: I say … I say nothing at all.

Ray's *light fades slowly and he disappears.*

29. DAVE AT SAMANTHA'S, MORNING

A light fades up at the other side of the stage to reveal **Dave** *leaning against the wall.*

Dave (*to audience*) Seiko tells me it's … Eh, Seiko doesn't tell me very much. Its battery is dead. So is mine. I'm staring at the red bricks of a wall. Seems like I've been here for ages. (**Dave** *stands up straight; he's very weak. He continues narrating to the audience*) Sam's apartment building. How the fuck did I get here? Fall through the door into the lift. Hit the button that most looks like a three. I stare at the pattern in the rubber floor of the lift. It's making me dizzy. I close my eyes. The lift *bings* loudly and it's like a laser beam through my brain. I find the key in my pocket and carefully unlock the door of Sam's apartment. I can feel the come-down rigor-mortis freezing me up and my hands and jaw are trembling uncontrollably. Sam's bedroom is a black hole. I feel my way across to the big double bed. (*To Samantha*) Sam. Sam … baby? (*To audience*) I can hear her murmuring and turning over under the thick duvet. I sit down on the edge of the bed and pull off my runners without opening the laces. I take off my jacket and get into bed without taking off the rest of my clothes. (*To Samantha*) Sam? Baby, are you awake? (*To audience*) She moans and turns over again. (*Samantha's voice*) 'I am now. Where were you? I waited at the club for half an hour.' (*To audience*) I reach my hands over to hug her. She squirms sleepily. (*Samantha's voice*) 'Do you still have your clothes on?' (*To audience*) I can't see her. I imagine her now. I imagine her with large breasts and wide hips. Swallowing me up in her warmth and softness. (*To Samantha*) Please baby, I'm … I'm scared. I … (*To audience*) I can feel her turning back toward me. (*Samantha's voice*) 'What's wrong Dave?' (*To Samantha*) I … I don't know. I'm not … I'm finished. Forget the drugs. I'm done. I'm sorry. I'm finished with the whole … drug thing. For good, I'm telling you now … (*Samantha's voice*) 'Yeah, right … You've said that before.' (*To Samantha*) Maybe, yeah. I have. But this time I'm serious. I don't want … Baby … (*To audience*) I reach out to her. She doesn't squirm this time. I put my arms around her. The glowing heat of her feels so good against my shivering corpse. She doesn't smell like Ralph Lauren anymore. She just smells like her. Safe … (*To Samantha*) Sam … (*To audience*) Then I say it. I say it to her. (*To Samantha*) I love you. (*To audience*) My eyes are getting used to the darkness. I can just see her eyes. They're open. Glinting. She smiles. Then she leans forward, kisses me on the forehead and whispers into my ear. (*Samantha's voice*) 'Dave … You're such a spa.'

Dave *smiles thinly and his light fades out; he disappears.*

Dave Doors close, motors hum excitingly and the lift rockets upwards. Through floors, ceilings, cables, pipes, air-conditioning vents.

Bernard Moving through the building like a multicoloured X-ray. Feel like I'm going to up to get into a space shuttle or something.

Dave Floor Four. Floor Five. Fuck me, this place is huge. Music's getting louder. Boom, boom, boom. Get ready.

Bernard Bing! Floor Six. Suuwwhish!

Dave A new track starts as the doors open and we step out of the lift. This is the shit and we are the men.

The music is now at its top volume; the lads have to shout to be heard over it.

Dave *and* **Bernard** *bop away to the music as another part of the stage lights up to reveal* **Ray**. **Ray** *is working behind a very busy bar. He talks directly to the audience.*

Ray Jesus. I think every fucking trendy is in here tonight. It's three deep at the bar. A platoon of Toni & Guy haircuts sway in front of me. And that prick of a supervisor Dermot is hovering around checking everyone's angle of pour. Got to keep an eye out for him.
Alright, s'pose I better serve some of these retards. (*To various customers*) No, sorry this is a Guinness-only bar. Cocktails are downstairs. Sorry, with you in a sec. Coming up right now … . Yes, it's free. No, all night. (*To audience*) All fucking night. Christ, what time is it? Where's me phone? (*To various*

customers) Coming now. No, Guinness only I'm afraid. (*To audience*) Fuck, it's only half eleven. Four missed calls. Surprise, surprise, fucking Linda. You have one new whinging message on your voice mail. (*To various customers*) Yeah, it's free.
No, the blue vouchers. The yellow ones are from last week. No, sorry. (*To audience*) Fuck, here's this cunt Dermot. (*To his supervisor, Dermot*) No, he had the wrong vouchers. I wasn't being cheeky. I was shouting over the music, man. Yeah, right. (*To audience*) Prick. Think he saw me messing with me phone. (*To customer*) Yeah, it's only Guinness. Twelve pints? OK, that's gonna take a while.

The light fades down on **Ray** *as he mimes pulling a pint. Our attention is focused back on* **Dave** *and* **Bernard** *left on the other side of the stage; they narrate directly to the audience.*

Bernard Jesus … This place is fucking mad. Feel like I'm in some ad or music video. One of those really colourful ones. Where everyone is a model or an android or something. Wish I was paying more attention when I was getting dressed. Don't think me socks match. Keep pushing my jeans down, hoping no-one will notice.

Dave Everyone here is drinking Guinness. I suppose you have to or something. But I don't drink Guinness. I tried it once when I was fifteen but to me it tasted like a milkshake made of cabbage or broccoli. Minging. Pity I don't like it. 'Cause it's free here tonight.

Bernard Ray is working behind one of the three bars in here. It's too busy to stay at his bar and talk to him so we walk around the club. We join a table with some people we apparently know.

Dave I'm talking about the war in Iraq.

Bernard I'm drinking.

Dave I'm talking about the new bar on the quays I haven't been to yet.

Bernard I'm looking at some chick's tanned tits.

Dave I'm talking about *Top Cat.*

Bernard I'm talking about *Top Gun.*

Dave I'm talking about Top Shop.

Bernard I'm staring at some guy's Hawaiian shirt.

Dave I'm walking downstairs. I'm passing some chick on a mobile phone. I'm noticing her g-string through her white trousers. I'm opening the door. I'm pissing. I'm checking that I look cool in the mirror. I'm checking the chick-with-phone's ass again.

Bernard I'm ordering a drink. I'm listening to a fat guy's joke. I'm getting Tequila Sunrise spilled on me by some hippy chick. I'm listening to another fat guy tell another joke. I'm watching Dave chat up some redhead. I'm finishing another Guinness.

Dave I'm on the phone to someone. I'm knocking back a shot of Aftershock. I'm outside bumming a cigarette off a chick with a fat ass. I'm ignoring her telling me how her mother might have breast cancer.

Bernard I'm asking Dave for more coke. I'm looking at the redhead whose thigh Dave is squeezing. I'm locking a cubicle door. I'm doing more coke.

Dave I'm eating crisps. I'm bumping into someone. I'm pissing.

Bernard I'm talking to the girl who spilled Tequila Sunrise on me. She's foreign. She's wearing a tiny, red boob tube and a long purple skirt that looks like it's been mauled to ribbons by a tiger. A large magnet is pulling my feet toward her. I'm looking at her lips.

I'm learning how to pronounce her name. I'm talking about Italy. I'm talking about Spain.

I'm talking about Prague. I'm talking about Finglas.

The light fades up again on **Ray** *at the bar; he's on the phone.*

Ray Linda, what is it? Did something happen? That message you just left. Fuck sake, I thought something happened to you. Well, I can't talk to you now. I'm working. And if I get caught on the phone to you I'll get a bollocking. I *am* working. I know what day it is. They called me in. Overtime. (*Realising he's being watched*) Oh fuck … (*Calling to his supervisor*) Yeah Dermot, I'll be off in a sec. I know man, yeah. (*Back to Linda on the phone*) I am not fucking out. I'm behind the fucking bar and I can't fucking talk. (*Calling to his supervisor*) Yeah, right. (*To customer*) Just coming there sir. With you in a sec. (*Back to Linda on the phone*) It's fucking mad here Linda. I'll be finished about three. Call me back then. (*Calling to his supervisor*) Look, man, would you have some patience? I'm doing my best. (*Back to Linda on the phone*) I can't, I still haven't got credit. I just forgot. (*Calling to his supervisor*) I know Dermot, I know. I'm hanging up now. (*Back to Linda on *the phone*) I finish at three, call then. Well, it'll have to do. That's when I'm done. Look it's mad here. I'm going. Bye. (*Calling to his supervisor*) Sorry, Dermot, sorry. (*To customer*) What can I get you? OK, coming up. (*To his supervisor, who has come over to him*) What, man? Can you not talk to me here? I had to take that call. OK, OK, I'll be with you now Dermot. Right, I'm fucking coming.

Bernard *bops away to the music. He's been chatting with the Foreign Girl.* **Dave** *is no longer with him.*

Bernard (*to audience*) I'm laughing. I'm chewing chewing-gum. I'm drinking Red Bull and vodka. I'm squeezing the Foreign Girl's shoulder. (*Talking to Foreign Girl*) Yeah. Well … Do you know someone here? Oh right. What do they do? What? Oh, web designers … sorry. Yeah. Just your accent … No, no, I really like it. It's different. Sure mine probably sounds weird as fuck to you. Really? You over here for long? A year? Oh, I thought you might be on holiday or something. Where do you work? Oh yeah? No, I know it. Really nice sandwiches. Me? No. Well, I've got sort of a part-time thing. Officey work. Trying to write a bit though. Ah, short stories, some poetry. Yeah? Really? Yeah, it's fun. Gives you a good feeling when you finish something and see all the words there on the page. I think … Ah sorry, I'm waffling. Ah, I am. Really, you think so? Thanks … I, eh, I like your skirt. Yeah, it's really cool …

Dave *reappears in the light. He's very coked up now, deranged in fact. He narrates to the audience aggressively.*

Dave I'm doing more coke. I'm pissing. I'm laughing. I'm looking at a painting on the wall. I'm listening to some guy talking about his da's funeral. I'm drinking. I'm singing.

I'm texting someone. I'm puking. I'm laughing. I'm tripping over a stool. I'm sitting on some girl's lap. I'm pissing. I'm looking at how white my dick is. I'm eating more crisps. I'm looking at some chick's fishnet stockings. I'm puking. I'm singing. I'm feeling a knee. I'm on the phone. I'm crying. I'm laughing. I'm talking to the bouncers. I'm having a laugh with the bouncers. I'm slagging the bouncers. I'm getting pushed by the bouncers. I'm outside. I'm outta coke. I'm dialling my phone.

Bernard (*to audience*) Me and this Foreign Girl are really talking a *lot*. About all sorts of stuff. Writing. Families. Art. All kinds of intense shit, you know? But what's funny is, this girl is *listening* to me. This is class. Really fucking class. It's like I'm ... *we're* ... making a genuine ... She leans in real close to me now and she's talking right into my ear and I'm thinking it's not just because the music is so loud ... I can see Ray having a bit of a shouting match with some bald guy with a tie. I think it might be his manager or something. The Foreign Girl puts her hand on my chest and without even thinking I lean forward and kiss her. And everything disappears. The heat. The other people. The music. Everything. Except her lips. And her hands on my chest. (**Ray** *crosses the stage to* **Bernard***; he looks angry*) Then she breaks away from me and the world reappears. She's smiling awkwardly and I realise Ray is standing beside us. (*To Foreign Girl*) Sorry. (*To Ray*) Nice fucking timing, man. What's up?

Ray Sorry to intrude, but I just quit my job and Dave's after getting kicked out. He's waiting outside. I think we should leave.

Bernard What? What about—

Ray Are you coming or what?

Bernard Ah fuck man, I don't know. I'm just after meetin'—

Ray Well, I'm fucking outta here.

Bernard Shit. (*To audience*) I tell the Foreign Girl I want to see her again. She says she'd like to see me too. I give her my phone number and another quick kiss. Then I'm following Ray towards the glass lift. I look back but a crowd of people has swallowed her up.

The lights and music fade; **Ray** *and* **Bernard** *disappear.*

20. VARIOUS CITY-CENTRE STREETS, NIGHT

Light fades up on **Dave**, *leaning against the edge of the stage.*

Dave (*to audience*) I'm leaning against the wall opposite the entrance of the Storehouse. Staring across at the two gorillas who fucked me out. One of them looks a bit like Steven Seagal. Prick. I take my silver pipe out of my jacket pocket and spark up a little bit of the Dutch weed Meehall brought me back from Amsterdam. I hold in a lungful for about thirty seconds, then let it all out with a big, wide toothy grin for the gorillas. (**Ray** *and* **Bernard** *join* **Dave** *in the light*) Ray and Bernard come out at last. I reach into the front of me jeans and pull me bag of Es from outta me jocks. I make sure the gorillas see me doing this. One of them talks into his walkie-talkie. Bernard looks a bit

nervous. I give him one of the Kennys. Ray snaps his out of me hand and swallows it down without a word. We start to walk away.
I shout back at the gorillas: Sorry cunts, no yokes for youse.

Bernard What do you think of your one?

Ray What?

Bernard What do you think of that girl I was with back there?

Ray She's not bad.

Dave Where's she from?

Bernard I, eh … I don't know. She's, eh … foreign.

Dave Oh right.

Bernard She's not bad, is she?

Ray She's a bit old for you.

Dave Where are we going?

Ray Any fucking where.

Bernard (*to audience*) Dave was right about those Kennys.

Dave Get you on a mad adrenaline buzz.

Bernard (*to audience*) They kick in and the night goes into fast forward.

Ray (*to audience*) My brain starts to stutter all over the fuckin'—

Bernard Apache Pizza!

Dave Three slices of pepperoni and three large Cokes.

Bernard (*to audience*) I only eat the pepperoni and leave the bread.

Dave Another slice of pepperoni and a pint in—

Ray Turk's fuckin' Head?

Bernard Heineken? Fuck Heineken! Er-ding-er!

Dave They've no Erdinger.

Ray Then what the fuck are we doin' here?

Bernard We should be in—

Dave Dakota won't let us in.

Bernard But I was there last week.

Dave Exactly, and you acted like a spare tit with gorillas at the end of the night.

Bernard I did? Oh, I did …

Ray Give me another E.

Dave Here, take two and run six miles before you call me in the morning.

Ray There's a big queue of people queuing to get into Q Bar.

Dave Do you know how fucking stupid that is?

The lads look around in horror, describing what they see to the audience.

Bernard Oh no, here comes the apocalypse.

Ray It's *Night of the Living Dead* on O'Connell Street.

Dave A river of puke and piss runs down the overflowing gutter.

Ray Streaky-faced girls stagger around blindly, carrying their new sandals and scratching their fat thighs through torn tights.

Bernard Three crew-cut lads throw up their Happy Meals outside McDonalds.

Dave Some English cunts in Ben Sherman shirts are playing chicken with the Luas in a shopping trolley.

Bernard An armada of ambulances and police cars roar past Clery's on their way to some unseen mill up.

Dave An ugly couple are screwing on a bench beside a homeless guy with a scarred face.

Ray A tornado of large seagulls swirls around a pile of half-eaten Supermacs, Burger King and Abrakebabra crap, fighting like vultures.

Bernard 'Elaine, come back!!!' screams some junkie and we cross the road towards the Ambassador.

Bernard *wanders off out of the light, disappearing for a moment.*

Dave (*to audience*) Ray stops at a set of traffic lights at, I think, Parnell Square.

Ray Wait.

Dave What?

Ray Where's Bernard?

Dave (*to audience*) It takes us a second or two to notice Bernard struggling to climb over a gate into some park or something. (*To Bernard*) What are you doing man?

Bernard I wanna get in here. Give us a push.

Dave (*to audience*) I hoist Bernard's second foot over the gate and he plonks down on the other side.

Bernard Are yez coming in or wha'?

Dave (*to audience*) Ray looks around a little. I get up onto the gate and hop over. Bernard runs down some steps that lead to a sort of fountain thing. I'm starting to recognise this place a little. Ray sighs loudly and looks at us through the gate.

Ray What if someone sees us? The cops always go past here.

Dave (*checking watch*) Seiko tells me it's … three a.m. Not at this hour?

Ray Especially at this hour.

Dave Ah you're a loser. (*To audience*) I follow Bernard down the steps. Ray follows after.
(*To the others*) What do you call this place again?

Bernard The Garden of Remembrance.

Dave What does it Rememberate?

Bernard I don't remember.

Dave (*to audience*) Bernard is taking off his shoes. I start to open the laces of me runners. I wonder why we're taking off our shoes.

Ray I think it's for 1916 or something. That's the Children of Lir.

Dave (*to audience*) Ray points down at a big statue at the other end of the water. It looks like a few people being attacked by some giant birds. It's pretty freaky. Bernard steps into the water and I climb in after him. Ah, now I get it. We're paddling. Deadly.

Ray *climbs in after them and they shiver and laugh together.*

Ray (*to audience*) The water is fucking freezing. But it feels mad. Like standing in electricity. It shoots up our legs, through our balls, zigzagging through our guts, opening up our lungs and reawakening the ecstasy in our heads.

Dave (*to audience*) It's all very crazy and the sky seems a weird purple colour and I wonder if I'm wired enough to be imagining this.

Bernard (*to audience*) When we get out of the water I can't feel the ground beneath my feet. The electricity zaps back down my legs and my feet feel like they're going to explode like a big sparkly firework.

Dave (*to audience*) I look down at my feet and then my hands. I'm all glowing, my skin is flashing and pulsing. I wiggle my fingers and toes and get these mad trails like car lights in a photograph.

Ray, Dave and Bernard together Off. Our. Tits.

Bernard I am King of Lir!

Dave (*to audience*) I turn and see Bernard waving down to me. He's about twenty-five feet in the air. He looks like he's flying in the purple sky. His bare feet wrapped around the neck of the big bronze bird at the top of the statue. (*The lads climb up onto the back of the booth, clinging to each other, arranging themselves in the shape of the statue. The light narrows to a single spotlight, highlighting them dramatically*) I see Ray climbing onto the shoulders of one of the figures. He's lighting up the joint he rolled earlier. Fucking nice one. One of the giant hands of the statue seems to reach out to me across the water and I step out onto it without fear. I think the statue bends and twists for me or something because suddenly without even noticing, I'm at the top. Sitting with the boys between the hard wings of the top bird. We smoke Ray's joint and look across at the back of the Rotunda and I wonder if any babies are popping out of their ma right now.

Bernard *turns and looks at him with mad, wide, cartoon eyes.*

Bernard This is deadly, isn't it?

Dave (*to audience*) I say yeah and look at Dublin. Taking it all in. Sucking the city up in a big breath of air.

Bernard We are legends.

Ray We are kings.

Dave We are wired out of our skulls. How are we going to get down?

Ray (*to audience*) Well, after a while we figure it out.

The lighting changes and the lads jump down, arranging themselves around the booth as it becomes Ray's living room again.

21. RAY'S APARTMENT, NIGHT

The lads move about doing various things as described. They're fairly wired; the pace is fast and manic.

Bernard (*to audience*) Then it's Ray's gaff. Next stop.

Ray Pit stop.

Dave Piss stop, more like. I'm first in the jacks.

Ray Then me.

Bernard Finally me. Why am I always last?

Dave 'Cause you're a loser. Any drink?

Ray Half a bottle of Smirnoff on the shelf.

Dave Class. Any music?

Ray Leftfield. Rhythm and Stealth in the machine.

Dave Nice one. Any joints?

Ray Under construction. First, due for completion presently.

Dave Glug-glug.

Bernard Boom-boom.

Ray Puff-puff.

Dave Primary needs taken care of?

Ray Uh, maybe.

Bernard Well, not really. Feet still itching.

Dave Mine too. Un momento, s'il vous plaît.

Dave *heads out of the light for a moment.*

Bernard (*to audience*) Dave goes into the jacks again. (*To* **Ray**) What will we do next?

Ray Eh? Dunno.

Bernard Will we go walking again?

Ray Uh, dunno.

Bernard Sun'll be up soon. Can't sleep now. Don't wanna sleep now. Lets walk.

Ray Wait a while.

Dave *returns.*

Dave Nah, fuck that.

Bernard (*to audience*) Dave comes back from the jacks. Holding three tiny, bright white Es.

Dave Dutch Angels. Been saving them. Drop of acid in each pill. S'posed to blow your nut off.

Ray Ah, no. Not now. A waste.

Bernard What ye call them?

Dave Angels. Come on loser. Fuck it. End it with a bang. Die on a high.

Bernard Yeah.

30. BERNARD AND THE FOREIGN GIRL, AFTERNOON

The light fades up on the booth, where **Bernard** *is sitting. He looks spaced, but happy. He talks to the audience cheerfully.*

Bernard I think Sufi's has best cappuccino in this city. So frothy. So much chocolate.
I watch the sprinkles dissolve gradually in the thick froth, then I dip my finger in ever so slowly and scoop out a big bit. I suck it off my finger with my eyes closed. My taste buds are starting to work again. I'm becoming human again. The monged monster is dying slowly and this coffee tastes damn good. It's quite sunny. But the light doesn't hurt my eyes now. I look at it for a while. Then a tall, thin silhouette comes between me and the light. Her. (*To Foreign Girl*) Hi. (**Bernard** *reacts as if she's sitting down with him; he continues to the audience*) I can feel my face spreading into a big, stupid grin as she sits down opposite me. The Foreign Girl … I mean, of course she has a name. And I do know it. I can even pronounce it if I try. Because it's right there. And I'm not going to forget it. Not going to forget her because … This girl is cool. I mean really cool. The best words to describe her are the type of words you see on magazine covers. Funky. Sexy. Hip. Cool. She's all of these things. She doesn't mind me talking, she seems to like it. She's looking at me with this incredible smile that just makes me want to smile back. It's almost hard to talk about anything sad or bad because that smile always makes me happy. But I can't tell her that right now. Because that wouldn't be cool. Or hip. Or funky. Her eyes narrow when she's happy, widen when she's serious. I don't know what they look like when she's sad. I wonder how come she's so skinny when she eats so much. You can see the

outline of the muscles on her stomach sometimes. I wonder was she ever bullied at school. I wonder can she sing. I wonder what her pubic hair looks like. I wonder how many tattoos she has. I wonder if she really loves her parents. I wonder what age she is. I wonder … why is she sitting here with me?

Bernard *looks a little confused. His light fades and he disappears.*

THE END

The Gist of It

BY RODNEY LEE

The Gist of It was first performed by Fishamble: The New Play Company at Project Arts Centre, Dublin, on 23 February 2006, with the following cast and production team:

Liam	Paul Reid
Orla	Amy Conroy
Gerard	Philip O'Sullivan
Voiceovers	Students of the Gaiety School of Acting
Director	Jim Culleton
Designer	Sonia Haccius
Lighting Designer	Sinead McKenna
Sound Designers	Vincent Doherty Ivan Birthistle
Projection Designer	One Productions
Producer	Orla Flanagan
Production Manager	Des Kenny
Stage Director	Anne Layde
Stage Manager	Aine Beamish
Stage Management Intern	Theresa Ebenhoeh
Assistant Director Intern	Eoghan Doyle
Script Development	Gavin Kostick
PR/Marketing	Cerstin Mudiwa
Photography	Colm Hogan
Graphic Designer	Gareth Jones

The Gist of It was subsequently presented as a staged reading by Fishamble in association with Origin in May 2006 at the Glucksman Ireland House in New York. This version was directed by Jim Culleton and produced by George Heslin.

CAUTION

'*The Gist of It* is a first play, part of Fishamble's splendidly productive project of introducing new voices to the Irish theatre … well-honed sense of structure … a good deal of well-worked fun' *The Irish Times*

'mastery of dialogue … knock out, funny lines' *The Sunday Tribune*

'**** Good timing is the play's essential ingredient, and the script has it in spades. This is a finely-tuned and thoroughly enjoyable debut' *The Sunday Business Post*

'A good first play … an original and imaginative plot-line' *The Sunday Independent*

'a nugget of true-life comedy gold' *rte.ie*

'sharp and highly entertaining … wonderfully wicked comedy … an entertaining night of contemporary theatre' *dublinks.com*

'very funny … fantastic … brilliant' *RTÉ 1, The View*

'an entertaining and quite accomplished debut … a lot of laughs … crackling dialogue … hilarious characters' *The Event Guide*

'fun, fast-paced and intimate drama … well worth seeing' *Dubliner*

CHARACTERS

Orla Cullen – *film-student, early twenties*
Liam Duffy – *film-student, early twenties*
Gerard Cullen – **Orla***'s father, an English teacher, forties*

The play is set in a house in present-day Dublin
Act 1 takes place on Saturday morning
Act 2 takes place on Saturday evening
Act 3 takes place on Sunday morning
It runs for approximately 90 minutes with no interval

Act One

Saturday afternoon. Coloured lights flash on the stage in time to atonal music. The sound of a baby crying plays over the music. Images are projected onto the walls; a close-up of butterfly wings, a worm crawling on an apple, a cow's heart in liquid. A spotlight illuminates an old Victorian dollhouse in the centre of the stage. **Liam**, *in a white shirt, appears behind it. He holds up a large plastic butterfly and walks around the dollhouse.*

Liam She has no future, no chance … to soar, her wings will become … dust. Behind a locked door, her heart is no more worn out by strife. Her taciturn scream lost … In the night, no more … Dreams know nothing … Know life …

Liam *pulls the plastic butterfly apart. A voice is heard from the darkness.*

Orla No, no, no.

Liam (*weary*) Jesus.

Orla That …

Liam What?

Orla Hmm …

Liam (*shrugs*) What?

Orla I don't … (*tries to find the words*)

Liam Don't what?

Orla It was … (*tries to find the words*)

Liam Christ Orla, come on.

Liam *holds up a clapper-board before the camera.*

Liam Do you want an end-board?

Orla Don't bother.

Orla *turns on the house-lights to reveal the ground floor of a small house. On the left, a living-room. On the right, a kitchen. In the living-room, on the right, there's a sofa at an angle, a small TV and video facing it and a coffee-table beside it. A coat-rack and waste-paper bin stand beside the door. A video-camera on a tripod is pointed at an angle in front of* **Liam**. *The room is cluttered with film-making equipment, props, etc. In the corner, against the wall, is a shelf of video-tapes, most with hand-written labels, others unlabelled. In another corner is a fish-tank filled with liquid. A cow's heart is suspended in it. In the kitchen, there's a table and chair. On the table is a telephone. At the back is a sink and washboard. The door, left, leads to the hallway.*

Orla (*sighs*) What am I going to do?

Liam What are *you* going to do? Just tell me …

Orla It's not that easy Liam.

Liam Tell me how you want me to say it. What's the big deal?

Orla That had no … (*struggles to find the words*)

Liam No what?

Orla No biological necessity.

Liam What?

Orla Make it more coruscating. Think about feelings of intense pain, sorrow, etcetera.

Liam What are you saying?

Orla Undulating anguish.

Liam Huh?

Orla You're too emotionally prosaic. You're not thinking about the meaning behind the words.

Liam What meaning?!

Liam *plonks down on the sofa, exhausted.*

Orla If you'd only do what I wrote in the script.

Liam I'm not doing that.

Orla The way I originally envisioned it.

Liam No.

Orla It's only a little one.

Liam (*firm*) I said no.

Orla It's Nicole, isn't it?

Liam What's Nicole?

Orla Why you can't concentrate. It must have been upsetting.

Liam Drop it, Orla.

Orla I've touched a nerve, I'm backing off.

Liam Orla, I couldn't give a toss!

Orla *lifts up a jar containing a live butterfly.*

Orla It probably won't even live that much longer. Butterflies have a very short life-span.

Liam Orla, I'm not killing it! How can you be so blasé about killing a butterfly for a student movie?

Orla Liam, while, from your point of view, this is only a student film, it's also a work of art and there's no point doing it if you're not going to commit 100%.

Liam I don't just mean student movies. I mean killing something for *any movie* is wrong.

Orla I'm not making *any movie.*

Liam (*tired*) I don't see how it helps my performance if I kill an innocent little butterfly anyway.

Orla It will help, Liam, because every time you say that speech you have all the gravitas of a sock-puppet. Killing the butterfly will add the extra ... frisson of existentialism you lack.

Liam But it's not just a prop Orla, it's alive.

Orla Look at it this way. If you don't kill it now, it'll only get eaten by a hungry Rottweiler or stamped on by some delinquent child.

Liam How can someone who cried at *E.T.* be so cynical?

Orla (*shocked*) I didn't cry at *E.T.*

Liam Yes you did. In Larry's class last Tuesday.

Orla Right Liam, a bug-eyed plastic turd on a magic bike truly makes my eyes water.

Liam I saw you.

Orla No, you didn't.

Liam *picks up a biscuit off the table and takes a bite.*

Liam Orla, you were weeping like a baby.

Orla (*annoyed*) Can you not eat when you're wearing that shirt Liam? You'll get it dirty.

Liam *slowly puts the rest of the biscuit down with exaggerated care.*

Orla Oh, and before I forget, taciturn sounds wrong coming out of your mouth. Like a retarded infant learning to speak. Can you practise saying it please?

Liam (*sighs*) Look, OK. Let's try this again. This scene is the climax of the movie, is it?

Orla It's not a movie, it's a film.

Orla *sits beside* **Liam**.

Liam Alright, Orla.

Orla This is the emotional apotheosis of the film. Broken Doll has spent her entire life trying to please Man in White, trying to placate him and cater to his whims but of course, he barely registers her existence.

Liam Why don't I have a name?

Orla What?

Liam Why am I Man in White? Why amn't I Tony or Donald or … Ruddeger?

Orla You don't have a name because you're not a real person.

Liam I'm not?

Orla No.

Liam What am I then?

Orla A Jungian construct.

Liam (*nods, taking this in his stride*) Go on.

Orla So Broken Doll returns home during the lunar eclipse only to find Man in White about to kill her butterfly. She cries out to stop him but her mouth falls off, which was the bit we shot this morning, and Man in White kills the butterfly. Broken Doll is shattered. She is desolate … She reverts to a pre-birth state of innocence and denial.

A beat. **Liam** *stares at* **Orla** *like she's crazy.*

Liam (*perplexed*) How do you plan on filming a pre-birth state of innocence and denial?

Orla By showing her blackened heart enveloped in amniotic fluid.

Liam (*pointing to the tank in the corner*) Oh, I get it! That's what the cow's heart in brine is all about.

Orla (*annoyed*) It's not brine, it's amniotic fluid … So what else do you not understand?

Liam (*thinks about it, then*) Well … what's the point in the butterfly?

Orla It supports a multitude of readings.

Liam Yeah, but … what does it represent?

Orla Whatever you want it to.

Liam That makes no sense.

Orla Life doesn't make sense. My art reflects that.

Liam *stares at her blankly.* **Orla** *stands up and goes to the camera.*

Orla You've no idea Liam, have you? Can't see beyond Friday night down the multiplex? Art is not the same thing as a Sandra Bullock movie.

Liam What's wrong with Sandra Bullock?

Orla I don't even know how to begin answering that!

Liam But how do you expect the audience to get anything from it if it doesn't even make sense?

Orla I'm not trying to sell popcorn Liam. This is not about entertainment, it's about expressing something of the human soul.

Liam But what's the point in making a movie if no-one gets it? Aren't you trying to communicate something? I mean, isn't that the point?

Orla (*confident*) My art will find its audience.

Liam Not if no-one can understand it.

Orla I can't believe you of all people are giving me lessons on film-making. By rights you shouldn't still be in the class.

Liam, *uneasy, gets up and walks away from* **Orla**.

Liam I never asked them to take me back …

Orla The only reason you're still here is because you can tell funny jokes and can drink a flaming sambuca while it's on fire. It is not because you know anything about making films. I, on the other hand, do.

Orla *tosses the jar to* **Liam**.

Liam I said no … Look, I know I've done some stupid things in my time but I'm not the kind of person who kills things on camera.

Orla No-one in the class will even know. You don't have to worry about that.

Liam That's not the point, Orla. It's wrong.

Orla What do you mean?

Liam What d'you mean what do I mean? And of course the class'll know. It'll be on camera.

Orla They're not going to watch my film.

Liam It'll be in the graduate screening with the rest of them. Everyone'll see it.

Orla I'm sure they'll all pop out for a cigarette when mine is on.

Liam No, they'll watch it just to laugh at me.

Orla Well, I won't tell them if you don't.

Liam *holds up the butterfly and studies it.* **Orla** *walks up to him.*

Orla (*impassioned*) Don't you think it would prefer to die for something important if it had the chance? Art is categorically the most important tool we have for expressing ourselves. Articulating the hidden depths of the unconscious and preserving that beyond time and space itself. Doesn't that sound important to you?

Liam It's already dead.

Liam *shakes the jar. The butterfly doesn't move.*

Orla What? Let me see!

Orla *snatches the jar off him, sits down and examines it.*

Liam You really should've put air-holes in it …

Orla *prods the butterfly.*

Orla Fuck! Don't do this to me. This scene is crucial!

Liam *strolls over to the dollhouse and picks up a piece of tiny furniture.* **Orla** *glances at him.*

Orla I told you not to touch that Liam. It's only borrowed and it's very, very expensive!

Liam OK.

Liam *walks away from it.*

Liam (*annoyed*) I can see why your original actor dropped out.

Orla His wife went into labour in a Dunnes Stores.

Liam (*over-lapping*) … labour in a Dunnes Stores. I know. Very believable.

Orla (*re. butterfly*) It moved! It's still alive. I'll let it breathe for a while.

Orla *puts the jar on the coffee-table and covers it loosely.*

Orla And for your information it's true. He spent hours on the phone telling me how guilty he felt. I actually had to convince him not to call round today … He's such a professional.

Liam OK, fair enough. He was telling the truth.

Orla Why would he have lied anyway?

Liam (*mutters*) Has he read the script?

Orla *glares at* **Liam**, *offended by his comment. She goes back to the camera.*

Orla (*casually*) I wonder what Nicole's up to tonight … Probably off into town with Bonnie and Miriam. Maybe Copperface Jacks? … All dressed up … On the pull …

Liam *glares at* **Orla**. *A beat.*

Liam Y'know, it's funny. All this time I've been wondering why I wasn't able to get your movie. I thought it was because I was thick but I just realised. The problem isn't me, (*he picks up the script*) it's your script. I don't understand it 'cause there's nothing to understand. It's just meaningless wank about nothing.

Liam *tosses the script on the sofa.* **Orla** *doesn't respond.* **Liam,** *tired and frustrated, walks away from her. He takes off the white shirt he's been wearing and hangs it over the sofa. Topless, he looks around for his t-shirt.* **Orla** *silently watches him. He finds it and puts it on, then goes back to eating his biscuit.*

Orla Liam, why are you here?

Liam Huh?

Orla Why did you agree to help me?

Liam (*uncomfortable*) I told you …

Orla What?

Liam You needed an actor so … that's why.

Orla All of a sudden you're my best friend?

Liam I just thought …

Orla You haven't said two words to me all year.

Liam (*shrugs*) I thought people have been giving you the silent treatment long enough.

Orla I don't need your charity Liam. If the class want to treat me like a leper, let them. I feel perfectly justified in what I did.

Liam Whatever, Orla, it's in the past now.

Orla Not that I give a damn but it probably never occurred to them there was another side to the story.

Liam (*tired*) You're right Orla, it really doesn't matter.

Orla (*ignores him*) Firstly, the time-table for the Sound-Room was completely unfair to me. My music had to be edited before I started shooting. How else could I choreograph the camera for Broken Doll's dance? It was absolutely vital I had access to the Pro Tools before this weekend.

Liam Yeah, OK, so the time-table was unfair.

Orla But you don't understand Liam. It was purely out of spite Nicole took that slot. And she was only messing about in the Sound-Room.

Liam But you never even asked her to swap with you. You could've at least talked to her.

Orla She'd never swap with me! I was outside the TV studio at Easter and I overheard her tell Joe she thought I was a lesbian.

Orla *waits for a response.* **Liam** *says nothing.*

Orla I'm not!

Liam So?

Orla (*shrugs*) She's a bitch.

Liam Still, Orla, you don't tell someone their mother's been taken to hospital 'cause you need to use their computer.

Orla But think of the relief when she found out her mother was fine.

Liam Did you even know Nicole's mum had cancer?

Orla Of course I did! It wouldn't have worked otherwise.

Liam You can't do things like that Orla. Nicole was really freaked out.

Orla I didn't know you still cared about her.

Liam (*sighs*) I just don't get how can you behave like that and think you'll get away with it.

Liam *goes back to the sofa, to get away from* **Orla**.

Orla Why did Nicole break up with you?

Liam I don't want to talk about it.

Orla Maybe you should Liam? Bring it to the surface rather than keeping it inside? It'll only fester and coalesce into a little black rock of bitter acrimony.

Liam Look Orla, I appreciate your concern but can we just drop it?

Orla No, no, you misunderstand Liam. I'm not concerned, I'm only thinking that the pain could be useful now … For your performance.

Liam (*shakes his head in disbelief*) I can't believe you cried at *E.T.*

Orla I did not cry at *E.T.*

Liam Orla, there's no shame in admitting it. So you cried at a movie; welcome to the human race.

Orla You're delusional.

Liam I saw you with my own eyes.

Orla I've never cried at a movie in my life!

Liam *nods.* **Orla** *saunters over to the butterfly jar.*

Liam I'm not killing it.

Orla *turns on her heel and saunters back to the camera.*

Orla Perhaps it would help you if I show you an example of what I'm after? There's a Maya Deren short that's simply superb.

Orla *goes over to the pile of video-tapes by the wall.*

Liam (*something occurs to him*) Orla? Earlier when you said I won't tell them if you don't, what did you mean by that?

Orla I won't tell anyone in the class that you're acting in my film. So if you don't tell them, your precious reputation among the herd will be more than safe.

Liam You didn't tell anyone I was going to help you?

Orla No.

Liam No-one knows I'm here?

Orla *stares at* **Liam**.

Orla What?

Liam Huh?

Orla You look like you've seen a ghost.

Liam I have to make a call.

Orla (*irritated*) Liam, we're in the middle of a scene.

Liam *goes into the kitchen, takes out his mobile phone and is about to dial when he reconsiders and puts it down.*

Gerard *enters, carrying a DVD player in its box.*

Gerard Knock, knock!

Orla (*surprised*) What are you doing here?

Gerard I have a little something for you.

Orla (*to* **Gerard**) We're in the middle of filming.

Gerard I didn't ring the bell …

In the kitchen, **Liam** *sits at the table and puts his head in his hands. He deliberates whether or not to make a phone call but eventually decides not to.* **Gerard** *puts the box down.*

Orla What's that?

Gerard A DVD player.

Orla What's it for?

Gerard Have you not heard, Orla? There are these shiny little discs, exactly like CDs only they—

Orla (*interrupts*) I mean what are you doing with it?

Gerard It's for you, Orla. It's a present.

Orla (*laughs nervously*) Sorry?

Gerard *sits on the sofa.* **Orla** *notices the script on the sofa. She quickly takes it and stuffs it in her pocket.* **Gerard** *opens up the DVD box.*

Gerard It's a top of the range model. Simply plug a lead into the TV and you're away in a hack. It won't take you long to set up at all.

Orla Why did you buy it?

Gerard Does a father need a reason to buy his daughter a present?

Orla No Dad, but I … I don't want it.

Gerard Why ever not?

Orla I'm sorry but we need to get back to work. We're in the middle of a vital—

Gerard What did you do with your hair?

Orla (*touches her hair*) What?

Gerard A new haircut, is it?

Orla (*surprised*) You're the first person to notice.

Gerard (*nods*) It's a haircut alright. (*He points at DVD player*) Why don't you want it? You've been talking about getting one for ages.

Orla I know, but—

Gerard How many times have I heard you complain about videos not being in widescreen?

Orla I know, Dad.

Gerard Now we can watch DVDs instead. Isn't that much better?

Orla *says nothing but then sits beside him.*

Orla Dad, please. I already explained. I only have the rest of the weekend to shoot and edit a whole ten-minute film. If it's not finished by Monday then I won't graduate and I won't have a show-reel.

Gerard *gets up and examines the dollhouse.*

Gerard Is this a prop? It's a bit shabby looking, isn't it?

Orla It's supposed to be like that.

Gerard You're going for a gritty texture to the film? A kind of cheapness? (*Nods*) Interesting choice.

Orla This film will open up a whole new world to me: film-festivals, arts funding, maybe even scholarships. So, Dad, it's very important I get it exactly right.

Gerard Who's that in the kitchen? A replacement for the creep who dropped out?

Orla Yes, he's from my class.

Gerard (*surprised*) Really? Someone from your class? A Gaahead or a bimbo?

Orla (*shrugs*) If I had any other options, I would have taken them.

Gerard Who is he?

Orla Liam Duffy.

Gerard Name rings a bell.

Orla He was the one who stole the trophy for cleanest college, dragged it around on the back of a moped and then put it back in its display case.

Gerard (*remembering*) Oh yes … I thought he was expelled.

Orla He was going to be but the class protested so the board reconsidered.

Gerard Typical. And does he like you?

Orla Dad, don't be silly.

Gerard But I'm glad your film's going well. That makes me happy. Glad to be happy … and happy to be glad … There's a spare Scart lead in my room …

Gerard *looks at* **Orla** *for a response. She says nothing. A beat.*

Gerard It won't take you a minute.

Orla I don't want it.

Gerard What?

Orla (*nods at the DVD player*) That.

Gerard Why not?

Orla *gets up and walks away from him.*

Orla No reason.

Gerard I don't understand.

Orla There's nothing to understand.

Gerard But what's the reason?

Orla (*shrugs*) No reason.

Gerard Simply pure irrationality, is it?

Orla (*thinks, then*) Yes.

Gerard (*blankly*) I have no response to that.

A beat.

Orla We absolutely have to get back to work now. So I'll see you on Monday, OK?

Gerard *sits down and looks at the DVD player.*

Gerard The shop-assistant in Dixons was one of my pupils. Isn't that a co-incidence? Last week I caught him chewing gum and made him swallow it. So when he saw me today I bet he was planning revenge … Either that or he's a patronising eejit to everyone. He assumed I knew nothing about technology and tried to foist the most expensive one on me. That's all they care about these days: money … And sex. Give them a copy of Shakespeare's complete works and they'd only try sell it on eBay … or have sex with it, am I right?

Orla (*quietly*) Dad, you promised me these few days.

Gerard (*irritated*) Now don't start Orla! A father does something nice for his child and she bites the head off him like a vicious black widow spider!

Gerard *angrily paces.*

Orla I'm not biting the head off you.

Gerard I never said you were. I'm talking about the black widow spider. It's a deadly predator in Central Asia … Orla, why is everything such hard work with you these days? This last year all we ever do is end up bickering … And you always seem to eat in college these days, never home for dinner. You used to love my cooking.

Orla It seems strange, that's all.

Gerard What?

Orla Buying me such a big present when I'm in the middle of shooting. All my concentration is on this film. I don't have the mental space to facilitate this right now.

Gerard It's times like these I wish your mother was still with us. She'd understand what you're on about.

Orla If I hook it up now will you go back to Carmel's?

Gerard Of course I will Orla. Have a look in the box of wires and things under my bed. I'm sure there's a SCART lead there.

Orla *exits.* **Gerard** *lifts up the DVD player and looks at it. A moment later,* **Liam** *enters from the kitchen.*

Liam Hi there. Where's Orla?

Gerard (*not looking at him*) Gone on an errand.

Liam Oh … Who are you?

Gerard (*re. DVD player*) Why didn't she want this?

Liam What?

Gerard Wouldn't you be happy if you got this as a present? It's a top of the range DVD player and yet she looked at me like I'd given her the Ebola virus. I know she doesn't want me here but I only wanted to do something nice for her.

Liam Oh. Are you the actor who dropped out?

Gerard (*hesitates, then*) That's right …

Liam God, you really dodged a bomb on this one.

Gerard Tell me, does Orla ever talk about her plans after graduation?

Liam We're not that close.

Gerard Does she ever talk about moving out of home? About getting her own place? (*Points at DVD*) Is that why she doesn't want this?

Liam I don't know.

Gerard What about her father? What does she say about him?

Liam She's never mentioned him to me. But, really we're not pals. We don't hang out.

Gerard Why has she been so tetchy and secretive lately? Is it because she's moving out? Is that her big secret?

Liam (*shrugs*) Don't look at me.

Gerard What did you mean I dodged a bomb on this one?

Liam *sits on the sofa and eats the rest of his biscuit, catching the crumbs in his other hand.*

Liam Man, you've no idea the crap I've put up with over the last few days. All for the sake of art with a capital A, as if that's some great gift to humanity. Thank God this is the last day.

Gerard Art is very important.

Liam Important to pretentious wankers who want to lord it over everyone else.

Liam *finishes his biscuit and looks at his handful of crumbs. He rubs them into the white shirt.*

Liam And you must be what? At least twenty years older than me? How can I be playing the same character as you? (*Remembers*) Oh yeah, I'm not a character, I'm a construct … You've read the script. Could you make any sense of it?

Gerard I haven't read it. Orla never shows me her work until it's complete.

Liam Have you seen her other movies?

Gerard Yes.

Liam And what did you think?

Gerard I think Orla's a singular talent whose art is exciting and different.

Liam Really?

Gerard (*shrugs*) No, I didn't understand them at all …

Liam (*chuckles*) Right.

Gerard But they're important to Orla so I'll support her in any way that I can.

Liam (*confused*) Hang on, how were you supposed to act in her movie without reading the script?

Gerard (*pauses and looks at* **Liam**) Is it any wonder I dropped out?

Liam *nods and looks down at the DVD player.*

Liam I can't believe you bought her a DVD player. It's not like you didn't have a good enough reason to drop out. You really didn't have to, y'know?

Gerard (*suspicious*) You'd like that, would you?

Liam What?

Gerard *walks over to* **Liam**.

Gerard If I wasn't here. If it was only you and Orla?

Liam What d'you mean?

Gerard You like her, do you? Hoping to make a bee-line into her pants?

Liam (*appalled*) What?! Jesus, no!

Gerard Why are you here?

Liam I'm helping her out … Actually it's a bit more complicated than that. It's because of my ex-girlfriend Nicole … (*Something suddenly occurs to him*) Listen, I know I don't know you but can I ask you a favour?

Gerard What is it?

Liam Well, Nicole, she broke up with me and I'm trying to get back with her.

Gerard Why did she break up with you?

Liam She said I only cared about myself.

Gerard The motto of your generation, I believe.

Liam Yeah, the thing is, nobody knows I'm working on Orla's movie. And it's Nicole's birthday today. So what I need you to do is ring Nicole, pretending to be someone else who's looking for me. But the real purpose of the call is to actually let her know that I'm helping Orla. Y'know, you could say something like you only just remembered where I was? You're an actor, you can improvise. So when Nicole finds that out … she'll ring me.

Gerard I don't understand.

Liam Which bit?

Gerard All of it. Ring her yourself.

Liam I can't just ring her.

Gerard Why?

Liam I can't go crawling back to her after being dumped. There's no way she'd take me back. I have to wait for her to ring me but she won't do that unless she knows I'm here helping Orla … I know it sounds nuts but it's really not.

Gerard Why would the fact you're helping Orla make Nicole ring you?

Liam Because Nicole hates Orla.

Gerard Excuse me?

Liam And it's like, the idea I'd work on Orla's movie rather than be around for Nicole's birthday will piss her off so much she'll have no choice but to ring me. And then when she rings I can explain to her that I don't only care about myself.

Gerard Why would she hate Orla?

Liam (*shrugs*) Oh, y'know …

Gerard (*offended*) I do not know … Simply because she doesn't follow the sheep watching *Big Brother* and smoking crack, the herd cuts her off! Is that it?

Liam Hey, Orla doesn't care about anyone else in the class, why should we care about her?

Gerard Every artistic genius was misunderstood in their own lifetime … Not that Orla's a genius yet, but you know what I mean.

Liam Anyway, will you ring Nicole for me then?

Gerard *sits on the sofa.*

Gerard Why on earth would I help you do that? You only want to make her jealous. You want to make her think you and Orla are an item.

Liam *stares at* **Gerard**. *A beat.* **Liam** *bursts out laughing.*

Gerard What's so funny?

Liam Nothing, nothing. Look, I'm not trying to make Nicole jealous. I just want to get back with her, that's all.

Gerard You only want to make yourself feel better.

Liam No, you don't understand. This will help me get her back.

Gerard Rubbish! You don't care about her at all!

Liam *sits down beside* **Gerard**.

Liam No, I do! It's like, y'know the way you go through life with a constant niggling feeling of dissatisfaction? Even when things are grand, there's this vague sense that there's more out there? That there's something better? That somehow you could be living the movie-version of your life where you say witty things and girls think you're sexy? And you don't stand in the kitchen for hours trying to decide what to have for breakfast? Well, that's how Nicole makes me feel. Like my life is a movie.

Gerard Is Nicole actually a girl? Or is it your pet name for cocaine?

Liam How can I make you understand?

Gerard I understand.

Liam If you understood, we wouldn't still be talking. You'd be ringing her. Please, she's the only thing in my life that's worth a damn.

Gerard You're barely out of your teens. How can any girl be so important?

Liam Look, let me show you what she's like. I have a video of her.

Liam *gets a video from his bag and puts it into the video player. He presses play and they watch it. Sounds of babies crying, atonal music and a self-important monologue can be heard.*

Liam That's Nicole there. Now can you tell me she's not the most beautiful thing you've ever seen?

Gerard She is pretty.

Liam And she doesn't care about making a fool of herself. How rare is that in a stunner?

They watch some more in silence.

Gerard What is this video?

Liam There was a free afternoon last week so Nicole and some of the class got Orla's script and we made a spoof of it.

Gerard Excuse me?

Liam We were really bored.

Gerard The class made a parody of Orla's script? But it was a joke? You showed it to her afterward?

Liam No, of course not.

TV (*in mock-serious tones*) Behind a locked door, her heart is no more worn out … by strife, her taciturn scream, lost in the night … no more.

Gerard This is appalling.

Liam I know, try saying it on camera!

Gerard (*staring at the TV*) Is this what Orla wants? To be a part of this idiotic rabble? She wants to abandon me for this?

(*Looks at* **Liam**) Everything I've done for her and now she throws it back in my face.

Liam (*confused*) What? Did you spend a lot of time rehearsing or something?

Gerard It wasn't just time. It was love.

Liam (*shocked*) Love?

Gerard Yes, love. What am I going to do?

Liam You love Orla?

Gerard Of course I love her.

Liam (*confused*) Does she know?

Gerard I try to tell her, I try to show her but she doesn't want to hear.

Liam And … what about your wife?

Gerard *stares at* **Liam**. *A beat.*

Gerard My wife is dead.

Liam (*mortified*) Oh God! I'm so sorry. I … I didn't know.

Gerard How would you have known?

Liam That's terrible, I … Wait, are you saying that you called in here to give Orla a DVD player even though your wife just died in childbirth … (*incredulous*) and Orla wouldn't forgive you?

Gerard What in the name of God are you on about? I'm Orla's father.

Liam (*horrified*) I thought you were that actor.

Gerard (*waves his hand dismissively*) That was a lie.

Liam Jesus! (*Quickly turns off TV*) We were just messing about. Really, it was just for a laugh.

Gerard (*realising*) They'll all laugh at her, won't they? At the graduate screening. The first public screening of her work and she'll be greeted with howls of laughter …

Liam It was just a joke. It doesn't mean anything.

Gerard What are you saying? It means everything to her! It's Orla's whole world. That's all she ever does. All she ever talks about. And now she'll be ripped to shreds like a pine marten in a den of panthers.

They sit in silence for a few moments.

Liam Do panthers live in dens?

Gerard That is absolutely irrelevant! … What am I going to do about her film?

Liam Maybe you could have a talk with her. I don't mean tell her about the video, but … I don't know …

Gerard (*thinking*) No, no, you're right. It's not too late. You're saying I should stop her finishing the film?

Liam No, that's not what I'm saying at all!

Gerard I could say something so that she'll let me stay … What if I was sick or something? Dying, even.

Liam (*appalled*) What?

Gerard No? Too much?

Liam You can't tell her that!

Gerard How can I be thinking this? But what kind of a father sits back and lets his only daughter be humiliated? Whatever my personal feelings or whatever the consequences, at the end of the day I'm her father and I have to protect her. Then the question becomes not how can I do this but how can I not? This film must not be made, (*points at the TV*) she must never see this and the pine marten might yet survive. Am I right?

A beat.

Liam So, anyway … will you ring Nicole for me?

Orla *enters.*

Orla There was no SCART lead in that box.

Gerard I must have been mistaken. Maybe I gave it to Carmel when she got her new TV.

Orla Dad, I'll go and buy a lead on Monday and connect it then, OK?

Gerard OK, Orla …

Orla I better get back to work. Liam's very dedicated to his craft … He'll get edgy if we don't get shooting soon, isn't that right, Liam?

Liam (*flustered*) Eh, yeah, sure … I have to use the jacks.

Liam *hurriedly exits.*

Orla Auntie Carmel will be wondering where you are.

Gerard I have all my books here and the television.

Orla Carmel has a television.

Gerard Yes, but she doesn't have my books.

Orla Take some with you.

Gerard Orla, she hates me. She thinks I'm a bore and an intellectual snob.

Orla That's not true Dad.

Gerard *gets up and walks over to the fish-tank. He taps the glass.*

Gerard I've spent the last four days listening to her complain about her sciatica and her rheumatism and the poisonous spider eggs nestled in her pancreas! Why can't I stay here?

Orla You could give someone a call. Go out for dinner with them.

Gerard Who?

Orla I don't know. Someone from school?

Gerard They don't like me either.

Orla Go to the cinema. Or a play.

Gerard On my own?

Orla (*starting to panic*) But Dad, you promised. I told you how important this film is to me.

At the mention of film, something suddenly occurs to **Gerard**. *He goes back to the TV.*

Gerard Orla, you're being irrational. It won't make the slightest difference if I stay here.

Orla (*pleading*) No Dad, it has to be only me and Liam this weekend.

Gerard Orla, it is *my* house.

Orla I asked you for this months ago and you said it was no problem.

Gerard Did I say that? Doesn't sound like me.

Orla You did.

Gerard I'll stay in my room and you won't hear a peep. You won't hear a pip.

Orla Dad please, I never ask you for any time to myself. All I'm asking for is this weekend. It's just for my film, that's all …

Gerard What would your mother say if she saw you treating me like this? She'd be horrified, Orla. Horrified! Kicking me out of our home to spend the weekend with someone who doesn't like me. Do you think Mum would do that if she was still with us? Do you think she'd be proud of you right now?

Orla *walks away from him, saying nothing.* **Gerard** *sees his chance and discreetly ejects the tape from the video player. He looks around and then sticks it under the coffee-table. He turns back to* **Orla.**

Gerard Well, do you?

Orla (*quietly*) No.

Gerard No … The only way we have of honouring her memory is to do what she would want. Am I right?

Orla *says nothing.*

Gerard Now, I'll go to my room and read my books. You make your film and the next time you see me, it'll be Monday morning … You won't even hear a puh!

Gerard *exits.* **Orla**, *seething with frustration, goes to the shelf of videos and makes herself busy looking for a particular one. She finds it and pulls it out of a stack but the rest of the tapes fall to the ground with a clatter.* **Orla**, *immobilised with frustration, stares at the mess. She then takes a deep breath, regains her composure and puts the video into the player. She goes to the hall.*

Orla (*loud*) Liam? Liam!

A few moments later, **Liam** *enters.*

Liam Is, eh … everything OK?

Orla Fine. Are you ready to go again?

Liam Oh. Sure.

Orla *throws the white shirt to* **Liam** *and goes to the camera.* **Liam** *puts the shirt on and stands at the dollhouse.* **Orla** *turns off the house-lights (leaving* **Liam** *in a spotlight) and goes behind the camera.*

Liam Will I slate it?

Orla Yes.

Liam *prepares the clapper-board then holds it up before the camera.*

Orla Rolling.

Liam Slate 40, take 32.

Orla Settle and … action.

Liam She has no future, no chance … to soar, her wings will become dust … Behind a locked door, her heart is no more worn out—

Orla You're trying to sabotage my film, aren't you?

Liam Huh?

Orla This is merely a sardonic joke to you.

Liam (*shocked*) What?

Orla *turns on the lights.*

Orla I get it now Liam. You're failing the year, so you want me to fail as well?

Liam Orla, don't be ridiculous.

Orla Why are you being so shit with this speech? Do you know what passion is Liam? Do you understand the concept? Maybe I have a dictionary around here somewhere …

Liam (*sighs*) Y'know Orla, you shouldn't get too obsessed with your movie … and y'know, whatever reaction it gets …

Orla I'm not obsessed. I'm committed.

Liam I'm just saying there's more to life than art, y'know?

Orla So, I have no life. Is that what you're trying to say?!

Liam (*under his breath*) No, that's what I'm trying *not* to say.

Orla I have a very full life, thank you very much!

Liam You never come to Bakers with us at the weekends.

Orla I write at the weekends. Besides, getting drunk and swapping fart jokes with a bunch of talking Nike logos is not high on my to-do list!

Liam You never even came to the Christmas Social.

Orla Actually, I was going to but … why are we even talking about this?

Liam (*shrugs*) I don't know.

Liam *sees the mess of video-tapes on the ground.*

Liam What happened over there?

Orla Nothing.

Liam Are you sure you're OK?

Orla Yes, Liam.

A beat.

Liam Well, can I ask you for a favour?

Orla What?

Liam Could you ring Nicole and ask her for my mobile number? And could you explain I'm working on your film this weekend and I've gone out of my way to help you? Maybe I've gone out to Bray to pick up some equipment for you but now you have to contact me 'cause you also need me to get a dioptre, or something. You got that?

Orla (*completely baffled*) Why do you want me to do that?

Liam Because I'm trying to get back … (*stops himself*) I mean, I want to … get back at her.

Orla What?

Liam (*lying*) I want revenge.

Orla For who?

Liam Me … eh, both of us.

Orla What?

Liam *walks over to* **Orla**.

Liam It's revenge for me 'cause she dumped me for being selfish, but this shows I'm not selfish 'cause I'm helping you with your film. And it's revenge for you because … she said you were gay.

Orla I don't care about that anymore.

Liam Please Orla? It'd mean a lot to me.

Orla I didn't know you were the vengeful type.

Liam Yeah, well.

Orla If anything I would've thought you missed her.

Liam Why would I miss her?

Orla I don't know.

Liam Having to wait hours for her to put on her make-up and then she looks exactly the same as before? Freezing up whenever I went to kiss her in public? What's to miss?

Orla Liam, I'm not in the mood.

Liam You were right. She's a bitch.

Orla You agreed to help me so can we focus on the film? I have that Maya Deren short I was telling you about. Hopefully it'll give you a sense of what I'm after.

Orla *turns on the TV.* **Liam**, *alarmed, goes over to her.*

Liam (*flustered*) Orla, I don't think that'd help, really!

Orla It has exactly the right mood of jubilant ferocity I'm after.

Liam Oh sure! Jubilant ferocity, I get it now.

Orla Are you mocking me?

Liam No! I mean it. I think I know what you want now. Let's shoot it while it's still in my head.

Orla Have you seen the remote anywhere?

Orla *looks around for the remote control.* **Liam** *tries to think of something to say. He stands in front of the TV.*

Liam Orla, what's the story with you and your dad?

Orla There's no story.

Liam *touches her arm.*

Liam Orla …

Orla (*nervous*) What?

Orla *hesitates but then walks goes over to the dollhouse.* **Liam,** *relieved, turns off the TV.* **Orla** *re-arranges the dollhouse furniture.* **Liam** *looks at her, genuinely concerned.*

Liam Y'know Orla, sometimes it is good to talk about things. You don't have to keep it all inside … I mean, if you don't want to.

Orla It's fine Liam. Dad's a bit of a handful sometimes, that's all.

Liam What d'you mean?

Orla He gets … anxious. It's funny. That's why I never made it to the Christmas Social. (*Chuckles*) Dad accidentally locked himself in the bathroom and we spent hours trying to open the door. Eventually he got it open but by that time it was too late to go out.

Liam How do you accidentally lock yourself in a bathroom?

Orla The lock got jammed or something. (*Shrugs*) I don't know.

Liam And has it ever jammed since then?

Orla (*suddenly irritated*) What's your point?

Liam (*embarrassed*) I don't know. It's none of my business.

Orla That's right. It's not …

Orla *goes back to the camera.*

Orla Maybe we should do the apple shots next. I haven't actually tried getting the worm to wriggle on cue but I have a hairdryer on standby …

Liam So, will you ring Nicole for me?

Orla Do I look like your personal secretary?

Liam Please, it'll only take a second.

Orla I don't want to hear that pudenda-head's voice.

Liam Come on, Orla.

Orla What difference will it make if I ring her?

Liam It'll make a difference to me.

Orla Jesus Liam, get over it.

Liam Don't you think I want to Orla? I watched *Disclosure* last weekend and there was shagging tears in my eyes by the end of it. I was never like that before I met her.

Orla Watched what?

Liam *Disclosure*. With Michael Douglas?

Orla Have I seen it? What's it about?

Liam Michael Douglas works in this big computer company and wants to get a promotion but then Demi Moore is made his new boss and sexually harasses him. And when he goes to make a complaint she's already said that he sexually harassed her.

Orla (*trying to remember*) What happens then?

Liam Well, it turns out it was all a plan to get Michael Douglas fired and he finds out because someone sends him these anonymous e-mails so he has to go into virtual reality and fight this robot Demi Moore. And then they announce who got the promotion and it turns out to be this woman in her 60s who's been with the company the longest and it was her who sent the e-mails and she's actually the person who deserved the promotion all along and Michael Douglas starts clapping and Jesus Christ, I'm getting fucking teary-eyed again!

Liam *starts to break down as he says the above.*

Orla Sounds like shit.

Liam *wipes his eyes.*

Liam It is! That's what I'm saying! So, please Orla, do this one thing for me and ring Nicole!

Orla Jesus Liam, what's wrong with you?

Liam I don't know! I don't know what the fuck is wrong with me. So come on Orla, I'm begging you.

A beat.

Orla OK Liam. On one condition.

Liam What?

Orla *holds up the butterfly jar.*

Orla You kill the butterfly.

A beat.

Liam OK.

Orla What's her number?

Liam *scribbles the phone number on the script and hands it to* **Orla**.

Orla Fine. I'll do it now and then we get back to filming, OK? Do you want to come and listen?

Liam (*something occurs to him*) Eh … no. No, you go ahead.

Orla *goes into the kitchen.* **Liam** *makes sure she's gone, then goes to the video player, ejects the tape and stuffs it down the back of the sofa. Tired, he sits down and sighs.*

Meanwhile, in the kitchen, **Orla** *rings Nicole.*

Orla Hi, is this Nicole? Hello, it's Orla … (*Annoyed*) Orla from your class. I was wondering if you had Liam's phone number? Only he's working on my film this weekend and he's gone out to Bray to … No, I'm not joking. He's acting in it … Why is that so hard to believe? … How can I prove it? I told you he's not here … Now, why on earth would I make up such a thing? … Fine you conceited little pillow-case, you want proof? I was talking to Liam earlier and he said the vast amounts of make-up you wear don't make any difference to your ugly mug. And he thinks you're a frigid bitch because you never kissed him in public. So, how else would I know about that? … Well, there you go. Now if you'll excuse me, I have to get back to my movie.

Orla *hangs up.*

Orla (*to herself*) I mean film.

Lights go down.

Act Two

Saturday night. The living-room is bare except for the dollhouse, fish-tank and the DVD player on the ground; all the film equipment is packed away in cases. The clapper-board is on top of them. In the kitchen, the white shirt is hanging on the back of a chair. **Gerard** *enters.*

Gerard Orla?

Gerard *looks around and sees there's no-one in. He looks at the equipment, picks up the clapper-board and exits. A few moments later,* **Orla** *enters. She goes into the kitchen and examines the white shirt, carefully holding it up to the light. Meanwhile,* **Gerard** *enters again without the clapper-board. He doesn't notice* **Orla** *in the kitchen. He tries to open the heavy-duty camera-case.* **Orla** *walks into the living-room.*

Orla Dad?

Gerard (*startled*) Nothing.

Orla What are you doing?

Gerard (*flustered*) I wasn't doing anything.

Orla Why were you at the camera?

Gerard I wasn't *at* it. What's that supposed to mean? I only wanted to check it was OK.

Orla Why?

Gerard (*sighs, then with infinite patience*) I was lying on my bed wracked with guilt about what happened at dinner, so I said I'd come down and check with Orla that everything was alright. But then you weren't here so I was going to check it myself. That's not a crime, is it?

Orla Dad … is there something you want to tell me?

Gerard What do you mean?

Orla You know the camera's fine. You saw me catch it.

Gerard I'm no expert on digital cameras! As far as I know, catching it like that may have jostled the inner workings and done serious damage. I was concerned.

Orla Dad, what are you doing here?

Gerard Orla, I live here.

Orla Why did you knock the camera over earlier and why were you trying to get at it now?

Gerard (*suddenly outraged*) Orla! What are you implying? I told you it was an accident, I didn't even see the camera!

Orla Dad, I'm not picking a fight. I'm only asking why you wouldn't stay at Carmel's today.

Gerard Is that what you wore out?

Orla Sorry?

Gerard Traipsing around on a Saturday night without a jacket? You'll catch your death of cold Orla, I'm telling you.

Orla I was only down the road.

Gerard If you want to catch pneumonia, don't let me stop you.

Orla If it was cold, I would've worn a jacket.

Gerard How would you clean curry out of a dollhouse? Answer me that?

Orla Well, you—

Gerard (*holds up a hand*) Wait, I'm making a speech … It's not easy juggling a plate of curry in one hand and a glass of Chardonnay in the other. I was so intent on saving the dollhouse that I involuntarily nudged the camera with my elbow. It's as simple as that.

Orla (*quietly*) You pushed it with your hand. I saw you.

Gerard (*interrupts*) So you're not going to put on a jacket?

Orla What?

Gerard At least warm yourself up before you catch a chill.

Orla But it's not only the camera. Was it really necessary to make a Thai green curry from scratch for dinner? And what about the Maya Deren tape that mysteriously vanished from the video?

Gerard Orla, what has gotten into you? What are you saying?

Orla I'm not accusing you, Dad. I just want to know how, when I told you to be extra, extra careful around Liam's white shirt, you somehow managed to spill wine all down the front of it.

Gerard *walks into the kitchen towards the shirt.*

Gerard Now, Orla. You can barely see the stain!

Orla *panics and runs in after him.* **Gerard** *goes to pick it up.*

Orla (*fearful*) Will you not touch it, Dad? Please?!

Gerard *gives* **Orla** *a look.*

Gerard Have you been drinking?

Orla (*defensive*) I had a few.

Gerard Ah yes, it all becomes clear! Do you even realise how paranoid you're being right now? Where were you?

Orla Liam and I went to McSorleys.

Gerard Tell me Orla, since when is getting intoxicated a necessary part of the cinematic process?

Orla *turns around and walks back into the living-room.* **Gerard** *follows.*

Orla I had no choice. Liam insisted. He needed Dutch courage to do the butterfly shot.

Gerard Orla, you don't have to explain yourself. You're free to do whatever you want.

Orla He'll be back any minute now and then we're going to start shooting again. So if you could finish what you're doing and go upstairs, I'd very much appreciate it. (*Notices the clapper-board is gone*) Where's the clapper-board? I left it right here.

Gerard Orla, what happened to your lip?

Orla (*embarrassed*) Nothing.

Gerard Did you burn it? Let me see.

Gerard *holds her head up to the light.*

Orla It's nothing. I burnt it on a glass.

Gerard You have to put some cream on it or it'll swell up.

Orla It's fine.

Gerard What were you doing?

Orla Liam was teaching me a trick.

Gerard What trick?

Orla (*embarrassed*) How to drink a flaming sambuca.

Gerard And how was your lip burnt?

Orla He's a shit teacher.

Gerard It's becoming increasingly apparent how much you didn't want to be there.

Orla Dad, I'm twenty-two. What's wrong with going for a few drinks with a friend? And no, at first I didn't want to be there but to tell you the truth, after a while, I actually started having a good time. It felt good to simply sit and chat with someone my own age for a change. Every night, all I do is stay in and watch films with you. Is it too much—

Gerard Your mother would want you to keep me company, Orla.

Orla But wouldn't Mum want me to have friends? To go out once in a while and—

Gerard I'm dying.

Orla Sorry?

Gerard I think I'm dying.

Orla What? How are you dying?

Gerard I have cancer.

Orla (*shocked*) What?

Gerard Now, I may not be dying. It could be benign. The

doctor said he'd ring me today to give me the news. Whether it's benign or … the other one. I'm still waiting for the call.

Orla But it's half eleven … And it's Saturday.

Gerard Those doctors are worked to the bone.

Orla (*laughs nervously*) Dad, why are you saying this?

Gerard I thought you'd want to know.

Orla Is … is this really the truth Dad? Really?

Gerard Yes Orla! Of course it is.

Orla *says nothing.* **Gerard** *stares at her.*

Gerard You do believe me, don't you?

Orla (*shrugs*) I don't know, maybe, sure.

Gerard (*serious*) I found a lump so I went to the doctor and he said he'd ring me today to let me know but he thought it was probably cancer.

Orla So why didn't you mention this before?

Gerard You've been so busy with your film Orla, and it might still be nothing. And so here I am, waiting for what is, without fear of exaggeration, the single most important phone call I will ever receive … And I don't want to be alone when I answer it. I wanted to be with you when I found out Orla. That's why I didn't stay at Carmel's today.

A beat.

Orla Is this because I didn't want the DVD player?

Gerard (*infuriated*) Jesus Christ, Orla! Do you think I would make up something like this after what we went through when your mother died? That black hole that nearly swallowed us up, those years of grey, meaningless pain? Do you honestly think I would use that for my own ends? That I would put you through that again?

Orla, *unsure, looks at* **Gerard**. *A beat.*

Orla You ... you should have said something.

Gerard It might still be ... (*trails off*)

Orla What?

Gerard Nothing.

Orla No, what?

Gerard No, it might still be nothing.

Orla How do you feel? Maybe you should sit down or something ... Will I get you ... anything?

Gerard *sits on the sofa.* **Orla** *sits beside him.*

Gerard Orla, I'm fine. There's no need to make a fuss.

Orla *feels something press into her back. She reaches around and pulls out the video from the back of the sofa.*

Orla Oh.

Gerard What's that?

Orla It's that Maya Deren video. How did it get down there? … Have you told Carmel?

Gerard No, no. I'll wait until I know for certain.

Orla I think we should tell her. She'd know all about this kind of thing. She'll know what's best.

Gerard Not just now, Orla. You better go and put some cream on that lip.

Orla What?

Gerard Otherwise it'll swell up like a balloon and everyone will think you're Mick Jagger.

A beat.

Gerard Well, go on then.

Orla OK.

Orla *hesitates, then exits. She puts the video on top of the TV as she leaves.* **Gerard** *holds his head in his hands. A few moments later,* **Liam**, *a bit drunk, enters.*

Liam Hi there. Where's Orla?

Gerard (*angry*) Why? So you can finish the job and set fire to the rest of her face?

Liam What?

Gerard Why not simply douse her in petrol and be done with it! You don't give a damn about her well-being, do you? Don't give a shit! What kind of a person are you?!

Liam Jesus, don't blame me! She begged me to show her that trick.

Gerard Begged you, did she? That's not the way Orla tells it. She said you had her trapped in that pub all night.

Liam OK, it was my idea to go but after one drink, you couldn't move her for love nor money.

Gerard Is that the truth?

Liam Yes.

Gerard (*sighs*) What has happened to us? … How did we end up like this?

Liam (*points to DVD*) Hey, since you're not that actor, why did you bring this over?

Gerard (*dismissive*) I just needed an excuse to call in.

Liam (*nods*) Does Orla cry at movies?

Gerard No.

Liam I mean, has she ever cried at a movie?

Gerard No.

Liam Never?

Gerard No.

Liam But I saw her cry at *E.T.* Why won't she just admit it?

Liam *shrugs and looks around the room for something.*

Gerard I've always valued Orla's honesty. Such a rare and admirable quality … I remember one Sunday when Orla was sixteen … We'd been out to Deansgrange that morning to visit Helen's grave and then spent the afternoon staring blankly at the telly. The world was just an out-of-focus blur back then, no rhyme nor reason to any of it … I asked Orla what she wanted for dinner and she had this odd look on her face and then asked me to make something different. Something wild and strange and exotic. So I did … And that evening we sat down to our catfish and prune risotto with grilled onion pudding and Orla took one bite, looked at me and said … This tastes like feet … And we laughed. And suddenly, just a little, the world came back into focus. And I knew we were going to be OK … That feels like a long time ago. Now she doesn't care about me anymore. Not really … all she cares about is her film.

Liam *stares at* **Gerard**. *A beat.*

Liam You do know what her movie's about, don't you?

Gerard What?

Liam You.

A beat.

Gerard Repeat that.

Liam The movie's about you. At least, that's what Orla said.

Gerard What? What do you mean?

Liam (*shrugs*) I think it was only tonight after a few drinks that she realised it herself. She was about to explain it but we got distracted when I eh, accidentally set the table on fire … It was only a little fire, just a few flames really …

Gerard (*shocked*) How is her film about me?

Liam I don't know … (*thinks about it*) I guess Broken Doll must be Orla and the butterfly represents you. In the movie, she doesn't want it to die and when it does she's heartbroken.

Gerard No wonder she didn't want me here this— (*Something occurs to him*) My God, I've been such a fool! All this time I thought her secretiveness, the arguments, everything, was because she planned to move out … but that wasn't it at all. Her secret is that the film is about me. And there I was, prodding and pushing and sticking my nose in. No wonder she's been so cranky. (*Laughs*) Oh, Gerard Cullen, what an idiot you are! … But if she isn't moving out, (*points to DVD*) why didn't she want this?

Liam *spots* **Gerard** *sitting on his jacket.*

Liam Sorry, can I just … ?

Liam *points at his jacket.*

Gerard Oh.

Gerard *stands up and hands the jacket to* **Liam**. **Liam** *takes it but then* **Gerard** *won't let go of the other end.*

Gerard (*suddenly realising*) Where are you going?

Liam Town.

Gerard But … what about the film?

Liam What about it?

Gerard I thought you needed Dutch courage to do the last shot?

Liam No, I needed to get so shit-faced I couldn't remember my own name. But that didn't work and then I wasted the twenty minutes trying to score some weed but no joy. So now I have to go and find her.

Gerard Who?

Liam Nicole.

Gerard She didn't ring?

Liam It just doesn't add up. Orla rang her this afternoon and told her I was here. I know Nicole, she can't ignore anything that gets on her wick … How is this not tearing her up inside? I have to find out.

Gerard But you have to stay and finish the film.

Liam I thought you didn't want her to finish it?

Gerard That was before.

Liam Before what?

Gerard Before I knew it was a tribute to me. All these years, everything I've done for Orla … this is her way of thanking me, of showing how much she appreciates our life together … You have to finish it.

Liam *yanks the jacket out of* **Gerard***'s hand.*

Liam I have to go.

Gerard Dublin's a big city. How are you going to find her?

Liam She always has her birthday in Doyles.

Gerard You don't get it, do you? Nicole doesn't want you. Not ringing is her way of telling you that the relationship is dead.

Liam I don't know that.

Gerard You have all the proof you need! She didn't ring. She doesn't care. Am I right?

Liam No. You're not.

Gerard It's a perfectly understandable mistake to make. You and this girl got drunk a few times, slept with each other, swapped heart-warming stories about growing up with low IQs … Of course you assumed you were soul-mates but that simply wasn't the case.

Liam No, me and Nicole was real. She didn't see me the way everyone else did, y'know? She wouldn't even go out with me until I'd written more of my script.

Gerard (*surprised*) Oh.

Liam What?

Gerard You write?

Liam (*annoyed*) Yeah, it's what I specialised in. Why is that so hard to believe?

Gerard (*shrugs*) You don't look the type.

Liam (*angry*) Jesus! You take one look at me and assume I'm some loser who's going to spend the rest of his life working in Supermac's, is that it? Is that what you think?

A beat.

Gerard Yes.

Liam *sits down on the sofa.*

Liam See, that's what I'm saying. Nicole didn't see me like that. She read the first ten pages of my graduate script and they made her laugh. She said they were hilarious. Then the next week I tried to kiss her at a social but she was having none of it. Ten more pages, she said, then I'll kiss you. I thought she was taking the piss but she was dead serious. Can you believe that? So I knocked out ten more pages but it's like, I didn't even have to *think* about them. My fingers touched the keyboard and they were off! The next time I looked at the clock it was 5 a.m. I loved that … staying up, on my own, writing till the sun came up … I started going out with Nicole after that and all that time, she kept encouraging me to write. So don't tell me that she never really cared about me, OK?

Gerard Did you finish the script?

Liam Nah, I haven't written since she dumped me.

Gerard *sits beside* **Liam.**

Gerard I'm sorry to hear that. What's your script about?

Liam I don't want to talk about it.

Gerard What's it called?

Liam Look, forget it. Nicole was wrong, it was probably shit. I should have done camera with the rest of the guys.

Gerard Don't be ashamed because you want to strive for something more in life. Art is how we grapple with the senseless chaos of existence. Art is always worthwhile. Never forget that.

Liam It's called *Goodnight Sweet Prawn.* It's about a prawn fisher who's mistaken for a famous Shakespearean actor and falls in love with a gangster's daughter.

Gerard (*blankly*) I have no response to that.

A beat.

Liam (*gets up to leave*) Say goodbye to Orla for me.

Gerard And what makes you think Nicole will take you back?

Liam (*shrugs*) That's how it works in the movies. The guy runs through the rain and get to the airport just in time to stop her leaving. There's a happy ending waiting for me out there, I know there is.

Gerard That's nothing but Hollywood claptrap. The world does not work like that.

Liam How do you know?

Gerard *stands up and faces* **Liam.**

Gerard I know because ten years ago, my wife slipped on the wet kitchen floor and cracked her head open on the sideboard. Do you think if I pray hard enough she'll magically reappear in a puff of smoke and a harp glissando?

Liam No, I don't but—

Gerard Or do you think a mature but attractive widow with a sharp and sassy nature will move in next door, whom I'll bicker with incessantly for years, until eventually discovering our mutual love for each other?

Liam Look, all I'm saying is—

Gerard Or do you think … (*Stops in his tracks*) I can't think of any other happy endings … But they're all equally preposterous and have absolutely nothing to do with real life!

Liam But I have a chance with Nicole, I know I do. I can't let it slip through my fingers.

Gerard (*laughs*) Now you even sound like the hero of a corny B-movie!

Liam So? What's wrong with that? (*Looks at his watch*) I have to catch the last bus.

Gerard (*shrugs*) No-one's stopping you.

Liam *puts on his jacket and heads to the door.* **Gerard** *sits down.*

Gerard (*casually*) But there's one thing you haven't thought of …

Liam *stops, hesitates, then turns around.*

Liam What?

Gerard What if you're not the hero?

Liam What?

Gerard What if you're actually the bad guy?

Liam What d'you mean?

Gerard You talk about dashing off and winning the girl back like they do in the movies. But it's always the hero who gets the girl. The good, virtuous person who deserves his happy ending.

Liam So?

Gerard So, what have you done that makes you the hero?

Liam I … OK, so I haven't done anything amazing but I'm not the worst person in the world.

Gerard The bad guy never thinks of himself as the bad guy, isn't that right?

Liam Yeah, but—

Gerard So you could be bad and not know it.

Liam No I know, but—

Gerard Nicole is a beautiful and funny girl who, no doubt, could have her pick of men. What makes you think you deserve someone like that?

Liam Well, because …

Gerard When you look at your life: the drunkenness, the vandalism, the drugs—

Liam (*unsure*) I'm not that bad.

Gerard Making fun of people behind their back, lying and using people for your own ends … Setting furniture ablaze?

Do you really think Nicole deserves to be with someone like that? Am I right?

A beat.

Liam I don't feel so good.

Gerard Because you know what will happen if you go and confront Nicole? You'll stagger into the pub and you'll find her in the corner, sitting close to another man, holding his hand, maybe even kissing him. And do you know who that man is? … *He's* the hero.

Liam, *depressed, sits on the sofa again.*

Gerard You wanted to know why Nicole never rang. I think you have your answer … So you'll stay?

Liam *takes off his jacket.* **Orla** *enters.* **Gerard** *takes Liam's jacket from him and hangs it up on the coat-rack.*

Orla How are you, Dad? Do you need anything?

Gerard A good night's sleep is all I need right now. I'll leave you two in peace to finish your film.

Orla Dad.

Gerard Now Orla, I don't want you to worry … OK?

Orla *nods.* **Gerard** *exits.* **Orla**, *concerned, watches him leave.*

Liam Is it OK if I crash here tonight?

Orla (*troubled*) Sure, if you want.

Liam Are you alright? You look a bit …

Orla (*forced smile*) I'm fine … too much sambuca, that's all.

Liam Ever feel like if you were never born, it wouldn't make any difference?

Orla Liam, what's wrong with you?

Liam (*shakes his head, embarrassed*) Forget it, I'm an idiot.

Orla You're the most popular person in the class, Liam.

Liam Just 'cause I can drink the most.

Orla Everyone loves you. You're not a loser.

Liam I never said I was a loser! What made you say that?

Orla, *mortified, doesn't respond.* **Liam** *puts his head in his hands. While looking down, he spots the video-tape under the coffee-table. He picks it up and puts it on the table.*

Liam Did Nicole say anything else to you earlier?

Orla Liam, don't waste your time thinking about her. She's nothing but a little shit. Shit from a bottom.

Liam How did she sound on the phone?

Orla I don't know. Bland, thick, bubble-headed.

Liam Was she upset?

Orla Liam relax, you got your own back. She probably burst into tears after I hung up. Isn't that what you wanted?

Liam Yeah … I just … sometimes I don't get her at all.

Orla What's to get? You might as well try to understand a sheet of paper or some belly-button fluff. You should try to take your mind off her … It was so funny when you spilt that flaming sambuca on the table. I couldn't stop laughing.

Liam (*glum*) Yeah, hilarious.

Orla *goes to the TV and picks up the tape she left on top of it.*

Orla I found that tape I was going to show you. It got down the back of the sofa somehow.

Liam*'s face turns white. He stands up.*

Liam Orla. Hang on.

Orla *puts the tape into the video player.*

Liam Orla, wait.

Orla (*turns and looks at* **Liam**) What?

Liam What about the last shot? Don't you want to finish the film? I really feel I'm ready to do it now. But *right* now!

Orla Oh. OK.

Liam Quick, go and set up the camera before I chicken out again!

Orla Right.

Orla *goes and sets up the camera.* **Liam** *breathes a sigh of relief, quickly ejects the tape in the player, puts it in his bag and then puts in the tape he found under the coffee-table. Just as he's finished,* **Orla** *turns around.*

Liam Actually … do you want to show me this video first?

Orla The what?

Liam (*points at the TV*) The Maya whatever movie. Jubilant ferocity?

A beat.

Orla (*shakes her head*) Forget it, it's not important. Let's just get this done and call it a night.

Liam *rolls his eyes, after all the trouble he's gone to switch the tapes.*

Liam OK. Whatever … (*looking around him*) Do you have the script?

Orla *takes the roof off the dollhouse and takes a script out from inside.* **Liam** *takes it from her, staring at her like she's crazy.* **Orla** *catches his look.*

Orla What?

Liam It's a script, Orla, not the bloody crown jewels.

Liam *shakes his head in disbelief.* **Orla** *looks troubled. She turns away. Behind her,* **Liam** *looks around for the white shirt. He spots it in the kitchen and goes to get it.* **Orla** *doesn't notice that he's left the room.*

Orla You know I was telling you in the pub how I realised my film's about Dad? Well, I never finished telling you … I suppose it was the drink tonight that made it suddenly clear to me, what I've been denying for so long … My film's about what a horrific, selfish man my Dad truly is … and tonight I learnt he might actually … have cancer. That's why I can't leave the script lying around Liam …

Liam, *in the kitchen, doesn't hear what* **Orla** *says. He holds the shirt up to the light, looking at the stain, then puts it on. He walks back into the living-room, looking down at the stain.*

Orla I have to do everything I can to keep it out of sight.

Liam (*rubbing the stain*) It'll be fine Orla. I'll keep it well hidden.

Orla (*touched, looks at* **Liam**) I didn't know you cared.

Liam Really, it's not a problem. I'll just hide it with my hands if I have to.

Orla (*puzzled*) OK …

Liam D'you want to do this then?

Orla *nods.* **Liam** *stands behind the dollhouse, takes the fluttering butterfly out of the jar and holds it in his hands.* **Orla** *turns off the house-lights* (*leaving* **Liam** *in a spotlight*) *and goes behind the camera.*

Liam (*looks around*) Where's the clapper-board?

Orla Forget it, it's the last shot anyway. Ready? (**Liam** *nods*) Rolling ... And action.

Liam She has no future, no chance ... to soar, her wings will become dust ... Behind a locked door, her heart is no more ... worn out by strife. Her taciturn scream ... Lost in the night, no more ... (*he holds up the live butterfly*) Dreams know nothing ... life know ...

Orla Wait!

Liam Yeah?

Orla I'm not sure.

Liam About what?

Orla The butterfly.

Liam Really? 'Cause it's funny but that take actually felt ... kind of good. Maybe it's just holding it in my hands or maybe it's the five pints of Heineken but I think I really got a flash of what you're going for.

Orla That's good but I don't know.

Liam What do you mean?

Orla I don't know if … you should kill it.

Liam I don't mind.

Orla It's not that.

Liam 'Cause I think I get it now. I get why you want me to.

Orla You do?

Liam Yeah, the scene's about the relationship between the two characters. Broken Doll keeps trying to please Man in White but really, the relationship's over. He kills the butterfly to prove this to her. The butterfly represents their relationship. He has to kill it.

Orla OK, yes, but just use the words. Convey the same feeling with the words.

Liam OK. No butterfly then?

Orla No.

Liam Fair enough.

Liam *puts the butterfly back in its jar but then pauses.*

Liam But Orla, the thing is …

Orla What?

Liam I think it'd be better if I did it.

Orla It'll work fine without it.

Liam But Man in White has to do something extreme.

Orla I don't want you to do it.

Liam You're not getting what I'm saying.

Orla Liam, I don't care.

Liam It says something about life then. When a relationship's dead, it's dead.

Orla It's fine the other way.

Liam But it's not Orla.

Orla You said killing something for a film was wrong.

Liam I thought you were just being arty-farty then. But I get it now.

Orla Use the plastic butterfly. It makes no difference.

Liam But that won't capture anything of the … the pain, the fuckin' … heartache of real life.

Orla Liam, it's my film and I'm saying no.

Liam Why?

Orla Because.

Liam You want it to be good, don't you?

Orla (*hesitates*) Yes.

Liam 100% committed, you said.

Orla I know what I said.

Liam Did you mean it?

Orla Of course I did.

Liam So why don't you want to do it?

Orla It's complicated.

Liam Why is it complicated?

Orla Why? Why? Why? It's always why with you! You're like a little child or something. This is my decision, Liam. There's a chain of command and I'm the director and that's how it works!

Liam Why?

Orla Christ, Liam!

Liam I just want an answer Orla. What's your problem?

Orla You're my problem.

Liam That's hardly 100% Orla.

Orla I said no.

Liam 70% and falling …

Orla Things are different now.

Liam 50 tops.

Orla Liam, I said no!

Liam But why?

Orla Because!

Liam Because what?!

Orla (*upset*) I don't want it to die, OK?!

Orla *sits on the sofa. A beat.* **Liam** *turns on the house-lights.*

Liam (*shrugs*) OK Orla. Jesus …

Orla *says nothing.* **Liam** *sighs and puts down jar. He sits beside her and sees how upset she is.*

Liam Sorry … It's just … (*shakes his head*) It doesn't matter …

Orla What?

Liam I don't know, it's weird but for the first time I felt like I was getting your film … Like it was all suddenly clicking into place and you catch a glimpse of the big picture, y'know? … Like … like when you realise Bruce Willis is dead at the end of *The Sixth Sense*?

Liam *looks to* **Orla** *for a response.* **Orla***, still upset, says nothing.*

Liam I like your haircut, by the way.

Orla (*touching her hair*) Sorry?

Liam Your new haircut. It's nice.

Orla (*touched*) I didn't think you noticed.

Liam It suits you.

A beat.

Orla Say that bit again. Lost in the night, no more.

Liam Why?

Orla Just do it.

Liam Lost in the night, no more.

Orla Ten years of writing poetry and watching films have led me to this moment right now. But here I am with you and … I'm not thinking about art.

Liam You've lost me.

Orla You've found me.

Orla *touches* **Liam***'s hand.*

Liam (*scared*) Eh, Orla.

Orla You're the only one in the class who understands me Liam.

Liam But I don't understand you.

Orla When you say it.

Liam Look Orla—

Orla Lost in the night, no more …

Liam Maybe we should—

Orla Your lips curl up …

Liam Orla, I don't—

Orla … in the cutest way.

Orla *stops. She sees how terrified* **Liam** *is.* **Orla***, mortified, gets up and walks away from him.*

Liam It's … it's not you, Orla.

Orla (*laughs nervously*) I'm sorry Liam, I don't know what I'm doing.

Liam *gets up and goes to her.*

Liam No really, I mean it.

Orla Everything was so different when I was younger. Even though it was just the two of us, I used to love coming home and finding what bizarre new recipe Dad had tried. Stuffed herrings with apples, dandelion and bacon salad …

Liam Orla … what are you talking about?

Orla (*laughs nervously*) God, all the time I've spent on this film and now it seems so unimportant, so meaningless in the face of Dad having … God, I can barely even say it.

Liam Say what?

Orla Cancer.

Liam Eh, Orla …

Orla (*shrugs, close to tears*) Baked halibut with a pumpkin crust. That was my favourite.

Liam Orla, your dad doesn't have cancer.

Orla Sorry?

Liam He made it up.

Orla (*bewildered*) But … What? How do you know?

Liam This afternoon, he told me he wanted to stay. And he said maybe he could pretend to be dying so that you'd let him.

Orla (*calls out*) Dad!

Liam I told him not to. I didn't know he was—

Orla (*calls out*)   Dad!

Gerard *enters, carrying the clapper-board.*

Gerard   Oops! I spotted this in my room. I must have accidentally used it as a tray when I was taking tea and biscuits up earlier. I only just noticed it now. What a nincompoop I am!

Liam *and* **Orla** *stare at* **Gerard** *blankly. A beat. He puts the clapper-board down.*

Gerard (*cheerful*)   So, I'll leave you to it!

Orla   Dad, don't go.

Gerard   Sorry?

Orla   How will I know when to wear a jacket?

Gerard   Excuse me?

Orla   How will I avoid catching my death of cold? I don't know when it's cold out or not.

Gerard   I'm not following you.

Orla   Of course most people simply look out the window and guess what to wear and they usually don't die of pneumonia but I'm not like that.

Gerard (*to* **Liam**)   What is she talking about?

Liam   Orla.

Orla (*to* **Gerard**) If you're not here, I won't know when to put it on. Should I wear it now? Should I put my jacket on now? I should, shouldn't I?

Orla *puts her jacket on and stands defiantly before a bewildered* **Gerard**. *A beat.*

Gerard (*blankly*) I have no response to that.

Orla You don't? Maybe I should wear two. Would that be better? Otherwise I might get a chill and fall down dead on the spot. Thanks, that's the kind of propitious advice I need.

Orla *puts* **Liam***'s jacket on over her own.* **Gerard** *and* **Liam** *stare at her.*

Orla It's not like you'd have to tell a grown adult to wear her jacket when she leaves the house. You'd only say that to a child, wouldn't you? Am I right? … (*Louder*) Am I right?

Gerard Orla, have you completely lost your marbles?

Liam (*to* **Gerard**) This is my fault.

Orla No, it's not, Liam. (*Pointing at* **Gerard**) It's his.

Gerard What is my fault? Will you please tell me what is going on here?

Orla Dad, you don't have cancer.

Gerard What? … What do you mean, Orla?

Orla Dad, give it a rest, please?

Gerard OK, Orla, OK. You're right … Maybe I don't have cancer but maybe I do. I won't know until the doctor rings with the results.

Orla Which doctor?

Gerard He wasn't a witch-doctor! He was a fully licensed cancer specialist.

Orla Dr O'Connell, was it?

Gerard No, no. This was a special clinic I went to. Out near Greystones. You wouldn't know it.

Orla What's it called?

Liam Orla, listen. Will you sit down and let me explain what's going on?

Orla *ignores him.*

Gerard Tell me, why would I make up something like this?

Gerard *waits for a response.* **Orla** *walks away, saying nothing.* **Gerard** *goes over to her and stands in front of her.*

Gerard (*serious*) No Orla, look at me. I want to know why you would think that. What kind of a man do you think I am?

Orla (*unsure*) Didn't you tell Liam that you were going to lie to me?

Gerard (*laughs*) You believe the word of this boy over your own father?! He's been lying to you all weekend!

Orla What?

Gerard He's not your friend, Orla. He doesn't care about you! He's only here because it'll help him get his ex-girlfriend back.

Orla *looks at* **Liam**.

Liam No, Orla, let me explain. I … I didn't want to hurt your feelings.

Gerard (*to* **Orla**) You see? I knew from the start you couldn't trust him!

Orla (*to* **Gerard**) Why did you lie to me, Dad?

Gerard Orla, you have it all wrong. Yes, I did say to Liam I was going to tell you I was dying. But I only said that because it's the truth. Liam assumed it was a lie but it's not. It's the truth Orla. The doctor will ring and then you'll see … (*He notices butterfly jar and picks it up*) Is this for your film? You'll need to get a bigger jar if you want it to live.

Orla What did you say the clinic was called?

Gerard My God Orla! Why all the questions? I tell you I'm dying and you hold a table-quiz!

Orla I'm in shock … What's the clinic called, Dad?

Gerard I don't remember. Did you know that butterflies taste through their feet? Can't be very hygienic, can it?

Orla When did you go to this clinic?

Gerard The Hartzell Clinic! That's what it's called. Out near Greystones. So now do you believe me, Orla?

A beat.

Orla (*quietly*) Yes, Dad. I do.

A beat.

Orla (*to* **Liam**) Well, that's a relief.

Gerard What?

Orla (*to* **Liam**) After getting my hopes up that he might be dying, it would've been awful if it wasn't true.

Gerard Orla, what are you saying?

Orla (*to* **Liam**) I was so disappointed when you said he was lying. But now I know it's true. You don't know how happy that makes me. Now all we have to do is wait. Fingers crossed!

Gerard *is stunned.* **Orla** *glances at him.*

Liam Jesus, Orla!

Orla What?

Behind them, **Gerard***, still holding the butterfly jar, goes into the kitchen and locks the door.*

Liam How can you be so heartless?

Orla *notices* **Gerard** *has gone into the kitchen. She turns to* **Liam**.

Orla He doesn't have cancer, Liam.

Liam But you just said …

Orla The Hartzell Clinic? Mr Hartzell is the name of the English teacher in *The Catcher in the Rye*, which Dad's teaching for the Leaving this year. He's making it all up.

Orla *walks over to the kitchen door.*

Orla Dad?

Gerard, *agitated, paces in the kitchen.*

Orla Dad, open the door.

Liam But why did you say those things to him?

Orla He started it.

Liam Jesus Christ! Will you listen to me, Orla? You don't know the whole story.

Orla And you do, right? The big game-player holding all the cards! … (*Realises*) Oh … something tells me your plan to get Nicole back isn't going to work.

Liam Why not?

Orla It's not my fault. You shouldn't have lied to me.

Liam What did you say to her?

Orla Only that you think she's a frigid bitch who needs lots of make-up.

Liam (*furious*) What?!

Orla I was only repeating what you said.

Liam Jesus Christ, Orla!

Orla I was trying to convince her because she wouldn't believe you were working on my film. I didn't know you wanted to get back together in copacetic bliss!

Liam You did this on purpose!

Orla No, you told me you wanted revenge.

Liam You were only supposed to tell her I was helping you!

Orla But Liam, sometimes it's good to talk. Better not to keep it all inside? Isn't that what you said to me, Liam? Isn't it?

Liam *grabs his jacket and heads for the exit. He turns to* **Orla**.

Liam Fuck you, Orla. Fuck you and your poxy movie!

Orla (*shouts*) It's not a movie, it's a film!

Suddenly the phone in the kitchen rings. Everyone freezes. A beat. **Gerard** *answers the phone.*

Lights go down.

Act Three

Sunday morning. The living-room is the same as it was last night. **Gerard** *sits in the kitchen, his head in his hands, the butterfly jar beside him.* **Orla** *enters, carrying a plastic bag containing a Scart lead.*

Orla (*jolly*) Brrr! Chilly out, this morning.

Gerard (*looks up*) Orla?

Orla *takes off her jacket and a script out of her back-pocket. She tosses it onto the table and goes to the kitchen door.*

Orla I have a little surprise for you, Dad. I went to Dixons and bought a SCART lead. So now I can hook up the DVD and we can watch films on it. Isn't that good news?

No answer.

Orla Could you come out and give me a hand with it?

A beat.

Gerard We don't have any DVDs to play on it.

Orla, *thinking, paces around the room. She goes to the kitchen door again.*

Orla How about some breakfast? Are you hungry, Dad?

Gerard Not really.

Orla I was hoping you'd make me some French toast.

Gerard Excuse me?

Orla (*loud*) French toast.

Gerard *says nothing.*

Orla You know I love the way you make it. With cinnamon and honey. How about it?

Gerard Did you know that French toast didn't actually originate in France? It was invented by an American called Joseph French in the 18th century.

Orla, *annoyed, throws the SCART lead onto the sofa.*

Gerard Did you say something?

Orla (*innocently*) No … Dad? … It's been ages since we've been up to Kilmainham. Why don't we go today? Wouldn't that be nice? Spending an afternoon strolling around the exhibits? You giving out about the art, me giving out about parents letting their children run around? Then we could go for over-priced cream-teas in the Westbury and both give out about that. Wouldn't that be fun?

Gerard It's been so long since we've had a day like that.

Orla Why don't we do it today?

Gerard When?

Orla Now.

A beat.

Gerard I thought it was cold out.

Orla Not *that* cold.

Gerard Chilly out, you said.

Orla I was exaggerating.

Gerard I don't want to catch a cold … Surely that wouldn't be wise when we still don't know what the diagnosis is.

Orla (*annoyed*) We can wear our winter coats.

A beat. **Gerard** *stands up and moves to the door.*

Gerard (*gently*) You know, Orla, whenever I suggest you put on a jacket, I'm not doing it to patronise you. I'm only saying it because I care about you.

Orla (*sighs*) Dad, will you open the door and give me the butterfly? … Please? I need it.

Gerard Is that what this rigmarole is all about? French toast and SCART leads! If you wanted the butterfly, why didn't you simply ask me for it?

Orla I asked you for it hours ago.

Gerard But you can't shoot it without Liam, so what difference does it make?

Orla Change of plan. I'll shoot a close-up of me killing the butterfly and intercut it with the footage of Liam.

Gerard So you still want to finish your film? … Even after last night?

Orla Dad, last night … when I said I was relieved you might die, you didn't think I was being serious, did you?

Orla *waits for a response.* **Gerard** *says nothing.*

Orla Because I wasn't. You know how I can get. I was annoyed because the film wasn't going right … I don't want you to die, Dad.

Gerard Honestly?

Orla (*paces as she talks*) Yes. I was … blowing off steam … I was being silly.

Gerard Then I hope you didn't get a fright when the phone rang last night.

Orla Oh no, I guessed it was Nicole. Who else would ring at that hour only a drunken twit desperate for a ride?

Gerard (*laughs*) And I couldn't make any sense of Liam's plan. It seemed like gibberish to me but he got the girl in the end …

Orla *goes over to the kitchen door.*

Orla (*glumly*) They're probably having breakfast at the moment, eating croissants and reading the Sunday papers …

or at least the *Beano*. God, he couldn't run out of here fast enough after she rang. Away from the freak-show … They're probably laughing at us right now.

Gerard (*gently*) Orla, they're beneath our contempt …

Orla Sorry?

Gerard. (*loud*) I said they're beneath our contempt!

A beat.

Orla So, can I have it? Dad, all I want to is to get this last shot.

Gerard (*unsure*) And you honestly didn't mean what you said last night?

Orla No, Dad. I didn't …

Gerard OK Orla, fine … So, can I read your script?

Orla *freezes.*

Orla What?

Gerard Your script. Can I read it?

Orla No.

Gerard Why not?

Orla You know I don't like showing my work until it's finished.

Gerard Orla, I know the film's about me.

Orla (*panicked*) No, it isn't!

Orla *paces nervously.*

Gerard It's not?

Orla (*laughs nervously*) No, why do you say that?

Gerard Why don't you want me to read it then?

Orla (*nervous*) But you always wait till my film's finished before watching it. Why change that pattern of behaviour now? Why introduce that element of random chaos into our lives when there's enough uncertainty in modern living as it is?

Gerard Orla, you're rambling.

Orla I'm trying to explain.

Gerard Well, stop explaining and simply tell me.

Orla *takes the script off the table and hides it under the dollhouse roof.*

Orla I can't find it. Liam must've taken it.

Gerard Orla, why won't you give me your script?

Orla *goes over to the kitchen.*

Orla Dad, I'm telling you the truth. Liam took the only other copy … Open the door and see for yourself if you don't believe me.

Gerard But why would he do that?

Orla Who knows? He was angry. Maybe he was going to burn it or wipe his arse or make a hat out of it. We may never find out.

The doorbell rings. **Orla** *freezes. It rings again, insistently.*

Gerard Are you going to get that?

Orla *anxiously exits.*

Liam (*offstage*) Well, here I am again!

A slightly drunk **Liam** *enters. He paces around the room, angry and hyper.* **Orla** *follows.*

Orla Liam. Wait a minute, my dad is going to ask you—

Liam (*ignoring her*) A glutton for punishment, that's me!

Gerard *gets up and goes to the kitchen door.*

Gerard Liam?

Orla (*to* **Liam**) Stop, I have to tell you something.

Liam Orla, I don't want to hear it.

Orla God, I can smell the drink off you. It's not even twelve.

Gerard (*loud*) Liam?

Liam *looks around him, not sure where the voice is coming from.*

Gerard (*loud*) Did you take Orla's script last night?

Orla (*to* **Liam**) Say yes. I'll explain later.

Liam (*to* **Orla**) Why should I do anything you ask me?

Gerard (*loud*) Well? Did you take it? Hello?

Orla Please, Liam.

Liam You know I said I liked your haircut?

Orla Yes?

Liam Well, I lied. Training day at barber college, was it?

Orla Take that back.

Liam It's a question. I can't take it back.

Gerard Excuse me?

Orla (*loudly to* **Gerard**) Dad, he's drunk. He doesn't even know where he is!

Liam I'm not drunk. I've been drinking. That's not the same as drunk.

Orla You drink too much.

Liam You don't drink enough.

Gerard (*loud*) Liam, did you take Orla's script last night?

Liam (*loud*) Yeah, I really wanted a souvenir of this tremendous weekend!

Orla (*loud*) Don't mind him, Dad. It's an in-joke we have.

Liam No, it's not. I didn't touch your precious script.

Gerard, *dismayed, sits at the table again.*

Orla Dad? … Dad?

Gerard *doesn't answer. He looks at the butterfly in the jar.* **Liam** *paces, agitated.*

Orla (*to* **Liam**) Thanks a bunch, Liam!

Liam All weekend I help you with your movie and what thanks do I get? You sabotage me and Nicole.

Orla You were the one who lied to me!

Liam (*ignores her*) But that wasn't enough. Couldn't let me have my happy ending, could you?

Orla *walks over to the exit and shows* **Liam** *the way out.*

Orla What a poignant synopsis, Liam, but if you don't mind, I have a film to finish.

Liam This isn't the way it's supposed to be. Nicole should be waking me up right now tickling my foot with her little toes … She liked doing that.

Orla Liam, what do you want?

Liam It's your fault.

Orla What is my fault?

Liam Acting in your movie, trying my best to say that ridiculous speech, making a fool of myself. And after all that, when it finally clicks why I should kill the butterfly, you go and change your mind. No wonder I was so screwed up.

Orla What happened last night?

Liam *looks at* **Orla** *and sighs. He sits on the sofa.*

Liam I went to Doyles where Nicole was having her party. She was in this tiny pink top and covered in sweat from dancing but God, she was a total vision. Like Katie Holmes in *The Gift* or Carla Gu-whatsherface.

Orla I get the picture.

Liam So I was explaining how I didn't really mean the stuff you told her I said when her favourite song came on. The Violent Femmes' 'Blister in the Sun'? (**Orla** *shrugs; she doesn't know it*) So she dragged me up on the dance floor and everyone was jumping so wildly, I could feel the wooden floor creaking and bouncing from the weight. And just when I thought we might literally bring the house down, she put her arms around me and we kissed. And I swear it was like fucking seventy-five-frames-a-second slow-motion. There we were, holding each other in the middle of the dance floor, heaving bodies flying around us, a strobe flashing above and the earth moving beneath our feet …

Orla (*glum*) Sounds like fun.

Liam Then we went back to her place. It was so perfect … or at least it would have been if it wasn't for you.

Orla What did I do?

Liam You got me so tangled up in your movie that I couldn't get it out of my head.

Orla I don't understand.

Liam Why? Because I don't have the big, intelligent words you use? Is that it? All the words you've been throwing at me this weekend, trying to make me feel like an idiot?

Orla I wasn't trying.

Liam *throws her a look. He gets up and faces* **Orla**.

Liam Come on. What are we waiting for? Let's do it.

Orla Do what?

Liam Finish your movie.

Orla (*incredulous*) You want to finish my film?

Liam Yes.

Orla Why?

Liam Because then the problem will be solved and I can go back to Nicole.

Orla What problem?

Liam *walks away from* **Orla.**

Liam It doesn't matter. Let's just do this so I can get out of here.

Orla What happened with Nicole?

Liam You don't need to know.

Orla I do.

Liam (*annoyed*) Can we just finish the movie please?

Orla No. Not until you tell me the whole story. You think I trust you for one second after last night? Now what was my fault?

Liam Fine Orla, you want to know? (*He puts his face into hers*) It was your fault I couldn't fucking get it up last night. Happy now?

Liam *walks away from her.*

Orla (*incredulous*) How on earth is that my fault?

Liam Because I couldn't get your movie out of my head, I couldn't relax and I couldn't … perform in the bedroom.

Orla I'm sorry, what?

Liam D'you know how long I'd been dreaming of that moment? That moment before sex where nothing else matters and all your worries melt away and time crawls to a complete stop? And last night, I was back on her bed with her lips on mine and my fingers on her back and Nicole popping the buttons on my jeans. And even though she'd been dancing all night, her skin still smelled like cherries. And if you were thinking more fully you'd wish that that moment would last forever but you don't care 'cause the only thing that matters is her body and the parts of it that are touching yours. Except … that's what I should have been thinking. Do you know what was actually going through my head?

Orla What?

Liam If Man in White doesn't kill the butterfly then Broken Doll will never realise how empty her life is and nothing will ever change for her!

Orla *stares at* **Liam**, *speechless. A beat. He continues.*

Liam No matter what I tried, I couldn't stop thinking about your movie. And when I tried to explain this to Nicole, she got it all wrong and thought I was saying I couldn't get you out of my head. And I told her I'd rather chew glass than be in bed with you but I couldn't make her understand so she kicked me out.

Orla And do you have this problem often?

Liam (*firm*) Don't start.

Orla (*innocently*) I'm only asking.

Liam Last night was so perfect. It wasn't supposed to turn out like this.

Orla Life's a fiasco, Liam. Get used to it.

Liam No, I can still make this right. This isn't me! This isn't how it goes.

Orla Liam, believe me, I know what I'm talking about. Life is not perfect.

Liam You're just giving up. But that's not who I am … So if we just get the movie in the can, it'll be complete in my head and I can forget about it. I'll have my closure and the problem will go away.

Orla Liam, I don't know why you think my film has anything to do with your impotence.

Liam I'm not impotent! This never happened to me before.

Orla But there could be any number of reasons for it. Why fixate on my film?

Liam Shut up, that's why.

Orla *throws her arms in the air.*

Orla Fine Liam. If you want to help me, that's great. Let's do it.

Liam You get the camera, I'll set up the lights.

Orla But we can't finish it.

Liam Why not?

Orla Dad has the butterfly in there and he's locked the door. We can't do the last scene without it.

Liam I thought you weren't going to kill it. What changed your mind?

Orla Finding out my dad is a selfish, fruitcake-ass bastard! I want the butterfly to die screaming in intense pain.

Liam I don't think butterflies scream.

Orla (*shrugs*) I'll dub it on later.

Liam (*looks at the kitchen*) Can you get in through the window?

Orla It's locked.

Liam Do you have a spare key for the door?

Orla (*surprised*) Oh, maybe. I never even thought of that.

Orla *exits.*

Liam (*to* **Gerard**) Hello? (*No answer*) Mr. Cullen?

Gerard Are you talking to me?

Liam What are you doing in there?

Gerard Excuse me?

Liam (*loud*) What are you doing in there?

Gerard (*shakes his head, weary*) God knows, don't ask me. Where's Orla?

Liam She's gone upstairs. Can I get the butterfly off you please?

Gerard Why? So you can finish her film, then take a front-row seat to laugh it off the screen?

Liam Look, if Orla wants to be an artist, she has to take a bit of stick.

Gerard It'll destroy her.

Liam You have to let her make her own mistakes. She's not … hang on! I thought you wanted the film finished.

Gerard What am I supposed to believe? Orla makes a tribute film to me but then wishes I was dead? She tells me she didn't mean it but then lies and says you took her script! How am I to make sense of it all? Why can't she simply be honest with me?

Liam Oh, come on! You lied about having cancer.

Gerard (*outraged*) I did not!

Liam Orla said you named the clinic after someone in *The Catcher in the Rye* or something?

A beat.

Gerard (*quietly*) Orla told you that?

Liam Yeah, look, she knows it's all a big lie. That's why she's been acting so crazy … But if you just open the door and let us finish the film, I'm telling you, everything'll be grand.

Gerard *leaps up and goes to the door.*

Gerard (*angry*) Everything will be grand, will it?! What do you know about life? What do you know about being a father? A girl ditches you and you think it's the end of the world. You've no idea what life is actually like. I've already lost my wife. I can't stand by and lose my daughter too!

A beat.

Liam (*confused*) What?

Gerard *walks away from the door. He paces in the kitchen.*

Gerard If I don't take steps now, she'll be gone and I'll be left here by myself. Year in, year out, on my own, watching *Countdown*, reading the obits and slowly, inevitably crumbling away into nothing.

A beat.

Liam That's the real reason you're doing this? But … that's nuts.

Gerard Your plan was crazy and it worked.

Liam What plan?

Gerard Getting Orla to ring Nicole.

Liam My plan wasn't crazy … So you stop Orla from graduating this year. What are you going to do next year?

Gerard (*shrugs*) I'll cross that bridge when I get to it.

Liam But … you're blackmailing Orla into staying with you. That's just wrong.

Gerard *sits down again.*

Gerard I'm not blackmailing her, I'm doing it for her own good.

Liam You're doing it for yourself, you nut-job!

Gerard (*chuckles dismissively*) No, no. You don't understand.

Liam (*incredulous*) But you just said ten seconds ago you didn't want to be alone.

Gerard You don't appreciate the relationship Orla and I have. Things are strained this weekend but they'll be back to normal soon enough. As long as I shield her from the humiliation. That's the important thing.

Liam But that's just an excuse because you don't want her to leave … Do you realise that after this weekend, Orla will never speak to you again?

Gerard You wouldn't understand … That's not an insult by the way, I mean it literally.

Liam How can I get it through to you?

Gerard (*laughs*) There's nothing to get.

Liam *paces, thinking.*

Liam You want to spare Orla humiliation? That's why you're doing this?

Gerard Yes.

Liam So why not come out and help her with the film? Make sure there's nothing in it to laugh at?

Gerard How can I do that when she won't even let me read her script?

Liam *looks around him for the script. He goes to the dollhouse, gets the script and slides it under the kitchen door.*

Liam There. Now you've no excuse.

Orla *enters, looking at her fingernail. In the kitchen,* **Gerard** *stares at the script a moment, then picks it up, sits at the table and reads it.*

Orla (*to* **Liam**) Any luck?

Liam (*weary*) I don't know. Did you find a spare key?

Orla (*holds up her nail*) All I got was a bloody broken nail from rooting around the top of the wardrobe. (*Sighs, weary*) God, I'm worn out by him!

Orla *goes over to the kitchen.*

Orla Dad? (*No answer*) Dad, will you please open up? … Are you not even going to talk to me now?

Gerard, *absorbed in reading the script, doesn't answer.* **Orla** *sighs, defeated. She turns back to* **Liam.**

Orla Why did you say it then?

Liam What?

Orla Why did you say you liked my haircut if you didn't mean it?

Liam Because at the time I thought you needed to hear something nice.

Orla (*listens at the door again*) What do you think he's doing in there?

Liam Reading.

Orla Reading what?

Liam Your script.

Orla (*stunned*) You gave him my script?

Liam Yes.

Orla. Dad?

Gerard, *absorbed in reading, doesn't answer.*

Orla (*to* **Liam**) Why did you do that?!

Liam So he'd open the door.

Orla I can't believe you'd do that Liam!

Liam (*baffled*) What do you mean?

Orla That you'd be this malicious!

Liam (*baffled*) I was trying to get the butterfly. Isn't that what you wanted?

Orla Don't plead ignorance! You knew exactly what you were doing! Getting me to look for a spare key so that you'd have your chance?

Liam (*incredulous*) I don't believe this.

Orla All part of your master plan.

Liam What master plan?!

Orla You had no right Liam! After I bare my soul and confide in you, what do you do? Betray me and fling it back in my face!

Liam Jesus Christ! Are we all on different fucking planets?! What the hell are you talking about?

Orla, *fuming, walks over to the fish-tank, pulls the cow's heart out of it and holds it up to* **Liam**. *She walks to the bin and throws it in. She gives* **Liam** *a defiant look. He stares back at her in disbelief.*

Liam What the hell is that supposed to mean?!

Orla (*calm*) You can forget about the film now Liam.

Liam Orla, you said.

Orla I changed my mind.

Liam Jesus, for once in your life will you do something for someone else?

Orla Liam, I *could* care less … but not much.

Liam Orla, I need this. It's important.

Orla I said no.

Liam You don't get it, do you? You can't comprehend how someone else can feel this much about another human being. What would you know about people with your Maya Deren videos and your amniotic fuckin' brine?

Orla And don't worry about your little problem Liam, I'll give Mr. Viagra your number next time I see him!

Liam Can't even admit you cried at *E.T.*? Can't deal with any kind of human feelings at all, can you?

Orla Get it through your thick fucking skull Liam, I did not cry at *E.T.*

Liam I was sitting right behind you! Why can't you admit it? What is wrong with you!?

A beat.

Orla OK Liam. Yes, I was crying. I was crying and you saw me.

Liam Thank you!

Orla But it had nothing to do with that moronic film. I wasn't even watching it … All day not one person said a single word about my stupid new haircut … Oh, I know what you're all like, and on the way in last Tuesday I was bracing myself for the reaction. For the quips and the jibes but then I get there and there's not a word. Not a snigger. Not even a look … The whole day went by and not one person in the class even noticed my hair. Because they don't see me … Because I'm invisible. I don't even exist … I'm nothing … That's why I was crying Liam … It had nothing to do with E bloody T.

A beat.

Liam Orla, we have to finish the movie. I can't go on without Nicole.

Orla God, Liam, will you listen to yourself?

Liam Are you going to do it?

Orla There's more chance of you winning an Oscar this year.

Liam *angrily knocks the dollhouse to the ground. The contents go sprawling.*

Liam I'm not kidding Orla! She's the only thing I care about.

Orla You don't give a shit about Nicole! Every time you talk about her, it's never how funny *she* is or how great *she* is, it's always about how she laughs at *your* jokes or how she encourages *you*. *I* can't keep going without her. *I* don't care about anything else. *I* deserve her. You don't even see her as a person. You don't care about her. You only care about how she makes you feel.

Liam (*unsure*) That's … that's not true.

Orla Tell me Liam, what's Nicole's graduate film about? Do you even know? And how was her shoot? Did you bother to ask her? Well, did you?

Liam *has no response. He sits on the sofa, the fight gone out of him.* **Orla** *leaves him and goes over to the kitchen.*

Orla (*scared but hopeful*) Dad? (*No answer*) … (*louder*) Dad?

In the kitchen, **Gerard** *finishes reading the script and puts it down.*

Gerard Yes, Orla?

Orla Did you … did you read it?

Gerard Yes, I did.

A beat.

Orla (*hopeful*) And …?

Gerard I'm not sure what to say.

Orla Dad, I can explain.

Gerard I have to say Orla, I'm disappointed.

Orla You were never supposed to see it.

Gerard That's no excuse.

Orla It's only made up. You shouldn't take it seriously.

Gerard No matter Orla, there has to be some sense to it.

Orla Dad, I'm sorry. I didn't … What? … What do you mean?

Gerard Just because it's fiction doesn't mean you can throw out the rulebook on logic.

Orla I'm not following. You read my script?

Gerard Yes.

Orla And you understood it?

Gerard (*shrugs*) The gist of it …

Orla What didn't you understand?

Gerard I don't know what I was expecting, really. I hoped it would give me some kind of insight into how you see me. How you see our life together. I wasn't expecting what reads, for all the world, like the … random thoughts of a paranoid Bedlamite.

Orla (*crestfallen*) You didn't understand it?

Gerard What's it supposed to be about? Is it a lament for lost youth? A diatribe against patriarchy? A polemic against cruelty to insects? What has all of that got to do with me?

Orla (*hurt*) How can you not understand it, Dad? Out of everyone in the whole world … if anyone was going to understand it, I thought it would be you.

Gerard If it's any consolation, I understand why you didn't want me to see it. But Orla, you can't blame your audience if they don't understand your film, am I right?

Orla (*defeated*) Yes, Dad … you're right.

Orla *sits on the floor, beaten.*

Gerard Now feel free to disagree but I think you should shelve this version altogether and perhaps aim to have a film ready for next year instead. I can help with it, give you guidance throughout the year … You'll see I'm right in the future …

Liam (*loudly*) She has no future!

Gerard *and* **Orla** *freeze in surprised bafflement.* **Orla** *looks at* **Liam**. **Gerard** *listens at the door.* **Liam** *lifts his head and continues, passionately.*

Liam No chance to soar!

Liam *stands up and continues.*

Liam Her wings will become dust behind a locked door, Her heart is no more, worn out by strife, Her taciturn scream, lost in the night. No more dreams, no nothing, no life …

The words strike a chord with **Gerard**. *A beat. He picks up the butterfly jar, and comes out of the kitchen.* **Orla** *stares at him, not knowing what to say.*

Gerard (*chuckles*) Once, when you were only small, I spent a whole afternoon taking apart a remote control when the TV suddenly stopped working. I had batteries and wires spread all over the kitchen table and then your mother walked in. And she asked me what I was doing with the remote for the CD player … You never see the wood for the trees, she used to say to me.

A beat.

Orla I miss her.

Gerard I do too, Orla … If she was here right now she would've understood your film in an instant. Would have seen how meaningful it is … And she would've called me a self-indulgent fool … Only she's not here anymore … But you are. You're all I have, Orla … And the thought of losing you makes me do stupid things. Stupid selfish things that even a child wouldn't do.

Gerard *looks to* **Orla** *for a response. She doesn't know what to say.*

Gerard You know I lied about having cancer, don't you?

Orla (*embarrassed*) Yes, Dad.

Gerard I don't know why I did that, Orla. It popped out of my mouth before I could stop myself and then I just kept digging myself deeper and deeper … I'm sorry for doing that Orla.

Orla I know, Dad.

Gerard And I'm sorry for locking myself in the bathroom at Christmas.

Orla I know, Dad.

Gerard And I'm sorry for scaring off your original actor.

Orla I kn— … what?

Gerard (*embarrassed*) I may have ever so slightly threatened him when he was here rehearsing last weekend. But he was a lecherous little creep, Orla, you can't deny that.

Orla *shakes her head in disbelief.*

Gerard But that … that kind of behaviour is behind me now. I promise.

Orla I'm not a child anymore.

Gerard Things will change around here, Orla. From now on. I mean it.

Orla Dad, I … I can't spend the rest of my life watching films here with you but that doesn't mean I don't want you in my life … You're all I have too … My life will change and so will yours but it'll be OK. It'll be different, that's all.

Gerard (*holds up butterfly jar*) Like a caterpillar changing into a butterfly?

Orla *smiles.* **Gerard** *hands her the jar.*

Gerard I think maybe I'll go and have lunch at Carmel's. Perhaps I should do it every weekend? Give the old bat someone to moan at … (*Nods at* **Liam**) Liam.

Gerard *starts to leave.*

Orla Dad?

Gerard Yes, Orla?

Orla It is a bit chilly out.

Orla *holds up Gerard's jacket.* **Gerard** *goes over to her and puts it on.*

Gerard Don't want to catch my death of cold now, do I? Liam!

Gerard *exits.*

Liam (*excited*) God, all this time it was staring me in the face and I didn't see it. How many times did I read it and all I saw was pretentious wank? But I wasn't looking hard enough. What the butterfly represents … It's you … And did you see the effect it had on him? It was your words that made him come out of the kitchen.

Orla No, it wasn't Liam … It was yours.

Liam But to be able to reach someone like that … really speak to them, y'know? It's amazing … I had no idea you could do that with words. With stuff you write yourself.

Orla (*surprised and delighted*) Hello? Isn't that what I've been saying to you all week? I told you Liam. Art is important.

Orla *puts dollhouse the right way up.*

Liam Sorry about that, by the way. Is it worth a lot?

Orla (*waves her hand dismissively*) I lied, it's a piece of junk.

Liam *holds up the butterfly jar.*

Liam So what are we waiting for? Let's do this.

Orla You'll stay for a while and give me a hand?

Liam (*looks at his watch*) Sure, lots of time. Shoot this scene, finish the film, call into Nicole's and shag the shit out of her.

Orla You get changed and set up the lights. I'll get the camera.

Liam *puts on the white shirt and picks up the clapper-board.* **Orla** *sets up the camera but then pauses and looks at the butterfly jar.*

Orla You know what Liam? Let's use the plastic butterfly instead.

Liam Yeah?

Orla Some quick editing and you'll never notice. (*Holds up the jar*) I think she's been through enough this weekend.

Liam (*shrugs*) You're the director.

Orla *and* **Liam** *go into the kitchen.* **Orla** *opens the kitchen window, then lifts up the jar.*

Orla That's a wrap for you, little one.

She opens the jar and lets the butterfly fly out through the window. **Orla** *and* **Liam** *watch it fly away …*

Liam (*concerned*) Oh. Look out for the …

Orla *and* **Liam** *wince …*

Liam Lawnmower.

A beat. They both stare out the window in embarrassed silence … **Liam** *looks down at the clapper-board.*

Liam Forty-seven slates. Not bad for a five-day shoot.

Orla (*getting back to work*) Let's make it forty-eight!

Liam *goes back to setting up the lights.* **Orla** *sets up the camera.*

Orla What do you talk about in Bakers?

Liam What?

Orla When you go for a drink with the class? What does everyone talk about?

Liam I don't know. Lots of things.

Orla Like what? Complain about lectures? Movies you like?

Liam (*shrugs*) Yeah, that kind of thing.

Orla Maybe next weekend, I'll come along. I mean, what do you think?

Liam (*working as he talks*) Yeah, you should …

Liam *positions a light-stand but the DVD box on the ground is in the way. He motions to* **Orla** *to move it. She moves the DVD out of the way.*

Liam Are you planning on moving out soon?

Orla (*shrugs*) I hadn't given it any thought. Why do you ask?

Liam Then why didn't you want that?

Orla I made a vow I wouldn't get a DVD player until I lost my virginity.

Liam (*blankly*) I have no response to that.

A beat. **Liam** *goes back to setting up the equipment.* **Orla** *looks at the box.*

Orla (*cheerfully*) What the hell!

Orla *unpacks the DVD and connects it to the television. Behind her* **Liam** *continues working.*

Liam Y'know what? I think I'll stay up late tonight and finish writing my script … If Milo somehow fakes his death while performing *Othello* then he could run away with Roxie and get the money to repair his trawler … So the prawn-fisher'll finally get his happy ending.

Orla *is about to unplug the video-recorder when she checks to see if there's any tape inside. She finds one and presses play. Liam's spoof video comes on.* **Orla** *sits back on the sofa and watches it.*

Orla (*on verge of tears*) When did you make this?

Liam *goes to* **Orla** *and is horrified to see what she's watching.*

Liam Last week. We were just messing about one afternoon. You weren't supposed to see it. I'm sorry Orla but it doesn't mean anything. It's just Harris didn't show up for the two o'clock lecture and Nicole got a copy of your script and … we were just bored. It was nothing personal though. If it was someone else's script we would have done that too. We were just having a laugh Orla, honest. It didn't mean anything.

Orla Relax Liam … (*She laughs, upset*) It's only a movie.

Lights go down.

THE END

Noah and the Tower Flower

BY SEAN McLOUGHLIN

Noah and the Tower Flower was first performed by Fishamble: The New Play Company on 17 May 2007, at Axis Arts Centre, with the following cast and production team:

Noah	Darren Healy
Natalie	Mary Murray
Director	Jim Culleton
Set and Costume Designer	Sinéad O'Hanlon
Lighting Designer	Mark Galione
Sound Designers/Composers	Ivan Birthistle and Vincent Doherty
Producer	Orla Flanagan
Script Development	Gavin Kostick
Marketing Officer	Ross O'Corrain
Graphic Design	Simon Dry
Production Manager	Des Kenny
Stage Director	Stephanie Ryan
Stage Manager	Jo Richards

Winner of the Best New Play Award 2007 at the *Irish Times* Theatre Awards

Winner of the overall Stewart Parker Trust Award 2007

Nominated for a Playwrights' and Screenwriters' Guild *ZeBBie* Award (formerly OZ Whitehead Award) for Best Theatre Script in 2007

'It's a little cracker ... Mary Murray and Darren Healy are as funny, endearing and accomplished as could be hoped for ... Jim Culleton directs with a great touch of liveliness and subtlety' *Sunday Independent*

'Sean McLoughlin has written a fairytale of Ballymun with all the edge of Shane MacGowan's New York version ... Mary Murray is stunning as Natalie; Darren Healy brings physical comedy, a manic energy and a superb De Niro impersonation to his portrayal of Noah ... Jim Culleton has clearly allowed the actors to nurse their characters into life ... exhilarating, clever and disturbing' *Irish Independent*

'McLoughlin demonstrates a keen eye for character and an ear for amusingly blunt dialogue' *The Irish Times*

'McLoughlin convincingly captures the desperation of obsession, addiction, loneliness and love, in a Dublin idiom laced with mordant humour. Darren Healy and Mary Murray make the intimacy of Fishamble's production almost difficult to watch ... the snappy Dublin banter in McLoughlin's play is beautiful, hard poetry ... ****' *Sunday Business Post*

CHARACTERS

Noah
Natalie

SCENE ONE

Natalie *sits on her bedside. Her hair is down, and she is wearing an Adidas tracksuit. She is barefoot. Her hands are clasped together. She is reciting the first verse of the serenity prayer, over and over again. 'God grant me the serenity to accept the things I cannot change; courage to change the things I can; and wisdom to know the difference.' After 15 or 20 seconds the stage lights come down. But we still hear* **Natalie** *recite her prayer, even in the second scene.*

SCENE TWO

A wooded area. **Noah** *is on his knees, digging up earth with his hands. He is wearing a three-quarter-length leather jacket, a red chequer shirt, blue jeans and white runners. There's a large blue plastic sack a few feet away from him. He eventually pulls a small wooden box out of the ground. He opens the box and takes out a hand gun. He inspects it. The voice of* **Natalie** *begins to fade, as do the stage lights.*

SCENE THREE

A public house in Ballymun. Two high tables, both parallel to each other. Between both is a space of about 10 feet. **Natalie** *is* *sitting at one. She is drinking a glass of G and T. She lights up a cigarette. Silence. Enter* **Noah**, *holding his dark blue sack and a bottle of Miller.* **Natalie** *glances at him for a second, then looks away.*

SCENE FOUR

Noah (*winks*) How's it goin'?

Natalie Alrigh'.

Noah *puts his sack down and sits. Pause.*

Noah First drink in eight months.

Natalie Yeah?

Noah *nods yes.*

Noah I was in the Joy. Only after gettin' out this mornin'. (*Hoists bottle*) *Sláinte.* (*He takes a large hit.*) Not bad. (*Short pause*) Not great now bu' … not bad.

Natalie What were ye in for?

Noah Stupidity. (*Pause.* **Noah** *smiles*) Are you a tower flower?

Natalie A wha'?!

Noah A tower flower. Do you reside in one of the Towers?

Natalie I do, yeah.

Noah (*surprised*) Which one?

Natalie Ceannt. (**Natalie** *exhales smoke, then stabs out her cigarette in ashtray*) I used to reside in Connolly, if that's any good to ye.

Noah (*small laugh*) Tower flower all the way! Wha'?

Natalie Tower flower.

Noah (*nodding his head*) That's what me and that … muppet Flynner used to call young ones from the Towers. (*Pause*) When are they comin' down?

Natalie Next summer.

Noah Is that for defo now?

Natalie (*sharp*) Yeah.

Pause.

Noah Are they blowin' them up?

Natalie I haven't a fuckin' clue what they're doin'. All I know is … I'm getting' an apartment out of it.

Noah Are ye gettin' an apartment?

Natalie Fuckin' righ' I am! Sure I've been livin' in Ceannt for two year.

Noah You go girl.

Natalie Shut the fuck up.

Noah laughs.

Noah Only buzzin' with ye. (*Short pause*) No but, that's rapid that's is. (*Short pause*) And like … are ye livin' with someone or … ?

Natalie I live on me own, I do.

Noah Aw righ'. (*Short pause*) And d'ye like livin' on yer own?

Natalie (*sharp*) I do yeah! (*Short pause*) Wouldn't have it any other way.

She takes a sip of her drink. Pause.

Noah So the towers are comin' down next summer.

Natalie Yeah.

Pause.

Noah It'd be rapid if they blew them up. (*Short pause*) They blow them up in Germany, they do.

Natalie Is that righ'?

Noah Yeah. And in England. (*Short pause*) It'd rapid if they blew them up. If they blew them up, I'd get a few cans for it, I would.

Natalie Big into destruction, yeah?

Noah Aw yeah. TNT, all the way.

Natalie Yer big into yer dirt as well.

Noah Wha'?

Natalie Yer hands.

Noah *looks at his hands.*

Noah Aw yeah. (*Shakes head. Pause*) Had a bit of a fall this mornin'.

Pause.

Natalie So where do you live anyway? Or should I say, where do you reside?

Noah Well, currently, at present, I don't reside nowhere. I used to reside in 26 Balcurris Avenue. Not anymore though.

Natalie Why?

Noah 'Cause I'm barred. Owl one doesn't want me livin' in the gaff anymore. (*Shakes head*) eight months in the Joy, and she wouldn't even invite me in for a cup of tea. All I get out of her … is a big dirty lecture … and ninety Euro. (*Impersonates his mother*) Here … take that and go. Go on! (*Wagging finger*) And don't you dare go anywhere near yer granny's. You go anywhere near yer granny's, I'll slap the guards on ye. (*Own voice*) Pppph. The fuckin' guards. (*Short pause*) Well I tell ye. She can go fuck herself 'cause … as soon as I've had a couple of these babies, (*lifts up the bottle of Miller*) I'm off to Sheridan Court, I am!

Natalie Is that where yer granny lives?

Noah Yip! Sheridan Court.

Natalie Will she put ye up?

Noah She'll put me up.

Natalie What if she doesn't?

Noah She'll put me up. That woman will put me up. Me and the granny are like that, we are. (*Crosses fingers*) Two peas in a pot.

Natalie Pod.

Noah Wha'?!

Natalie Nuttin'.

Pause.

Noah Lookin' forward to seein' her now, I am. (*Sniffs*) Always have great conversations, we do. She's a great owl skin. eighty-three years of age, she is! Hope she lives till one hundred and three, God bless 'er. (*Short pause*) She was the only one who visited me when I was in the Joy, ye know tha'? The only one. She'd come in every once in a while, with a big smile and twenty John Player Blue. (*Short pause*) Didn't see any of me buddies from Balbutcher do tha'. Visited me the first few weeks alrigh'. Bu' tha' was abou' it. Muppets. (*Pause*)

Tell ye somethin'. Ye quickly find out who yer buddies are when yer in the slam.

Pause.

Natalie What was it like?

Noah What was what like?

Natalie The Joy!

Noah Aw it was lovely. Absolutely lovely. Best eight months of me life. (*Short pause*) The fuck ye think it was like? It was fuckin' disgustin'! Nappers (*heroin addicts*) all over the place. Dirty filthy nappers! (**Natalie** *looks away*) I tell ye somethin'. Before I went into the Joy, I didn't mind nappers so much. Now I fuckin' hate them. Messy bastards, the lot of them.

Pause.

Natalie (*not looking at him*) I reckon you're a spoofer.

Noah Wha'?!

Pause. **Natalie** *glances at him for a second.*

Natalie You weren't in the fuckin' Joy.

Noah I was in the Joy!

Natalie No ye weren't.

Noah I fuckin' was!! Whatcha think that's all abou'? (*Points at sack*) Think I'm bleedin' Father Christmas or something?

Natalie I think yer a spoofer, that's what I think.

Short pause.

Noah I was in the fuckin' Joy, righ'!

Natalie No ye weren't.

Noah I fuckin' was!

Natalie Ye weren't! Ye weren't in the Joy! You're a fuckin' spoofer, ye are!

Pause. **Noah** *grits his teeth.*

Noah Are you some sort of professional head wrecker, or something?

Natalie No. But I know spoofer when I see one. (*Pause*) You were kicked outta yer gaff, ye were.

Noah Excuse me?!!

Natalie (*fast and angry*) You were kicked outta yer gaff. You were kicked outta yer gaff, and yer in here now mouthin' outta ye. Actin' the hard man. (*Short pause*) If I was Big Juddy Woods though ye wouldn't be actin' the hard man.

Noah Who?!

Natalie Juddy Woods!!

Noah Never heard of 'im.

Natalie *nods at him a couple of times.*

Natalie Yeah well, he's someone who has been in Mountjoy. (**Noah** *throws his hands up*) And he's someone who'd kick the livin' fuckin' crap outta you in 0.3 seconds.

Noah I was in the fuckin' Joy, righ'!

Natalie No ye weren't.

Noah I fuckin' was! I done eight months in Mountjoy for GBH and vandalism. And if wasn't for that fuckin' … prick of an owl fella of mine, I wouldn't have done any time at all.

Short pause.

Natalie How's that?

Noah 'Cause … I smashed up his car and he wouldn't drop the charges! The fuck bag knew I was on a suspended sentence and he wouldn't drop the charges.

Short pause.

Natalie Why did ye smash up his car?

Noah I had me reasons.

Pause.

Natalie And what were ye on a sus … sus … can't even talk. What were ye on a suspended sentence for?

Noah *ignores her.* **Natalie** *looks away.*

Noah I had a scrap with a bouncer one night and I got done for it. Any more questions?

Pause.

Natalie Look. I'm sorry for givin' ye grief whatever yer name is. It's just … I was very offended by what ye said a minute ago.

Noah What did I say?

Natalie Ye know what ye said. You were slaggin' heroin addicts.

Noah They're bad news though.

Natalie Ye don't have to tell me that. I fuckin' know. I was a heroin addict meself, I was. Strung out for three and a half year. (*Short pause*) Wha'?! Ye don't believe me?! Ye want me to roll up me sleeves and show ye me track marks?!! I still have them ye know. They're still there. And they always will be. Reminding me of me fucked-up past.

Pause.

Noah Look … I'm sorry if I offended ye, OK. (*Pause*) I'm sorry, righ'?

Natalie (*sharp*) OK.

Pause.

Noah By the way, the name's Noah.

Natalie Noah?

Noah Yeah. It's me nickname like. Me real name is Noel, bu' like … ye know … Noel, Noah. Ye know wha' I mean?

Natalie I think I do. (*Pause*) Where's yer boat?

Noah It's not a boat. It's an ark. It's outside, it is. (**Natalie** *gives a small laugh*) I'm short a few giraffes. Gonna have to go up to Dublin Zoo, sort it ou'. (*Pause*) Bu' come 'ere. Don't mean to be a wet blanket or anythin' bu' … how long are ye off the smack?

Natalie Fourteen month.

Noah *gives her a slow reassuring wink.*

Noah And ye just gave it up like?

Natalie Well … I had a massive OD like and …

Noah That snapped ye out of it.

Natalie Yeah. (*Pause*) I was dead for over a minute (**Noah** *looks at her in shock. She nods at him*) Doctors told me it was a miracle I survived. And with me brains intact.

Noah Fuck snakes. (*Short pause*) You were actually dead?

Natalie Yeah.

Pause. **Natalie** *looks upset.*

Noah Are ye alrigh'?

Natalie Yeah.

Short pause.

Noah Bu' come 'ere. (*Walks over to her and shakes her hand*) Fair play.

Natalie Ye don't have to shake me hand.

Noah No.

He walks back to high table. Takes slug of bottle. Pause.

Noah *goes to say something but stops. Again he goes to say something, and again he stops.*

Noah If I'm Noah, well then you're Lazarus.

Natalie (*smiling*) Jesus.

Noah No, no. Jesus has nuttin' to do with this. He's in Coolock curin' lepers. (**Natalie** *gives a small laugh*)

Pause.

Noah And come 'ere. Ye know when you were dead? Did ye experience anything?

Natalie I did, yeah.

Noah Wha'??!!

Short pause.

Natalie I just remember … now this isn't a spoof.

Noah Go on! Go on!

Natalie I just remember … movin' towards somethin' mad bright. It was like … I don't what it was like … it was … it was mad bright it was and … I kept movin' towards it and … whoosh! All of a sudden I was sucked away from it and … that's when I woke up in the ambulance. (**Noah** *is nodding his head enthusiastically. He's been doing this the whole time she has been speaking of her experience*)

Noah That was yer soul moving towards God.

Natalie Ye reckon?

Noah Yeah. That was yer soul movin' towards God. (*Short pause*) D'ye not believe in God?

Natalie I do, yeah. (*Half smiling*) Sure I do say me serenity prayer every day.

Noah Yer wha' prayer?

Natalie Me serenity prayer. (*Short pause*) It's a prayer for recovering addicts.

Noah Aw righ'. (*Pause*) Nah but … that was yer soul movin' towards God.

Natalie *nods her head a couple of times.*

Natalie Maybe.

Noah It was! Tellin' ye.

Pause.

Noah If you didn't have that OD, d'ye reckon ye'd still be a smack-head?

Natalie Yeah. I'd be out there now, by the swimming pool with the rest of them. Skagged ou' of it. (*Pause*) They all hate me they do.

Noah Who?

Natalie Me old mates. They all think I'm an ignorant bitch. They don't understand though. I can't have nuttin' to do with them anymore.

Noah I know what you're sayin'. I understand.

Natalie I wish they would.

Noah Ah fuck them!

Natalie No! (*Short pause*) They're on the H-train, ye see.

Noah The H-train?

Natalie The heroin train! Doesn't stop for no one. (*Pause*) Waved at Wheelie the day the other day. Didn't even wave back. He just went like tha' (*sticks out lower lip*) and turned his back on me. And this was someone I used to get on great with. Me and Wheelie were like … you and yer granny. (**Noah** *holds in his laughter*) Wha'? Wha' are ye laughin' at? (**Noah** *shakes his head, slightly embarrassed*) I'm not takin' the piss.

Noah I know.

Pause.

Natalie I think that's lovely by the way.

Noah Wha'?

Natalie (*slow to answer*) The friendship ye have with yer granny. There's somethin' really lovely about it.

Noah Ah she's a good owl skin. (*Pause*) This Wheelie character …

Natalie What abou' 'im?

Noah I think I know who he is.

Natalie The whole of Ballymun knows who he is.

Noah He's in a wheelchair isn't he?

Natalie (*sarcastic*) Yeah.

Noah I know him!

Natalie Ye know 'im?

Noah Not personally or anythin' bu' … I know who yer talkin' abou'. (*Short pause*) Does he still be with them two young ones? Whenever I use to see him before, he was always with two young ones.

Natalie Yeah. They're his sisters. Benita and Val. (*Short pause*) It was … it was in Val's cousins gaff … that I had me OD

Noah Aw righ'.

Pause.

Natalie Val has the flee.

Noah Yeah?

Natalie nods yes.

Pause.

Natalie (*sharp*) I don't have the flee. (**Noah** *nods*) I don't!

Noah I believe ye. (*Pause*) Does Wheelie have the flee?

Natalie (*purses lips*) He didn't when I was hangin' round with him.

Noah He's a mad-lookin' thing, isn't he? (**Natalie** *sniggers*) The wheelchair helps.

Natalie Yeah well, he wouldn't be able to do much without it.

Noah No I mean, it helps him look madder lookin'.

Natalie Ow. (**Natalie** *sniggers*) (*Pause*) There was a fella in the Joy who was in a wheelchair. (*Coughs*) Traveller. Mad fuckin' pikey. (*Short pause*) Always singin'. Fair owl voice on 'im. (**Natalie** *starts laughing*) I know ye always hear tha' abou' pikeys, bu' this fella could sing. (**Natalie** *is still laughing*) He used to … what are ye laughin' at?

Natalie Keep talkin'.

Noah *smiles.*

Noah He used to sing that ballad … I don't know whether ye know it or not … On this our wedding day. (**Natalie** *bursts out laughing*) that's what he used to sing. (*Sings in a mock traveller voice*) 'On this our wedding day.' (**Natalie** *is still laughing*) The cunt's probably been married sixty times. That's why he loves singin' it. (**Natalie** *continues laughing.* **Noah** *gets up out of his seat and imitates being in a wheelchair*) 'On this our wedding day.'

Natalie *continues laughing.* **Noah** *returns to his seat and sits.*

Natalie Awww. (*Shakes head*) Yer a funny bastard.

Noah Ye think so?

Natalie I do, yeah.

Short pause.

Noah So ye think I'm funny?

Natalie Yeah!

Noah Well, I always had a knack for makin' people laugh. (*Short pause*) Half the time I think they're laughin' at me, mind you.

Natalie I'm not laughin' at ye.

Long pause.

Noah So what's the story with ye, anyway?

Natalie What's the story with me?

Noah Yeah.

Short pause.

Natalie Sorry … what exactly are ye askin' me here?

Noah I'm askin' ye, what's the story with ye? (*Short pause*) Why … are … you … in here?

Natalie 'Cause I'm havin a drink. Like yerself.

Noah Yeah bu' … it's early like.

Natalie Aw so does that make me a dipso now, does it?

Noah Did I say that?

Natalie No bu' … that's what you were thinkin'.

Noah No it wasn't.

Natalie It fuckin' was. (**Noah** *opens his mouth and shakes his head*) Look! I drink in here every Wednesday mornin', OK?! I collect me labour on a Wednesday mornin', and then I come in here and have a couple of drinks. The only other time I drink is on a Saturday nigh'. So I'm not a bleedin' dipso, OK?

Noah I never said ye were! I was only wonderin' what you were doin' in here.

Natalie Yeah well, now ye know.

Pause.

Noah D'ye ever have yer drink next door?

Natalie (*sharp*) No.

Noah I used to drink next door. Meself and … them … fuckin' muppets used to have a couple of scoops in there on a Saturday nigh', before we got the thirteen into town.

Natalie Me owl fella drinks next door. (*Short pause*) Fuckin' dirt bag.

Noah Ye don't like yer owl fella?

Natalie No, I don't. Don't like 'im at all. Fuckin' adulterer. (**Noah** *has a confused look on his face*) Walked out on us a few years ago he did. Left me ma for some slapper from Poppintree. (*Short pause*) Joan. That's her name. Slapper. (*Short pause*) He's still with her, he is. Dirt bag. (*Short pause*) Broke me poor mother's heart, so he did. (*Pause*) Me poor mother's had it rough I tell ye. What with that bleedin' … dirt bag walkin' out on 'er and … (*sighs*)

Noah Wha'?

Natalie *sighs.*

Natalie I was a fuckin' pig when I was on the smack. (*Short pause*) When I think of some of the stuff I done to her … Jesus. (*Short pause*) I took a knife to her once. I took a knife to me own mother.

Noah Did ye stab 'er?

Natalie No I didn't … fuckin' stab 'er! Jesus! Jesus Christ I don't know why I'm even tellin' ye this!

Noah It's alrigh'.

Natalie It's no' alright. Who are you to bleedin' say it's alrigh'?

Pause.

Noah Look. When ye done all that stuff you were on the gear. You were …

Natalie So that makes it alrigh'? Does it?

Pause.

Noah Look. If this makes ye feel any better. I was a nightmare meself, I was. A fuckin' terrible nightmare at that. Fuckin' … don't know many times me ma and da had to go court with me. Fuckin' … court 44 and 45 were like another home away from home. If that be the expression. And like … what I'm tryna say is … there was all that jazz … and I wasn't even on the smack!! Whacked the owl Bally out of it alrigh' … and the E's and all that stuff … bu' … (*flaps*) who hasn't? (*Pause*) You were on the H-train Natalie. 'Member what ye said abou' the H-train?

Natalie *smiles and looks away.*

Natalie You should be a counsellor, ye know that?

Noah Me arse.

Natalie Ye should.

Pause.

Noah Hmmmph. Counsellor. (*Pause. He puts on a southern U.S. accent*) Counsellor! Counsellor! Where are you counsellor?

Natalie Are ye OK there Noah?

Noah Sound. Just doin' me Max Cady impersonation.

Natalie (*sarcastic*) Righ'.

Noah (*southern U.S. accent. Not to Natalie*) 'I ain't no white piece of trash. I'm better than you all! (*Pause*) I can out-learn you. I can out-read you. I can out-think you. And I can out- (*stresses*) philosophise you. And I'm gonna out-last you'. (*Laughs*) All I need is the big cigar, and one of them Hawaii t-shirts.

Natalie (*sarcastic*) Yeah ye'd look great in one of them. The bee's knees.

Noah No bu' … .ye gotta agree. It's a great owl film.

Natalie Wha'?

Noah *Cape Fear*!

Natalie Never seen it.

Noah Ye never seen it?!!!

Natalie No. Heard of it alrigh' bu' … never seen it.

Noah Man! I can't believe ye never seen it.

Natalie Get over it Noah.

Noah Fuckin' love that film. (*Short pause*) That film used to be in me head twenty-four seven.

Natalie I think it still is Noah.

Noah De Niro's best film. After *Raging Bull* that is. Can't top *Raging Bull*. (*Puts arms down by his side. Impersonates De Niro doing Jake La Motta*) 'Ya never knocked me down Ray. Ya never knocked me down.'

Natalie Safe to say, yer a fan of Robert De Niro.

Noah Aw it's safe to say alrigh'. (*Takes a slug from his bottle*) Bobby Milk.

Natalie Who?

Noah Bobby Milk.

Natalie Yer losin' it Noah.

Noah No. (*Smiles*) Bobby Milk.

Natalie Bobby Milk.

Noah That's what they used to call De Niro when he was a chisler.

Natalie Aw righ'. Did he like his milk?

Noah Do you like yer milk?

Natalie Fuck off.

Noah He was mad pale as a chisler.

Natalie Aw righ'.

Noah D'ye want a gas of milk?

Natalie D'ye wanna kick in the balls?

Noah Wouldn't mind. (*Pause*) No bu' … no buzzin' … d'ye wanna a glass of milk?

Natalie *flings a beer mat at him.* **Noah** *laughs. He finishes off his bottle. He walks away from his table.*

Noah (*points at her glass*) G and T?

Natalie No tanks.

Noah Shut up, would ye?

Natalie I don't want one Noah. Honest to Jesus. Soon as I'm finished this … I'm off to do me shoppin'.

Noah Fair enough. Are ye sure now?

Natalie Positive.

Noah Fair enough.

Noah *goes to the bar and orders. We do not see or hear him make his order. He should be off stage or in darkness. He returns about a minute later.* **Natalie** *finishes off her drink and prepares to leave.* **Noah** *sits.* **Natalie***'s exit is a reluctant one.*

Natalie It was nice meetin' ye Noah.

Noah Same. Same.

Natalie See ye. (*She exits*)

Noah See ye. (*Pause*) Stay off the H-train now!

Natalie I will. Tanks. (*Just before she exits*) Tell yer granny I said hello.

Noah I will.

Noah *smiles to himself. It's a sad smile. He fingers bottle and reminisces. He's thinking about* **Natalie**. *He mutters something to himself. Silence. He picks up bottle and takes a slug. Instead of resting it back down on the table he holds it and looks straight ahead. Silence. Enter* **Natalie**.

Natalie D'ye wanna buzz back to me flat for a few bevies?

Noah (*nods and purses his lips*) Sounds good to me.

Natalie Just for a few bevvies now. Nuttin' else.

Noah Sound.

Natalie Yer into that so?

Noah Big time, yeah.

Natalie (*smiling*) Righ'. (*Short pause*) I'll buzz back here after I done me shoppin' … then we'll hit the offo.

Noah Sound. Sound. How long will ye be?

Natalie 'Bout twenty minutes. Is that alrigh'?

Noah Sound, yeah. What's yer name by the way?

Natalie Natalie.

Noah Righ' Natalie. I'll see ye in twenty.

Natalie Sound. (*Pause*) I hope ye like Elton John.

Noah Wha'?!

End of Scene 4. As the lights are coming down, we hear the end of Elton John's 'Bad Side of the Moon' When the lights come back up again Scene 5 begins.

SCENE 5

A flat. Sparse. **Natalie** *is dancing to the song, 'Bad Side of the Moon'. She sings the chorus. The song is ending.* **Noah** *is seated. He is drinking a can of beer. Before him is a table. On it is a large bottle of gin and a carton of orange juice.*

Natalie Me favourite song of all time, that is. (*Short pause*) That song sums up my life, it does. That's my song. (*Sits*) What's your song? (*Short pause*) That's an Elton John song.

Noah Wha'?

Natalie 'Your Song'.

Noah My song isn't an Elton John song ye mad thing.

Natalie *sniggers.*

Natalie No. What I'm sayin' is … there's an Elton John song, called 'Your Song'.

Noah Aww righ'. (*Short pause*) Is there an Elton John song called 'Your Song'?

Natalie Yeah. D'ye wanna hear it?

Noah (*quick and sharp*) No. (*Smiles*)

Natalie So what is it anyway?

Noah Wha'?

Natalie What's yer favourite song?

Noah Dunno. Don't have one.

Natalie Ye must have a favourite song.

Noah I don't.

Natalie Ye have a favourite actor.

Noah True.

Natalie Aw yer not gonna start doin' 'im now, are ye?

Short pause.

Noah Migh'.

Natalie Aw Jaysus. Me and me big gob.

Noah *purses his lips and stares at* **Natalie.**

Noah (*impersonating Travis Bickle*) You lookin' at me?

Natalie Aw here we go.

Noah (*still impersonating*) I said, are you lookin' at me? (*Looks around*) I don't see anyone else here.

Natalie Fill me up Robert.

Pulling the well-known De Niro face, he uncaps bottle and pours gin into her glass.

Natalie More.

Noah (*posh voice*) More??!!

Natalie Yeah. (*He pours*) That's enough. (*She adds orange juice to her drink*)

Pause. **Noah** *is smiling.*

Natalie What are ye smiling at?

Noah Nuttin'.

Natalie Go on tell me. What are ye smilin' at?

Short pause.

Noah I do have a favourite song.

Natalie What is it?

Noah If I tell ye yer just gonna break yer shit laughin'.

Natalie I won't, I promise. I won't! I swear to Jesus.

Noah I don't actually know the name of the song …

Natalie Ye don't know the name of it?!!

Noah Cool the jets there Natalie.

Natalie How could ye not know the name though?

Noah 'Cause I don't. I know how it goes though. D'ye wanna me to sing it for ye?

Natalie (*excited*) Yeah, go for it!

Noah Yer not to laugh now.

Natalie I won't. I promise.

Noah OK. Here goes. Yer not to laugh now. (**Natalie** *touches her heart and nods.* **Noah** *begins to sing*) 'No matter what they tell us, no matter what they say, (**Natalie** *sniggers*) No matter … (*Hums the rest of the line because he doesn't know the words*) … please make them go away'. I knew ye'd start laughin'. That's very rude, that is!

Natalie I'm sorry Noah.

Noah Fuck ye.

Natalie Noah!

Short pause.

Noah Probably think I'm a pufter now, don't ye?!

Natalie I don't.

Noah Ye don't have to be a teeny bopper to like boy-bands, ye know.

Natalie D'ye like boy-bands?

Noah Fuckin' love boy-bands. (*Short pause*) Westlife are me favourite.

Noah *starts laughing.*

Natalie Fuckin' wind-up merchant ye.

Noah I had ye there.

Natalie Gee-bag.

Pause.

Noah When I was in the slam I used to joke about Westlife the whole time. Hmmph. One time in front of all the lads I asked The Gov could he arrange to have the fab five in to do a … ye know … play a few songs. For the lads like. Ye know. Like what they do with plays in there. Hmmph. He laughed. Told me that it wasn't such a good idea. That if he done that, they'd have to sing in a big metal cage. (*Sniggers*) That was a clever one to come up with. (*Pause*) One band that would go down rapid in there would be Aslan.

Natalie Ah they're great.

Noah Go down a storm they would. Actually … any one of their songs could be me favourite song.

Natalie I seen them play live before.

Noah Same here. The Somethin' Head in town. Where d'you see them play?

Natalie The Castle.

Noah The Castle in Finglas?

Natalie The very one.

Noah Never frequented it meself.

Natalie The hassle in The Castle.

Noah Well believe it. (*Short pause*) Did he go barefoot?

Natalie Who?

Noah Christy of course.

Natalie Can't remember.

Noah He went barefoot in the Something Head.

Natalie Can't remember much about that night. I was bleedin' twisted. Meself and cunt face lashed back a load of vodka in the stables before we left.

Noah Who's cunt face?

Natalie Me old boyfriend. (*Short pause*) Cunno. (*Short pause*) I rue the day I met that fucker. (*Short pause*) He was the one who got me on the gear.

Noah Yeah?

Natalie *nods yes.*

Natalie One night in The Stables he forced me to chase the dragon with 'im and …

Noah He forced ye?

Natalie Yeah. He told me, if I didn't chase the dragon with 'im, he'd break it off with me. So … love sick fool that I was, I chased the dragon with 'im.

Noah Why didn't ye just tell him to fuck off?

Natalie 'Cause I loved 'im. I didn't want to lose 'im.

Pause.

Noah That's fucked up.

Natalie Ye see … up till then … I was only doin' coke and drinkin', ye know. Bu' eh … Cunno wasn't happy with that. Ye see, Cunno's mentality was … we done coke together and … we done yokes together, why aren't we chasin' the dragon together? That was his mentality.

Noah Fucked-up mentality.

Natalie Greedy mentality. (*Pause*) Few weeks later, what does he do? (*Short pause*) He blows me out. Hmmph. Gets me hooked on gear, and then he blows me out.

Noah Gee-bag.

Natalie I went to bits, after he blew me out. Chased the dragon like mad. (*Short pause*) Then I gave up chasin' and started bangin'. World was too much for me. Had to get out of orbit. And if there's one way of doin' that … (*Pause*) I'll never forget me first hit. It was beautiful. Killed everything. All me sadness. All me … It was beautiful. (*Short pause*) Never quite got that same hit again.

Noah (*enraged*) That cunt deserves a hidin'. (*Pause*) D'ye want me to give him a hidin'?

Natalie Yer only outta jail Noah.

Noah Doesn't matter. I'll still give 'im a hidin'.

Natalie You'd do that for me?

Noah I would yeah.

Natalie *smiles at him.*

Natalie Yeah well … yer gonna have to go to England so. 'Cause that's where he is.

Noah What's he doin' in England?

Natalie Owed out to a load of dealers. Scarpered over there. (*Pause*) So are ye gonna go over?

Noah It's a bit out of me way to be honest with ye but … if he was still livin' here … .(*points finger in the air*) that man would be in for a serious hidin'.

Natalie *smiles at him.*

Natalie That's one of the nicest things any one's ever said to me. Ye know that?

Noah I'd do it I would.

Pause.

Natalie So what are ye gonna do with yerself, now that yer a free man?

Noah Dunno.

Pause.

Natalie Have ye ever thought about bein' an actor Noah?

Noah I'd love to be an actor.

Natalie See how I knew that. (*Short pause*) Ye'd be good at it as well.

Noah Ye reckon?

Natalie I do.

Noah This isn't like the counselling thing now, is it?

Natalie Wha'?

Noah Back in the pub ye said … I should be a counsellor.

Natalie Ah that was only a buzz. I'm not buzzin' with ye now though. Honest. I definitely think ye should be an actor.

(*Short pause*) Them impersonations ye do of De Niro are gift, they are. A bit scary now but … they're good.

Noah Tanks.

Natalie 'Cause like … ye don't just do the voice good. Ye do the face and hands good as well.

Noah Tanks.

Natalie Ye should do a drama course or somethin'.

Noah I might, yeah. Soon as I get me shit together that is.

Natalie And if …

Noah They done a …

Natalie Go on.

Noah They done a drama workshop in the Joy they did.

Natalie Yeah?

Noah Didn't do it though.

Natalie Why not?

Noah Bottled it.

Natalie Ah, that's no good.

Noah I know, I know bu' … .ah sure, soon as I get me shit together, I'll do acting classes or somethin' like that.

Natalie Do now. Don't bottle it.

Noah I won't.

Natalie And if ye ever become famous, don't forget me.

Noah I won't. I'll buy ye a car and a bottle of G and T.

Natalie You'll buy me a car and a gaff more like it. And a nice big gaff at that. (**Noah** *smiles*)

Noah Whatcha want a gaff for when you're gettin' an apartment?

Natalie I want a gaff Noah.

Noah OK. I'll get ye a gaff.

Natalie Oh yeah! One more thing. (**Noah** *rolls his eyes*) When yer makin' yer Oscar speech, I want ye to mention me. And … tank me … for … encouragin' ye to be an actor.

Noah I will. (*Makes speech*) I'd like to give a big shout out to …

Natalie Stand up if yer gonna do it.

Noah OK.

Noah *stands up.*

Noah I'll like to give a big shout out to … what's yer surname?

Natalie Dunne.

Noah I'd like to give a big shout out to Natalie Dunne. (*Wagging his finger*) You don't know who she is but … she lives on the … what storey is this?

Natalie I won't be livin' here. I'll be in me new gaff. Remember?

Noah Aw righ'.

Natalie Start again. (**Noah** *shakes his head*) Go on.

Noah I'd like to give a big shout out to Natalie Dunne. Who's livin' in her new gaff. The gaff I bought her …

Natalie Ye can't say that!

Noah Fuck snakes.

Natalie Ye can't though.

Noah Who's livin in her new gaff. I'd like to tank 'er 'cause … she was the one who told me I should be an actor. Tank you Natalie. Good night. God bless. Safe home. (**Natalie** *cheers*) Hold on a minute! (*Points a finger in the air. Silence*) Not finished. (*Silence*) Better bein' a king for a night, than a schmuck for a life time.

A puzzled **Natalie** *shakes her head.*

Natalie Go on. Take yer bow.

Noah No.

Natalie Take a bow. Ye have to take a bow.

Noah *bows. It's more like a court jester's bow than a proper one.* **Noah** *sits.*

Noah That deserves a whopper of a slug. (*Takes one*)

Natalie If you're gonna take a whopper of a slug, I'm gonna take a whopper of a slug.

Noah Yehaay!

Both laugh. Pause.

Noah So what storey is this anyway?

Natalie The 5th. The 5th storey of the big ECT.

Short pause.

Noah Eamonn Ceannt Tower.

Noah *nods at her.*

Natalie Yer a clever bastard, ye know that?

Noah Fuck off. (*Moronic voice*) Fug off.

Natalie Shut up you.

Noah (*moronic voice*) Fug off.

Natalie How long are ye gonna keep this up for?

Noah *grins. He looks around.*

Noah D'ye like livin' here?

Natalie (*purses her lips*) It's alrigh'. I don't have much option to be honest with ye.

Noah Whatcha mean?

Natalie Well like … I wouldn't be able to live anywhere else. Well I could actually. I could live with me ma but … ye know what I mean.

Noah Would she take ye back?

Natalie Course she fuckin' would!! Why wouldn't she?!

Noah No it's just … the vibes you were givin' me in the pub … I though' … yerself and yer ma … were like … finito.

Natalie No! Far from it! Me and me ma get on great now, we do. Sure I do be up to her most nights. (*Short pause*) If I wasn't for me ma I'd be a total loner.

Noah *nods a couple of times.*

Noah Where does she live?

Natalie Connolly Tower.

Noah Aw that's righ'. Ye told me that. (*Pause*) Connolly was the little fat guy with the tash.

Natalie I know. I know me history as well. Don't you worry. One of the best in me class at it, I was.

Noah *grins.*

Noah Who was Eamonn Ceannt so?

Natalie (*gives him a strange look*) He was one of the rebels.

Noah That's not what I'm askin' ye. I'm askin' ye, what did he look like?

Natalie Haven't a clue what he looked like.

Noah *gibes at her.*

Natalie Shut up you. (**Noah** *continues to gibe*) Anyway, Celtic history was more my thing, it was! (*Short pause*) Cuchulainn and Maeve. (**Noah** *laughs*) What are ye laughin' at?

Pause.

Noah As far as I know, Ceannt was the skinny one with the glasses.

Natalie Yeah! That was him. (*Sniggers*) Haven't a fuckin' clue.

Pause.

Noah Yer ma must be chuffed to bits that yer off the gear.

Natalie She's happy alrigh'.

Pause.

Natalie She has me head wrecked about gettin' a job.

Noah I know all abou' that. I've had fuckin' years of that.

Natalie Every time I go up to her, it's the same deal. (*Impersonates her mother*) 'Would ye not get yer self a little job?' It's always a little job. (*She shakes her head*) I keep tellin' 'er, 'Look Ma! As soon as I move into the new apartment, that's when I'll get meself a job!' And I will! 'Cause like … I'll have the right mentality then, so I will. Don't have the right mentality now, ye see. Don't want a fuckin' job now. (*Nods to herself*) But as soon I move into that new apartment … I'll want a job then. New apartment. New job. New life. Ye know what I mean?

Noah I know what ye mean, yeah. (*Short pause*) But I still think yer ma's righ'.

Natalie Why?!

Noah 'Cause like … if ye get yerself a job now …

Natalie But I don't want a job now!

Noah Bu' … if ye don't want a job now, what makes ye think ye'll want one when yer in yer new apartment?

Natalie 'Cause I'll have a different mentality when I'm in me new apartment! That's what I'm tryna tell ye. That's what I keep tryna tell me ma, but she won't listen. She never bleedin' listens. (*Short pause*) Ye see righ' now, I'm in Limbo.

Noah Yer in wha'?

Natalie Limbo! It's like … (*Sighs*) Look! I like the life I'm livin' righ' now, OK?!

Noah Cool.

Natalie I know I'm not workin' or anythin' bu' … I'm still off the smack and … that to me is more important than havin' any fuckin' job!

Noah Yer righ'! Yer dead righ'! But all I'm sayin' is … if ye got yerself a job now, by the time ye get over to yer apartment, ye'll be in the swing of things.

Natalie But I don't want a fuckin' job now! When I'm … Look! I'm a fuckin' tosspot! OK?! And the few months I've left here, I'm gonna stay that way! So please just … back off with this one, OK?!

Noah OK. (*Hoists up can*) Tosspots forever!

Natalie Are you takin' the piss outta me?

Noah No! Sure I'm a fuckin' tosspot meself. Always have been.

Natalie Pppphh. (*Short pause*) If anyone's earned the righ' to be a tosspot, it's me. (*Short pause*) Not everyone beats heroin Noah. I did though. I bet it!

Noah And fair play to ye. And come 'ere, I'm sorry for givin' ye grief.

Natalie *looks at him with a half smile on her face.*

Natalie Yer alrigh'. I'll forgive ye.

Pause.

Noah So what type of work will ye be lookin' for when yer in yer new apartment? (**Natalie** *laughs*) Wha'?

Natalie I dunno. Cleanin' or somethin'. Somethin' basic. (*Pause*) Ye don't know any jobs where ye can sit on yer arse all day and smoke work cigarettes, do ye?

Noah I do as a matter of fact.

Natalie Ye do?

Noah Yeah. Me old job.

Natalie Which was?

Noah Dublin Corporation. Worked in the Corpo, I did.

Natalie You worked in the Corpo?

Noah I did. D'ye want me to put in a word for ye?

Natalie (*smiling*) Yer alrigh'.

Noah Sure? All it takes is a phone call.

Natalie Ah sure, I'll think I'll give it a miss.

Noah Fair enough.

Natalie Besides, I don't think I'd really fit in.

Noah I think ye would. (*Short pause*) I can just see ye now ... sittin' in the depot with Dessie and Vinny. Playin' cards and ... talkin' abou' football ... (*laughs*)

Natalie Aw yeah.

Noah ... then gettin' up on Vinny's shoulders. (*Bursts out laughing.* **Natalie** *is lost.* **Noah** *continues laughing*) One day righ' ... (*Laughs*) One day ... (*Laughs*) One day ... I got up on Vinny's shoulders ... (*Laughs*) and the gaffer walked in. There's me on Vinny's shoulders. Vinny's swayin' all over the place ... and the gaffer walks in. But the thing about it is ... it was a beautiful day outside. That's what made it funnier. We should have been out cuttin' ... (*Starts laughing*) And there I was ... (*laughing*) up on Vinny's shoulders. Swayin' all over the place. (*Laughs*) Ah ye had to have been there. Fuckin' gas. (*Short pause*) Aw I tell ye, that job was a buzz ... I was only there for a couple of months, but it was a buzz.

Natalie D'ye get the sack?

Pause.

Noah Someone give this woman a hundred pounds!

Natalie (*nodding to herself*) Ye got the sack.

Noah Yep. Some stupid little owl one seen me drinkin' in the Babog and grassed me to the gaffer.

Natalie The Babog?

Noah The little tractors.

Natalie Aw righ'. I thought ye meant a pub or somethin'.

Noah No.

Natalie Shouldn't of been drinkin' on the job.

Noah It was a fuckin' Friday.

Natalie Still.

Short pause.

Noah Owl fella went mad went I lost that job. Keep goin' on about it for months.

Natalie Is that why ye smashed up his car?

Noah No, no. Sure this is ancient history. This happened bleedin' years ago. (*Short pause*) I smashed up his car 'cause he kicked me outta the gaff.

Natalie Why did he kick ye outta the gaff? (*Short pause*) If ye don't want to talk about it, it's cool.

Noah No I'll tell ye, I'll tell ye. (*Short pause*) I freaked out at me sister one nigh' in the gaff, righ'? She was in the jacks … she's always in the jacks. She has like … obsessive … compulsive … disorder. Ye know what that is?

Natalie Haven't a clue.

Noah It's like … it's a disorder of the brain. Your brain tells ye to do things that ye don't necessarily want to do. But ye still do them. Stupid little things like … foldin' things … and washin' yer hands the whole time and … rituals like. That's what they're called. Rituals. So anyway … she does these rituals in the jacks righ' and … sometimes they keep her in there for ages. Half an hour sometimes and … this particular night, righ', I was in a fucking ferocious mood. I had that fuck bag of a bouncer in me brain and … when she wouldn't come out of the jacks … I bleedin' exploded. Any other night I would of just gone out the back and had a jimmy riddle behind the tank. But that night I wasn't havin' any of it. Started roarin' and shoutin' … kickin' the door. Callin' 'er all sorts of names. Callin' 'er a mentaller and stuff like that. Owl fella legs it up the stairs. Big evil grin on his mug. Lays into me. Verbally like … not physically. Owl fucker couldn't fight his way out of a ladies' jacks. Anyway, he's layin' into me. Tellin' me I have no rights. That I shouldn't be in the gaff. That I'm lucky to be in the gaff. That I'm a scumbag. Heard it all before. Used to it. So it's like … me pikin' at him, and him shoutin' at me. But that's all it is. But then what does he do? What does the owl fuck bag do? (*Short pause*) Starts yakkin' on about the bouncer. That fuckin' stupid no-brain bouncer.

Natalie *points at him.*

Natalie Is this the bouncer ye had a scrap with?

Noah Yeah.

Natalie And what happened there anyway?

Noah I fuckin' battered 'im. That's what happened. (*Short pause*) D'ye know what the fucker done?

Natalie Wha'?

Short pause.

Noah Spat in me face!

Natalie Scumbag.

Noah I was givin' 'im stick 'cause he wouldn't let me into the night club, and the fucker spat in me face! Done a big gobber in me face! Fuckin' … .I got 'im back for that though. I got 'im back for that big time. (*Makes a clucking sound and at same time head butts the air*) Stitched 'im, right in the nose.

Natalie Nice one.

Noah Didn't stop there. Started layin' into 'im more. (*Punches the air*) Boom! Boom! Boom! Then fuckin' … two no brainers popped out of no were and flattened me. Pinned me down on the ground, and kept me down on the ground until the pigs came. Ppph. Bad night. Very bad night. (*Short pause*) So anyway, when the owl fella start yakkin' on abou' no brains … I fuckin' flipped. Ye see … I had *no brains* in me head all day. Ow my God. Did ye hear what I just said there?

Natalie (*half smiling*) I did yeah.

Noah *shakes his head.*

Noah I had 'im in me head all day so … when the owl fella start yakkin' on about 'im I flipped. I got 'im in a head lock and … I kept 'im in a head lock for ages. Then when I let 'im out of the head lock, he told me to get the fuck out of the gaff and never come back. (*Pause*) Two nights later I *came* back. With a hammer. Coked outta my fuckin' eye balls. Done a load of coke that night in Flynner's shed. That's where I was livin'. (*Short pause*) Now, there's two things in this world that me owl fella loves, righ'? Liverpool F.C. is one. And the other, is his 95 D Honda Accord. So, when I arrived up to the gaff that night, I fuckin' destroyed that 95 D Honda Accord. Fuckin' blitzed it! Took everything out! Windows! Bonnet! Doors! Front lights! Back lights! You name it. Fuckin' … .(*Short pause*) Sure at one stage I was up on the bleedin' roof. (*Short pause*) Great entertainment for the neighbours though. Great entertainment. (*Short pause*) The last bit of entertainment they had like that was bleedin' … Boyler pullin' wheel spins up and down the road. But this was better. This was much better. This was … Noel Murray smashin' up his owl fella's car. Where's the bleedin' popcorn?!! (*Short pause*) Owl fella came out he did. For about two seconds that is. I told 'im to get back into the gaff or I'd do a job on him! (*Nods and smiles*) He went back into the gaff. So, I continued smashin' up the car, the neighbours continued watchin', and the owl fella got on the blower to the pigs. (*Short pause*) It felt good smashin' up that car. Felt real good. Felt like salvation. If that be the righ' word to use. When the pigs came I was still workin' on the fuckin' thing. Lot slower. But still workin' on it. Soon as they got out of the squaddy I gave them a wave. 'How's it goin' lads?' Gave the car one last whack, chucked the hammer on the lawn. Then I put me hands out for the cuffs. No arguin'. Best customer of the nigh'. Neighbours were very disappointed I'd say. I mean … (*Impersonates neighbour*) 'He smashes up his owl fella's car, and then when the guards come, he doesn't even put up a fight. I mean, what's that all about? That's not good entertainment. I didn't get up at two o'clock in the mornin' to watch half a show.'

Natalie Ah fuck the neighbours.

Pause.

Noah I really thought the owl fella would of dropped the charges. (*Short pause*) I mean … the fucker knew I was on a suspended sentence. He knew it! He knew somethin' like this would fuck me up big time. (*Pause*) I mean … even the pigs in Ballymun tried to get 'im to drop the charges.

Natalie And did yer ma not try and stop him?

Noah Me ma? Sure she probably put 'im up to it.

Natalie D'ye not get on with her either?

Noah No. I used to. When I was about three or somethin'.

Pause.

Noah I'm a stupid cunt I am.

Natalie Yer not a stupid cunt.

Noah I am. I'm a stupid cunt! Me whole life's one big fuck up.

Pause.

Natalie D'ye know what you need now? (*Short pause*) You need a girlfriend. When was the last time you had a girlfriend?

Noah Long time ago. (*Starts smiling*)

Natalie Wha'? Wha'?!

Noah I've never gone out with a bird in me life. Went out with Debbie Lyons for six days when I was fourteen. But I don't think that really counts.

Natalie Are you winding me up here Noah?

Noah No. Never had a bird in me life. I've been with birds alrigh' but … I've never gone out with one.

Natalie That's mad.

Noah I'm only bein' honest with ye.

Natalie Yeah, yeah. And … I respect that, I do. I respect ye for bein' honest.

Noah I was never really good in that department. The lads were good in that department bu' … Ppph. The lads.

Natalie Forget about them.

Noah If I meet them now on the street I'd ignore them. I would. I wouldn't even have a straightener with them. I'd just keep walkin'. (*Pause*) Flynner though! I can't believe Flynner would abandon me.

Natalie Well he did Noah. He abandoned ye.

Noah Why though?!! Why?!

Natalie He's not such a good friend? (*Pause*) Yer granny's a good friend though.

Noah You said it.

Natalie I'd love to meet her sometime.

Noah That can be arranged. Just one thing though. When yer with her. Don't mention blacks.

Natalie Does she not like black people?

Noah Hates them. Every time she was into me, she was moanin' about them. 'They're everywhere! They're everywhere!'

Natalie They are though! They're all over the place. Walkin' down the North Circular Road the other day I seen bleedin' loads of them.

Noah You and me granny would definitely get on. (*Short pause*) Yez are both racist …

Natalie I'm not racist!

Noah Yez have both brown eyes.

Natalie What?!!

Noah Yez have both brown eyes.

Natalie You're fuckin' mad, ye are.

Noah I know yeah.

Short pause.

Natalie You weren't in the Joy. You were in a mental home.

Noah I was in the Joy! Only jokin'. Remember tha'?

Natalie Yeah.

Noah I hope yer proud of them brown eyes!

Natalie What's this brown eyes buzz yer on?

Noah I've been on a brown eyes buzz all me life, I have. (*Short pause*) Love brown eyes I do.

Natalie Ye must love my eyes so.

Noah I do yeah. Yours are particularly dark.

Natalie They are. (*Short pause*) Yer own eyes are nice.

Noah I'd rather they were brown.

Natalie *shakes her head.*

Natalie Hold on a minute! I know why ye like brown eyes. Robert De Niro has brown eyes.

Noah That's not why I like brown eyes.

Natalie It is!

Noah It's not! I just love brown eyes. Always have, always will.

Pause.

Natalie What age are ye, Noah?

Noah Twenty-seven.

Natalie Yer two years older than meself.

Noah You're twenty-five?

Natalie Don't look it, sure I don't?

Noah Ye do.

Natalie Go on ye spoofer.

Noah Ye do! Maybe a bit older …

Natalie A lot bleedin' older. Bleedin' ancient lookin', I am. That's what the smack does to ye.

Noah Yer not ancient lookin' Natalie. (*Pause*) Yer very good lookin' ye are.

Natalie Tank you.

Natalie *refills her glass, looks him and smiles. She stands up and walks towards the couch.*

Noah What are ye up to?

Natalie I'm gonna sit beside ye. Is that alrigh'?

Noah Cool.

Natalie *sits. She takes a sip of her drink.*

Natalie What would ye do if I kissed ye? Would ye scream?

Noah I won't scream, no.

They move closer and kiss. It lasts about 15 seconds. **Natalie** *is smiling.* **Noah** *is blushing.*

Natalie Yer a nut bag. But I like ye.

Noah *smiles.*

Pause.

Noah When I get sorted in me granny's, I'll invite ye over for dinner. Meself, yerself, and the granny …

Natalie Shut up about yer granny.

Natalie *pulls him in to her and kisses him. Pause.* **Noah** *blushes.*

Natalie Are ye glad I invited ye back?

Short pause.

Noah Very much so, yeah. (**Natalie** *laughs*) What are ye laughin' at? (**Natalie** *shakes her head as if so say, 'nothing.' Pause.* **Noah** *grins*) You get a mad buzz off me. Don't ye?

Natalie I do yeah.

Pause.

Noah Is that why ye invited me back?

Natalie No. Well it is yeah, bu' … (*Short pause*) I invited ye back Noah 'cause you were nice to me.

Noah I was nice to ye?

Natalie Yeah. And 'cause I fancy the balls off ye.

Noah *grins.*

Noah D'ye fancy me, do ye?

Natalie I don't fancy ye. I fancy the balls off ye.

Noah *gives a small laugh.*

Noah Yeah well, I fancy the balls off you as well I do.

Natalie How d'you know I'd balls? (**Noah** *laughs*)

Pause.

Natalie You're the first young fella I've ever invited back here since I've been clean, d'ye know that?

Noah Really?

Natalie Yeah. I've never had another young fella back. (*Short pause*)

Noah And how long have ye been off the smack?

Natalie Two and a half year.

Noah Ye must really fancy me so?

Natalie I don't just fancy ye Noah. I fancy the balls off ye.

Natalie *cackles.*

Noah I fancy the balls off you as well, I do.

Natalie How d'you know I'd balls?

Noah Aw here we go again. (**Natalie** *laughs. Pause*) No bu' ... jokin' aside ... Natalie ... I'm mad about ye, I am. (**Natalie** *smiles at him*) Any chance of another kiss?

Natalie Of course there is.

They kiss. It's a short kiss.

Natalie Lets have a dance Noah.

Noah Wha'?

Natalie Lets have a dance. Have a song and all, I do.

Natalie *gets up and walks to the stereo in the kitchen.*

Noah I can't dance Natalie.

Natalie Relax! I'm not talkin' about boogie-in'.

Natalie *takes out the old CD and replaces it with another. There are several scattered around the stereo. She presses play. We hear the start of Elton John's 'Mona Lisas and Mad Hatters'. It's a slow song.* **Natalie** *walks back into the sitting room.*

Natalie Come on, get up!

Noah *gets up slowly. They both embrace and the dance begins. Halfway through the second chorus the light gradually comes down.*

SCENE 6

Morning time. **Noah** *is lying on the couch. He is awake, and still has all his clothes on, including his runners. He uses his leather jacket as a quilt. It's up to his chin. All we hear is the hum of the fridge and every so often the wind rattling the lift outside. A can of beer and the bottle of gin are on the table.*

Natalie (*from her bedroom*) Noah?

Noah Helloooo.

Natalie Just wonderin' if ye were still here.

Noah I am. I'm still here.

Pause.

Natalie Noah?

Noah Yeah?

Short pause.

Natalie High-heels and stilettos forever.

Noah High-heels and stilettos forever! (*Laughs*) Gonna get a spray can and spray that on a load of walls, I am. (*Pause*) D'ye remember the other one? (*Short pause*) D'ye remember it?

Natalie No.

Noah Ah ye must remember it?

Natalie I don't!

Noah *grins.*

Noah I smell …

Natalie Aw I remember it. (**Noah** *laughs*)

Noah Say it.

Natalie No.

Noah Go on. Say it.

Natalie No, I'm not sayin' it. It's bleedin' disgustin' it is.

Noah Just say it.

Pause.

Natalie I smell cunt! Now are ye happy?

Noah *laughs.*

Noah Aw Jaysus. (*Laughs*) Can ye imagine seein' that sprayed on a wall. (*Laughs*)

Natalie It's disgustin' it is.

Noah That's from *Silence of the Lambs*, that is.

Natalie I know. Ye told me. It's fuckin' disgustin'.

Noah *laughs.*

Noah (*evil voice*) I smell cunt.

Pause.

Natalie Is there any vodka left Noah?

Noah *looks at the bottle on the table.*

Noah No.

Natalie Wha'?!!

Noah There's none left.

Natalie Fuck! There goes me bleedin' curer.

Noah Yer wha'?

Natalie Me curer.

Pause.

Noah D'ye want me to pop over to the offo for ye? Get ye a bottle?

Natalie Yer alrigh'.

Noah Nay bother Natalie.

Natalie Nn na na na. Yer alrigh'. Stay where ye are.

Short pause.

Noah Ye wouldn't have to give me any money or nuttin'. I'll like ... I'll buy it for ye like. My treat.

Natalie That's very, very sweet of ye Noah. But ... yer alrigh'. Stay where ye are.

Noah Nay bother Natalie.

Natalie Stay where ye are Noah! Yer grand.

Noah Nay bother.

Natalie Noah! I'm hung over. But I'm not that hung over.

Noah Fair enough.

Short pause.

Natalie Anyway. Yer not exactly in a position to be forkin' out for bleedin' ... bottles of vodka.

Noah I am as a matter of fact.

Natalie Yer not! You've only a small bit of money and yer gonna have to hang on to it.

Noah Not nesses ... not ... not necessarily.

Natalie Wha'?

Short pause.

Noah Come this Saturday, I'm gonna be loaded, I am.

Natalie How's that?

Noah Ah now. (*Short pause*) Don't be nosey. Are ye gettin' up, or wha'?

Natalie I'll be up in a minute.

Noah *rubs his face. A minute passes. Enter* **Natalie**. *She has a lit cigarette in her mouth. She is wearing an Adidas tracksuit which is way too big for her. She stretches.* **Noah** *smiles at her.*

Natalie How was the couch?

Noah Grand. Did I just pass out last nigh'?

Natalie Yeah. One minute you were mumblin' abou' … yer man …

Noah Who?

Natalie Yer man …

Noah De Niro?

Natalie No! Yer mate that ye have the hump with.

Noah Awww. Flynner.

Natalie Yeah. You were mumblin' abou' him and … next of all … you were out for the count.

Noah *shakes his head and throws up his eyes.*

Noah Sorry.

Natalie Yer alrigh'.

Noah That's what happens when ye haven't had a drink in so many months.

Natalie True. It's a pity though. I was really up for a fuck. (**Noah** *is surprised*) I'm only jokin' with ye. I'm not that sort of girl. (**Noah** *wears a crooked grin*) I'm not!

Noah I believe ye.

Natalie Ye'd never catch me hoppin' in the sack on the first night.

Pause.

Noah D'ye still wanna go out with me?

Natalie Dunno. (*Pause*) Course I do!

Noah Nice one!

Natalie But Noah …

Noah Yeah?

Natalie Lets take things nice and slow, OK?

Noah Sound.

Natalie We'll have a few drinks today like we planned and … we'll meet up in a couple of weeks or somethin' like that, OK?

Noah Sound.

Natalie So are ye happy with that?

Noah Very happy. Very, very, very happy.

Natalie Good.

Noah *makes a very loud fingerless whistle.*

Noah That's how happy I am.

Natalie Jesus.

Natalie *spots a full glass of vodka and OJ beside her sink.*

Natalie Aw Jaysus! There's me curer. There's me curer.

Natalie *walks into the kitchen and picks it up.*

Natalie You probably think I'm a creamer drinkin' this?

Noah No.

Natalie I fuckin' need it, I tell ye. (*She drinks*) Nice bit in it as well.

Pause.

Noah Ye know wha'?

Natalie Wha'?

Noah I think I'll join ye. (*Grabs can of beer and cracks it open*) *Sláinte*!!

Natalie *Sláinte.*

Noah *takes a slug from his can.*

Natalie Mutton head ye. (*Laughs*)

Noah *puts a fake angry look on his face.*

Natalie I'm only jokin' with ye, ye mad thing.

Noah I know ye are. (*Belches*) Wouldn't normally do this but sure … fuck it! (*Pause*) Rejoice in thy youth, O young man.

Natalie Righ'.

Natalie *nods back at him.*

Pause.

Noah Brown eyes?

Natalie Yes blue eyes?

Noah Any chance of a fry?

Natalie Aw ye don't want a fry, do ye?

Noah Nay bother. Don't worry about it.

Short pause.

Natalie Ah fuck it. I'll do ye one.

Noah Nay bother Natalie.

Natalie No I'll do ye one. (**Natalie** *stubs out her cigarette in an ashtray close by. She then walks to the fridge. She opens it and looks in*) Can I do ye a rasher sandwich instead?

Noah Yes! That would be sweet. (*Short pause*) Are ye gonna have something to eat yerself?

Natalie Nah. Not till later. (**Natalie** *takes a packet of rashers out and puts them on kitchen work top. She then takes a frying pan from out of one of the presses below and then cooking oil from above. She puts the frying pan down and opens the packet with her teeth*)

Noah Lookin' forward to this now. (*Claps hands together and rubs them*) Aw man I tell ye. Ye wanna check out the food we used to get in that dump.

Natalie Yeah I heard it was fairly dodgy alrigh'.

Noah Dodgy? Pppph. I wouldn't feed it to a bleedin' dog, I wouldn't.

Short pause.

Natalie (*oiling the frying pan*) So what's the story with this money yer gettin' on Saturday?

Noah Ah now. (*Taps his nose.* **Natalie** *shakes her head, half smiling*)

Natalie How much are ye gettin'?

Short pause.

Noah Ten grand.

Natalie Fuck off.

Noah Ten grand. Ten g's.

Natalie Ten grand?

Noah Me hole. 250 quid more like it.

Pause.

Natalie Does someone owe ye?

Noah No.

Natalie Yer not givin' anythin' away, sure ye aren't?

Noah *winks at her.* **Natalie** *turns her back on him and puts three rashers on the pan. She turns around and sees* **Noah** *grinning.*

Natalie Wha'?

Noah Nuttin'.

Natalie Wha'?

Noah Nuttin'.

Natalie *goes back to the frying pan. She is shaking her head.*

Natalie D'ye want toast with these?

Noah Natalie?

Natalie (*turns around and faces him*) Yeah?

Noah *flicks his head up.*

Noah Check this out.

Noah *moves to the end of the couch and grabs his prison sack.* **Natalie** *watches him. She is slightly spooked.* **Noah** *has his hand in the sack. He is looking for something.*

Noah Come out ye bastard. (*Feels it. Looks up at* **Natalie** *and grins at her. He pulls out a small wooden box. He slowly puts the box on the table.* **Noah** *looks at her. Pause. He nods towards the box*) Have a look in there.

Short pause.

Natalie What's in it?

Noah Have a look.

Natalie Just tell us. What's in it?

Noah Have a look.

Natalie *walks towards the box. She looks at the box.*

Noah Have a look in there now.

Natalie Just tell us. What's in it?

Natalie Open … it … up … and have a look. It's nuttin' gory if that's what yer worryin' about.

Natalie *looks at the box.*

Natalie Just tell us. What's in it?

Noah Take off the lid and have a look.

Natalie *takes off the lid and looks down into the box. A shocked expression comes over her face. She drops the lid and steps back.*

Natalie Is that real?

Noah Course it's bleedin' real. Wouldn't be getting' 250 smackers for it, if it wasn't.

Noah *reaches over and puts his hand into the box. He takes out the gun.*

Natalie What are ye doin'?

Noah Relax, will ye? I'm just havin' a look at it.

He weighs it in his right hand. He knows he has her spooked.

Natalie Will ye put it back in the box please?

Noah *smiles at it.*

Noah Wha'?

Natalie Would ye please put it back in the box?

Noah *smiles at it.*

Noah Alrigh'. (*Goes to put it back in the box. Stops*)

Noah Fancy a game of Russian roulette? (**Natalie** *opens her mouth. She is scared*) Like in *The Deer Hunter*. Now don't tell me ye haven't seen *The Deer Hunter*?

Natalie (*very shaky*) Noah …

Noah (*impersonating De Niro. Grips the hand gun tighter*) I do three bullets, huh? We do three. One, two, three. (*He stares with crazed eyes at* **Natalie** *and spins chamber.*)

Natalie Will ye just put the fuckin' thing back in the box, will ye please?

Noah (*still impersonating De Niro. He laughs*) Now we got ourselves a game! You and me. (*A beat*) You and me.

Natalie I don't like this Noah. This isn't funny Noah.

Noah (*in his own voice*) It's not meant to be funny Natalie. It's Russian roulette. Biggest thrill ye'll ever get in yer life.

He spins the chamber.

Natalie Is that fuckin' thing loaded?

Noah Last time I checked it was, yeah. Two bullets I think. (*Spins the chamber one last time and puts it to his temple*)

Natalie Noah …

Noah Will I go for it?

Natalie Stop this Noah, please!

Noah Fuck it! I might as well. (*Exhales deeply*)

Natalie (*screams*) Noah!!!

Noah Relax the cacks! There's only two bullets in the fuckin' thing. I'll be alrigh'!

Natalie (*roars*) Put it in the fuckin' box now!!

Noah *roars for a couple of seconds. Stops roaring. Then pulls the trigger. While he does this* **Natalie** *watches him in absolute shock. She is frozen with fear. She puts her hand to her mouth and gasps. He then turns the gun on* **Natalie**.

Noah Your turn. (**Natalie** *screams.* **Noah** *stands and blocks off any sort of escape route*) Your turn Natalie. I've had mine, now it yours!

Natalie *is still screaming.*

Noah Relax will ye? I'm only buzzin' with ye! (**Natalie** *is frozen to the spot*) There's no bullets in it. Look! Look! (*He stands up and opens up the chamber*) Look! (*He holds the empty chamber up to her face. She looks for a second*)

Natalie Put it back in the box please.

Noah It's not loaded.

Natalie (*roars*) Put it back in the fuckin' box!!

Noah OK! OK. I'll put it back in the box. I'll put it back in the box. (*He puts it back in the box*) It's in the box. (*Pause*) Are ye alrigh'?

Natalie Do I look alrigh'? Do I look alrigh'?

Pause.

Noah Look ... I'm sorry righ'. I'm really sorry. I shouldn't of done that.

Natalie Fuckin' righ' ye shouldn't of! Fuckin' psycho ye.

Noah Look I'm sorry Natalie. OK? I'm a fuckin' eejit. I shouldn't have done that. I'm sorry.

Pause.

Natalie (*pointing at the box*) The fuck are ye doin' with that thing?

Noah I told ye. I'm sellin' it to a bloke who I was in the Joy with.

Natalie That's not what I'm askin' ye. I'm askin' ye ... (*Sighs*)

Noah Relax Natalie.

Natalie No, I won't relax! I won't relax! There's a fuckin' gun in me flat. So don't tell me to relax.

Noah *sighs. He flops back down on the couch again.*

Short pause.

Natalie What the fuck are ye doin' with a gun Noah?

Noah I own it.

Natalie Yeah, why? Why d'ye own a gun? Most people don't own a gun Noah.

Noah (*very vicious*) Yeah well I'm not most people, am I?! Only buzzin'.

Natalie Ye weren't.

Noah I fuckin' … Look Natalie … Ye see that? (*Points at box*) That's nuttin'!

Natalie That's a fuckin' gun Noah!

Noah Yeah I know bu' … it means nuttin' to me! That's what I'm tryna tell ye. (*Casual*) See that fuckin' thing? (*Points at box*) I bought that thing two and a half year ago, righ'? And the only reason why I bought was because … I was goin' through a mad phase, I was. I had De Niro in me head the whole time and … .

Natalie Ye still do!

Noah No, I don't!

Natalie Ye do Noah.

Noah No, I don't. I don't! OK?! (*Points at head*) He's in there alrigh' bu' … not half as much as he used to be. (*Short pause*) Two and a half years ago Natalie, he was in here (*points to his head and stresses*) the whole fuckin' time. I was obsessed with 'im. (*Stresses again*) That's why I bought the gun. (*Short pause*) I don't give a fuck about that fuckin' thing! See this fuckin' thing … (*Reaches for the box*)

Natalie I don't wanna fuckin' see it!!

Noah OK! OK! I'm just tryna get somethin' inside yer head. (*Steps back from box. Pause*) Look Natalie. That fuckin' thing righ' … that fuckin' thing … has been buried in the woods for the last two and half year. And it'd be still in the woods, if I didn't have that little chat with Paul White outside me cell that day. We got chattin' about guns and …

Natalie Have you ever used that thing?

Noah Loads of times, yeah. (*Shakes head.* **Natalie** *stares at him*) What have I just been tellin' ye? It's been buried in the woods for the last two and half year Natalie! I've never used it once! Well actually. Tell a lie. There was one time. (**Noah** *sees the shocked expression on* **Natalie***'s face*) Relax the cacks, will ye?! I didn't fuckin' shoot anyone if that's what yer thinkin'. (*Short pause*) 'Bout a year ago, meself and the lads went down to Devil's Glen for the weekend, righ'! And … I brought the gun down with me and … we had a buzz with it. (*Short pause*) Shot a few trees. Trees Natalie! Trees! Not people.

Natalie I don't want that thing in me flat.

Noah *gives a small laugh.*

Noah Wha'?

Natalie I don't want that thing in me flat. (**Noah** *gives a small laugh*) I want it out of me flat Noah!

Pause.

Noah D'ye not think yer bein' a bit dramatic here Natalie?

Natalie No, I don't.

Noah *sighs.*

Noah Look, what if I just …

Natalie I want it out of me flat Noah! This is my flat Noah. And I don't want that fuckin' thing in it. OK?

Noah Ye don't seriously expect me to walk all the way over to the woods again, do ye?!

Natalie Yes I do!

Noah Jesus CHRIST!

Pause.

Natalie Look Noah …

Noah OK fuck it! Fuck it! (*Stands up*) Anythin' to keep ye happy! (*Grabs his leather jacket and puts it on*) Have ye gotta plastic bag?

Natalie Wha'?

Noah Have ye gotta plastic bag? (*Points at box*) I'm not fuckin' carryin' that on its own. (**Natalie** *does nothing*) Have ye got one?

Natalie *goes into the kitchen and gets him a plastic bag. She gets it from one of the presses. She walks over and hands it to him. He snatches it from her and puts the box in it.*

Noah Righ'! I'll be back in about half an hour. (*Begins to make exit*) If I get bleedin' caugh' with this thing, it'll be all your fault.

Natalie Wha'?

Noah And with my bleedin' record ... only buzzin'. See ye in a bit. (*Makes exit*)

Noah *opens door and exits. He closes door.* **Natalie** *is staring at the ground. She stares at the ground for several seconds. She looks up and sighs. She walks over to her glass of vodka and finishes it in one. The lights begin to fade. End of Scene 6.*

SCENE 7

We hear someone trying to open **Natalie***'s door. The stage lights come up again.* **Natalie** *is sitting where she was sitting the day before. She is very worried looking. We hear someone trying to open the door. It is locked. There's a knock at the door.* **Natalie** *tightens up. There's another knock at door. The knocking continues. We hear* **Noah** *shouting* **Natalie***'s name. More knocking.* **Natalie** *tries to ignore it. The knocking and roaring continues.* **Natalie** *stands. Again we hear* **Noah** *roar* **Natalie***'s name. Once again we hear* **Noah** *roar her name and pound on the door. This continues.* **Natalie** *closes her eyes and screws up her face. She sighs. More pounding and roaring of her name. She quickly walks to the door. She stands before it. She looks very anxious. She unlocks the door and opens it. Enter* **Noah**. *He walks right by her into the kitchen area. He is holding his sack.*

Noah What's goin' on?! (*Silence.* **Noah** *is still holding his sack. He hoists it up a bit*) Why d'ye put me sack outside?!

Natalie *sighs.*

Natalie Look Noah …

Short pause.

Noah Wha'?! Wha'?!

Pause.

Natalie Look Noah, I don't want to go out with ye, OK?

Noah Ye don't want to go out with me?

Natalie No. (**Noah** *dumps his sack down on the ground. He puts his hand on his head and walks into the sitting room.* **Natalie** *takes small steps into the kitchen area.*)

Pause.

Noah Ye don't want to go out with me?

Natalie No.

Short pause.

Noah Has this anythin' to do with the gun? (*No response*) It fuckin' has, hasn't it?! Yer still spooked abou' that fuckin' gun. (*Grits teeth*) Fuckin' hell! I should never of shown ye the fuckin' thing!

Natalie It's not just the gun Noah, it's … it's the other stuff, the bleedin' … (*Short pause*)

Noah What other stuff?

Natalie The fuckin' … Look Noah! I don't want to go out with ye, OK. So now will you please just …

Noah What other stuff Natalie? (*No response.* **Noah** *groans*) OK, OK. Just … just answer me this. Why don't ye want to go out with me? Simple question Natalie.

Natalie 'Cause I'm scared! OK! I'm scared!

Noah Scared of wha'?

Natalie Scared of havin' another bad relationship, that's wha'! The last relationship I had was a fuckin' disaster and …

Noah Yeah 'cause the cunt you were goin' out with was a disaster. He was a fuckin' scum bag he was. Am I a scum bag?

Natalie No bu' …

Noah But wha'? Bu' wha' Natalie?

Natalie *sighs.*

Natalie Look Noah, it wouldn't work out, OK?

Noah Why? (*Short pause*) Why wouldn't it work out Natalie?

Natalie 'Cause yer a mad bastard and if I went out with ye, ye'd end up layin' into me.

Noah *sits back and stares at her.*

Noah Is that what ye think?

Natalie Yeah.

Pause.

Noah Natalie. I wouldn't … lay … a finger on ye.

Natalie Ye say this now Noah bu' … two … three months down the line it'd be a different story.

Noah No, it wouldn't.

Natalie It fuckin' would!! Ye'd end up beatin' the shit outta me.

Noah I don't believe this.

Natalie And then I'd end up back on the smack again.

Noah Ah shut the fuck up!

Natalie That's what would happen.

Noah Yer talkin' through yer hole Natalie.

Natalie Ow am I? Am I?

Noah Ye are yeah.

Short pause.

Natalie A few weeks ago … (**Noah** *goes to say something*) Just fuckin' listen to me here!! (*Short pause*) Five weeks ago, I got a bad bout of depression. See! You don't know fuckin' anythin' about me! I've depression, I have! Ye didn't know that, sure ye didn't?!! See? Ye don't fuckin' know anythin' about me! I've depression, I have! I've depression and … fuckin' … a few weeks ago, I got a bad bout of it and … I was (*makes an inch with her finger and thumb*) that much away from goin' back on it again. (*Makes inch again*) Only thing that stopped me was … ye know what it was? The new apartment. The new life! (*Short pause*) That's what stopped me. (*Short pause*) Now! If a bit of depression almost sent me over the edge, a fuckin' relationship with you definitely would!! I'd end out there again, with the rest of them. Skagged out of it. And God knows where you'd be. You'd probably be in the Joy, doin' impersonations of Robert De Niro.

Pause.

Noah I don't know what to say.

Natalie Don't say anythin'! Just get yer sack and go! Go on! Get out!

Noah No.

Natalie Get out of me fuckin' flat Noah!

Noah No! Not fuckin' goin' anywhere! Ye think I'm just gonna walk out that door, do ye? Bollix. Not goin' anywhere. (**Noah** *sits on the couch and crosses his arms. He uncrosses them*) If I walked out that door now, I'd be pissin' in the face of destiny.

Short pause.

Natalie What the fuck are ye talkin' about?

Noah I'm talkin' about you and me Natalie. You and me!!

Natalie There is no you and me.

Noah Yes there is! We're meant for each other Natalie. Ye even said so yerself last night.

Natalie *sighs.*

Natalie That was piss talk Noah.

Noah No, it wasn't.

Natalie It fuckin' was!

Noah It wasn't!!! It wasn't piss talk! (*Short pause*)You told me last night …

Natalie (*fast and angry*) Aw will ye shut the fuck up about last night? Last night I was pissed outta me brains.

Short pause.

Noah Were ye pissed outta yer brains this mornin'? 'Cause … as far as I remember Natalie … (*nodding to himself*) ye did say that ye wanted to go out with me.

Natalie Yeah and what else did I say to ye?

Noah Ye said ye wanted to go out with me.

Natalie And what else ye bleedin' …? I said to ye … that I'd go out with ye, but that I wanted to take things slow.

Noah Yeah.

Natalie And the reason why I said that to ye was 'cause … I wasn't sure of ye. But now I am. Ye see … when you were makin' yer little trip over to the woods that time … all that mad stuff you were tellin' me yesterday came back to me.

Noah What mad stuff?!!

Natalie The fuckin' … mad … violent stuff. The fuckin' … thing with the bouncer. The fuckin' …

Noah You were backin' me up on that one yesterday.

Natalie Wha'?!

Noah When I was tellin' ye what happened …

Natalie Look Noah! I don't want to go out with ye, OK? So now, I'd appreciate it …

Noah I'm not goin'.

Natalie *sighs.*

Natalie I don't want to go out with ye Noah!

Noah Yeah! 'Cause yer scared. You've got all these crazy notions in yer head that … I'm gonna give ye the slaps and … you're gonna end up on the smack again.

Natalie That's what will happen! And I tell ye something Noah! Ye wouldn't want to know me when I'm on the smack! I'm an evil bitch when I'm on that stuff! I'd end up stabbin' ye, I would! (*Short pause*) Aw ye don't think I'd do somethin' like that, do ye not?!! I fuckin' would I tell ye! Very nearly done it to me own mother! So why the fuck wouldn't do it to you?!!

Noah Any chance of knockin' off the dramatics Natalie?

Natalie Right that's it! Get out of me flat! Get out of me fuckin' flat, Noah!! (*Short pause*) If ye don't get out of me flat, Noah, I'm gonna start screamin'!

Noah Go for it.

Natalie Ye want me to start screamin'?!!

Noah Yeah. Might even join in. Love screamin' I do.

Natalie Ow my God.

Pause.

Noah Look Natalie! I know I have a bit of a rep for straighteners. But there's no fuckin' way I'd give ye the slaps. Love and respect! That's what ye'd get from me! Not slaps! (*Short pause*) If I was to go out with you Natalie Dunne … See how remembered yer surname? See how I remembered that? If I was to go out with you Natalie …

Natalie I don't wanna go out with ye!!! How many times do I have to tell ye! (*Sighs*) Look Noah … (*Sighs*) The only reason why I invited ye up here was because I was lonely. OK?! I did the exact same thing a few months ago. I met a young fella I used to go out with and … I invited him back. So yer not the first young fella I've invited back here! I lied to ye!

Noah OK! Big deal! Ye lied to me.

Short pause.

Natalie *sighs.*

Natalie Get outta me flat, Noah.

Noah No.

Natalie *sighs.*

Natalie So yer just gonna sit there like a spanner head all day, are ye?

Noah Yeah. (*Pause*) I wouldn't give ye the slaps, Natalie.

Pause.

Natalie Ye wouldn't give me the slaps, would ye not?

Noah No.

Natalie *moves closer to him.*

Natalie Ye wouldn't give me the slaps?

Noah *looks at her suspiciously.*

Noah No.

Natalie *spits in his face.* **Noah** *keeps his eyes closed. He slowly opens them and starts to slowly wipe away her spit.* **Natalie** *looks away. She is disgusted with herself. Pause. She looks at him.*

Natalie Why ye still here? The fuck are ye still here?!! Am after spittin' in yer face!

Short pause.

Noah (*still wiping*) Ye could spit in me face a hundred times, and I still wouldn't budge. (*Short pause*) I'm not walkin' out that door Natalie. If I walk out that door, I'm walkin' out on the best thing that ever happened to me. And that's not gick talk. Yer the best thing that's ever happened to me Natalie. (*Pause.* **Natalie** *is looking down at her feet*) Yesterday was one of the best days of me life, ye know that? (*Short pause*) I mean … there I was, fresh out of the Joy. (*Short pause*) No fuckin' … no prospects. No … no fuckin' nuttin'! Just a bleedin' sack and a head full of dreams. (*Short pause*) Then I walk into the Towers and I meet you. Ye invite me up here and … we have the most amazin' day. And ye know what the most amazin' thing about yesterday was? (*Short pause*) Ye know what it was? (*Teary*) Ye listened to me. Ye listened to me Natalie. Nobody … (*Breaks down a bit. Puts hand to his face*)

Natalie Are ye OK?

Noah *composes himself. It takes a few seconds.*

Noah Nobody ever listens to me. (*Short pause*) Me family don't listen to me. Me mates don't listen to me. Even me granny doesn't listen to me. She listens to me alrigh' but she doesn't really. But you, you listened to me! And that made me feel like … It made feel like I was somebody and not just some … stupid muppet. And I've never said anythin' like this to anybody before in me life. (*He sighs. Pause*) D'ye still want me to go? (*Short pause*) Fuck it! I'll go. (*He stands up, walks over to his bag and picks it up.* **Natalie** *looks very sorrowful. She doesn't make eye contact with him*)

Noah Goodbye.

He makes exit.

Natalie Noah?

Noah Wha'?

Short pause.

Natalie D'ye wanna go to the offo?

Noah Wha'?

Natalie D'ye wanna go to the offo?

Noah Are ye serious?

Natalie Yeah! (*Short pause.* **Noah** *is glowing*) So d'ye wanna go over or wha'?

Noah Yeah! Yeah! I'd love to go over.

Natalie Righ'.

Natalie *trots into her bedroom. A few seconds later she trots back out holding a note.*

Natalie Here. (*Handing him the note*) Get us a shoulder of that cheap stuff … and get yerself a couple of cans.

Noah That's very nice of ye Natalie bu' … this one's on me.

Natalie Take the fuckin' money Noah.

Noah My treat Natalie.

Natalie Take the fuckin' money, would ye?!

Noah My treat.

Natalie *sighs.*

Natalie OK, fair enough. Your treat. (*She reaches up and wipes away a bit of spit from his hair*) Sorry for spittin' at ye.

Noah Yer alrigh'. D'ye want smokes?

Natalie No I'm alrigh'. I have some. I've loads actually. Me sister brought me back a load of duty free last week.

Noah Where was she?

Natalie Santa Ponsa.

Noah Ballymun in the sun.

Natalie Yeah.

Short pause.

Noah So are we back on track again?

Natalie Look Noah. (*Sighs*) Let's not even think about havin' a relationship, OK? Let's just have a few drinks today and see how things go. OK?

Noah OK.

Short pause.

Natalie Ye see, ye have to understand Noah. (*Short pause*) I'm very nervous about havin' another bad relationship.

Noah But it wouldn't be!

Natalie Ye don't know that! We could have a relationship righ' and it could start off great. Like a lot of relationships do. Bu' … somewhere along the line, it could turn ugly and … if it does turn ugly …

Noah It's not gonna turn ugly.

Natalie (*stresses*) It might! I mean, we're both highly strung individuals. There's every chance in the world it could turn ugly. And if it does Noah, I don't think I'll be able to hack it. (*On the verge of tears*) I'd reckon I'd end up goin' back on the smack again and … that's the last thing I want. I've had to work so hard to get where I'm at and … (*Sighs. She puts her hand to her face*) Sorry …

Noah *moves towards her.*

Noah Yer alrigh'. (*He holds her hand and puts his other hand on her opposite arm*) I know what yer sayin'. (*Pause*) Are ye alrigh'? (**Natalie** *looks up at him, teary eyed. She rests her head on his chest. They stay like that for a short while.* **Natalie** *moves her head away. She sniffs.*)

Natalie What are we like?

Short pause.

Noah Two highly-strung individuals … being tender to each other.

Natalie *gives a small laugh. She rests her head back down on his chest.*

Natalie I like ye Noah. I like ye a lot. It's just …

Noah Ye don't want to have a relationship with me.

Natalie No I do! I do want to have a relationship with ye! It's just … Look! Let's just have a few drinks today and see how things go, OK?

Noah OK.

Natalie Righ' go on. Fuckin' gaspin' for a drink now I am.

Noah Yeah?

Natalie Yeah.

Noah *looks at her and smiles.*

Noah Righ'! I'll head over so.

Natalie OK. See ye in a few minutes.

Noah *makes exit.*

Noah (*smiles back at her as he opens door*) I'm gonna buy ye a big bunch of flowers I am.

Natalie Don't you dare get me flowers, Noah!

Noah I'm gettin' ye flowers, Natalie.

Natalie Don't, Noah.

Noah *opens door.*

Noah No. (*Steps outside*) I'm getting ye flowers Natalie. Flowers for the tower flower! (*He shuts the door.* **Natalie** *stands in the same spot. She shakes her head.* **Noah** *yelps.* **Natalie** *puts her hand to her hand and shakes her head. She has a half smile on her face.*)

Natalie Ah fuck. I forgot to tell him to get orange juice.

THE END

Happy Endings

BY RÓISÍN INGLE

Happy Endings was first performed by Fishamble: The New Play Company on 5 March 2005 as part of the production *She Was Wearing …* presented for Amnesty International's *Stop Violence Against Women* campaign with the following cast and crew:

Woman	Fiona Condon
Director	Jim Culleton
Producer	Ciara Flynn
Design Advisor	Sabine Dargent
Costume Supervisor	Sinead Cuthbert
Costume Assistant	Sarah Jane Shiels
	Stephanie Jensen
Lighting Designer	Debbie Behan
Production Manager	Sinead Wallace
Stage Directors	Miriam Duffy
	Marjolijn Venema
Stage Management Intern	Alice Maurel
Assistant Director	Joanne Beirne
Marketing and PR	Cerstin Mudiwa
Script Development	Gavin Kostick

A woman in her late twenties wearing a dressing gown stands barefoot centre stage. It's the early hours of the morning. She can't sleep. Has too much on her mind. She is waiting for someone to appear. Rummaging absentmindedly, nervously in her pockets. Lights go up.

Woman We can't go on like this. I've been down George's Street three times this month. In the medicine centre Mr Chang kept going on about the side effects of (*takes small medicine bottle from pocket and squints to read the tiny label*) Some Enchanted Evenings. He was after receiving another batch from Phuket. I didn't want to miss out. I know from what Mr Chang says that Some Enchanted Evenings is supposed to inject (*adopts vaguely Asian accent*) 'much spice and pepper into your loving life'. So far it's done nothing for me. I told Mr Chang this but he just rolled his eyes like he did the last time I was here. You'd think I was after drugs. Ecstasy, maybe? (*Thinks*) I suppose I am.

I told him I was desperate. There must be reasons for that, he said, which I ignored. (*Pause*) I'd heard he had a new product. Something special. I stood there waiting like I had all the time in the world. I have the patience of a saint. After a few minutes he realised I wasn't going anywhere. He looked both ways, cupping a smooth hand around his mouth. Come round the back, Mrs Julie, he whispered. He disappeared behind a threadbare curtain and emerged with a bottle filled with speckled green muck.

Mr Chang talked for a few minutes about how this stuff was so powerful he only administered it in special cases to people like his wife who was at 'that changing time of life'. Great. I'm a newly married twenty-seven-year-old woman and apparently

I have the sexual appetite of a menopausal fifty-five-year-old. Mr Chang said he didn't want it to get into the wrong hands. I assured him the only drink I'd be spiking was my own. He laid my hand on a velvet cushion, giving me the bottle as though he was passing on some exotic Eastern treasure. Know what it was called? Open Sesame. (*Grimaces*) Desperate times. Desperate measures. I put in my rucksack before he could change his mind. Take five drops for happiness and energy, lady, said Mr Chang. Ten drops if you want 'Happy Endings'. (*Pause*) 'Happy Endings'. (*Pause*)

What does he mean 'Happy Endings'? I've taken eight drops so far and I don't feel a thing. I can't go on like this. We can't. Bill will be back soon. We've been working this out together. We've been trying to work it out. (*Pause*) I think I might have reasons. I think it might help to tell. But I love him too much to take him there. (*Long reflective pause*) To a football field at midnight where a thirteen-year-old girl lies spread-eagled between goalposts floodlit by a guilty moon. The older boy is talking even as he moves on top of her about the goal he scored last week in that very spot. He praises her for staying so still. You have the patience of a saint, he says. The girl says nothing, just grits her teeth in silent thanks.

Maybe there *is* a way. Maybe Bill could hide in the bushes and read her thirteen-year-old mind. He'd understand why she did it. Wouldn't he? That she was sick of the taunts. They called her kitten behind her back. Purred and made catcalls as she walked past. She wanted to grow up overnight like the other girls had. In fields and parks and stolen cars. She didn't want to be a kitten. She wanted to be a woman. She wanted to know what that meant.

She found out later. It was the slamming of beds against walls, it was the sleek-sounding promises of approval that lured me there. Bill could put a glass up against the soiled wall of the past and hear everything for himself. It might help. Only (*Pause*) I don't want to lead him there. Down all those hidden lanes, into all those gloomy bedsits. The mornings after were strange and suffocating, washing teeth with someone else's toothbrush over a sink full of dirty dishes. Struggling with the lock on another unfamiliar door. I don't want him to understand the gratitude I felt after every surreptitious thigh stroke, every loaded compliment. I don't want him to hear the thud, thud, thud of beds against thin walls. I don't want to. (*Pause*) I can't. (*Pause*) Take him there. (*Mood lifts slightly as her thoughts are jogged back into the present*)

Me and Bill are everything I ever dreamed of. When he's around I feel solid. Safe. Like I'm curled up under a duvet and it's lashing outside. It's as though he was the only one who ever saw me. Not just some version of me. And still I can't bear to let him see it all. (*She brightens with forced optimism*) But it's all going to be fine. I can feel it. We just need Open Sesame or Some Enchanted Evenings or (*smiles*) Love Potion Number Nine and a Half Weeks to complete this fairytale. Here he comes now. (*Takes bottle of Open Sesame out of pocket and takes off dressing gown to reveal Ann Summers-style lingerie/nightgown underneath*) I'll keep on trying until Bill and I get everything we deserve. Nine drops, ten drops. For happy endings. Just don't turn on the light.

Light goes out.

THE END

Game

BY STELLA FEEHILY

Game was first performed by Fishamble: The New Play Company on 7 May 2003 at Project Arts Centre, Dublin, with the following cast and production team:

Woman	Jasmine Russell
Man	Charlie Bonner
Director	David Horan
Set Designer	Sinéad O'Hanlon
Costume Designer	Niamh Lunny
Lighting Designer	Mark Galione
Sound Designer	JJ Vernon
Artistic Director	Jim Culleton
Producer	Ciara Flynn
Script Development	Gavin Kostick
PR/Administration	Cerstin Mudiwa
	Kathy Scott
Production Manager	Marie Tierney
Stage Director	Tara Furlong
Stage Managers	Pamela McQueen
	Marella Boschi
Photography	Colm Hogan
Graphic Design	Gareth Jones

'a major and meritorious undertaking … the performers are something of a roll of honour, and it shows'
The Irish Times

'one of those fantastically simple ideas that works so well, you wonder why it hasn't been done before … bold, innovative and entertaining work by a new generation of playwrights'
Unison.ie

CHARACTERS

Woman – *Eva*
Man – *Robert*

A stroke (/) marks the point of interruption in overlapping dialogue.

A wine bar. A woman sitting, looking out a window. She is drinking a large glass of red wine. She waits, looks at her watch, and drinks. A man at the bar is watching her. After some time he makes a decision to walk over.

Man May I?

She looks up.

Woman Please yourself.

Man Thank you.

He sits.

Man Would you / like a drink?

She looks at her watch.

Woman Twenty-three minutes.

Man What?

Woman That's how long you've been watching me for.

Pause.

Man Are you sure?

Woman Quite sure.

Man (*laughs*) I'm sorry. I didn't mean to stare, I wanted to …

Woman Yes?

Man I wondered if you'd like …

Woman Do you speak in such quiet tones as a form of torture or for effect?

Man What?

Woman You could be saying all manner of things to me. But I can barely hear you.

Man I wasn't aware of it.

Woman If you insist on talking to the women you stare at, you should at least speak up.

Man I'm sorry, it was rude of me.

Woman Yes it was.

Man This is a bad start.

Woman You could always begin again.

Pause.

Man May I?

Woman Please yourself. (*She laughs*)

Man Would you like a drink?

Pause.

Woman No. Thank you.

They smile at one another.

Man What's your name?

Woman Guess.

Man What?

Woman You've stared for long enough, you must have an idea.

He laughs.

Man Well I'll try.

Silence.

Woman I can't hear you.

Man I haven't said anything.

Pause. They stare at one another.

Man Rebecca.

Woman Rebecca … biblical, interesting.

Man Well?

Woman Wrong, try again.

Man Angela?

Woman Angela … glacial – disappointed.

Man Glacial? No, Angela – angel.

Woman I see. Well, you're wrong.

Man Perhaps I'm not the right man for this game.

Woman You are.

Silence.

Man Eva.

Woman Eva. I like it.

Man Is it yours?

Eva I'll take it. Robert.

Robert How do you know my name?

Eva Your tag.

Robert My …? (*He looks down and unclips a security tag*) Oh yes … I thought … For a minute …

Eva No. (*Pause*) Does anyone call you Bob?

Robert Just Robert. Not Robbie or Bert or … (*Pause)* Though I seem to remember my father …

Eva Yes?

Robert … calling me Bobby. Perhaps I misremember.

Eva He's dead?

Robert When I was small.

Eva Small?

Robert I was four, nearly five when he died.

Eva What did he die of?

Robert Kidney failure, dialysis.

Eva I used to save the rings.

Robert What's that?

Eva On the cans, Coke tins. For dialysis. Do they still do that?

Robert What?

Eva Collect?

Robert I don't know.

Eva I'm not sure how they use them. I've always imagined a large exercise bike made from aluminium.

Robert I doubt that's what / they're used for.

Eva Yes, doubtful.

She smiles. Pause.

Robert I'd like to take you home.

Eva Where's that?

Robert Not far from here, five minutes in a taxi.

Silence.

Eva I'm not sure.

Robert I'd like to get to know you. We could talk. You know so much about me already.

Eva You haven't called me by my name yet.

Robert Eva.

Silence.

Eva It's always nice to hear one's name for the first time.

Robert I'd like to take you home Eva.

Eva You should stop saying home. You should say house or a hotel or something. When you say 'I'd like to take you home' I could almost believe I've been there before.

Robert Come with me now.

Eva Tell me more about your father.

Silence.

Robert He was a doctor, he's dead, my mother remarried, I have a half-sister.

Eva Do you love her?

Robert My sister?

Eva / Half.

Robert I'd like to get to know you, Eva.

Eva You're not trying very hard. You've spent the time talking about yourself. And insisting I come home with you.

Robert You forgot to mention the staring.

Eva And the staring, which I have to say was disconcerting.

Robert I'm sorry about that but I noticed you were alone and …

Eva Yes?

Robert And, I think, lonely.

Eva Oh … lonely.

Robert And I would just perhaps like to …

Eva To?

Robert Come with me. Now.

Eva I think you should fuck off now.

Silence.

Robert When I was watching you I made a decision.

Eva I thought as much.

Robert I'm going to follow you when you leave here and push my knife in your spine.

She laughs.

Robert Why are you laughing?

Eva Where's your knife?

Robert It's in my briefcase.

Eva What kind of a knife is it?

Robert It's a bread knife. And then I'm going to rape you, you fucking cocktease.

She laughs.

Eva You have a way with women.

Robert Take off your jacket.

Eva I want to see the knife.

He opens his briefcase; she looks inside. He closes it. She takes off her jacket; she is wearing a silk shirt.

Robert I've never told anyone about my father before.

Eva What about him?

Robert That he called me Bobby.

Eva Life is just full of surprises.

Robert Eva's not really your name is it?

Eva You could always threaten me with the knife. I might tell you all sorts about myself.

Robert Tell me your name?

Eva You are not playing by the rules Robert.

Robert What rules? You said my name. You know my name.

Eva You didn't refuse. That's not my problem.

Robert I want your name.

Eva You're starting to sound like Rumpelstiltskin. And I want to laugh. Laugh my fucking head off at you.

Robert Don't laugh at me.

Eva And I am now imagining you doing your little dance. And stamping your foot through the floor.

She laughs.

Robert Don't laugh.

Eva Your bread knife is blunt. You should always have a decent bread knife. Anything else is just plain rudeness.

Robert This is a bad start.

Eva There are no more beginnings allowed Robert.

Robert I like the way you say my name.

Eva It means nothing to me. I won't remember it after a while.

Robert It's possible to begin again.

She gets up. She picks up her jacket and puts it on.

Eva There were dogs barking, I slipped on the rug because the floors had just been waxed, my lip was split. I remember noise. Was that sound in *my* head? It was very loud. I thought, this is someone else's hearing not mine. And there were people on the landing watching. I remember the laughter very well. Very well.

She goes to exit.

Robert I'd say it was only one dog.

Eva What?

Robert One dog making a lot of noise.

They stare at one another.

Eva It was more than one definitely. Three I think.

Robert It's not necessary to exaggerate; the game is over.

Eva The game is not over till I'm gone.

Blackout.

THE END

Tara Has Written a Play

BY TARA DAIRMAN

Tara Has Written a Play was first performed by Fishamble: The New Play Company on 7 May 2003 at Project Arts Centre, Dublin, with the following cast and production team:

Isabel	Geraldine Plunkett
Bob	Des Cave
Director	Ronan Leahy
Set Designer	Sinéad O'Hanlon
Costume Designer	Niamh Lunny
Lighting Designer	Mark Galione
Sound Designer	JJ Vernon
Artistic Director	Jim Culleton
Producer	Ciara Flynn
Script Development	Gavin Kostick
PR/Administration	Cerstin Mudiwa
	Kathy Scott
Production Manager	Marie Tierney
Stage Director	Tara Furlong
Stage Managers	Pamela McQueen
	Marella Boschi
Photography	Colm Hogan
Graphic Design	Gareth Jones

'an impressive evening of theatre ... a novel way of showcasing new writing and directing ... Fishamble's emphasis on capturing new talents continues to produce fascinating results'
Sunday Tribune

CHARACTERS

Isabel
Bob

The stage is bare except for one item—a small couch. **Isabel** *and* **Bob**, *a middle-aged couple out for a night at the theatre, sit in the first row of the audience. They are dressed smartly, but it's a thin veneer.* **Bob**, *who would rather be anywhere else, flips through his programme listlessly.* **Isabel**, *attempting to be the picture of serenity, is failing miserably, crossing and uncrossing her legs compulsively and scanning the audience. Finally,* **Isabel** *can stand it no longer. Just as the lights begin to go down, she bursts out.*

Isabel Tara has written a play!

Bob (*not looking up from his programme*) Really? What's it about, then?

Isabel I don't know. But we'll know soon.

Bob How so?

Isabel It's about to be performed.

Bob What, tonight?

Isabel She said it would start at 9.30. What time is it?

Bob Almost 9.30. (*A pause*) Well, I'll just nip out to the bar then.

Bob *begins to stand up.* **Isabel** *sits him back down.*

Isabel You'll do nothing of the sort!

A pause. Legs cross and uncross, programme pages are flipped. **Bob**, *out of sheer boredom, begins to fold his programme into a paper aeroplane. The lights are down now, and* **Isabel** *and* **Bob** *are spotlit in the audience, though they don't seem to notice.*

Isabel (*whispering*) So … what do you think it's about?

Bob (*in his normal voice*) What? Didn't I just ask you that?

Isabel (*whispering again*) Shhhh! But I don't know what it's about.

Bob (*giving in and whispering*) How the hell should I know what it's about?

Isabel (*loud*) You're her father.

Bob (*louder*) You're her mother.

Isabel (*loudest*) Oh fine! (*A pause*) I wonder what it could be about.

Bob Christ, it's probably about love, sex, death, whatever people write about … stuff and things.

Bob *lets the paper aeroplane fly. It lands in the middle of the stage.*

Isabel Did she tell you that?

Bob No.

Isabel Did she tell you it's about stuff and things?

Bob No, I made that part up.

Bob *gets up and begins to climb up onto the stage to retrieve his aeroplane.* **Isabel** *rises and follows him to continue the argument.*

Isabel She's always telling you things.

Bob She didn't tell me anything. I didn't even know she'd written a play.

Isabel (*to the audience*) I just hope it's not post-modern. I hope it's a real play with a plot and characters. Anything but post-modern.

A pause. Now, even though they're on stage, **Bob** *and* **Isabel** *are no longer at the theatre. It's as if they're in a room in their own house.*

Bob Hey Isabel.

Isabel Yes.

Bob Wanna have sex?

He grabs her.

Isabel Oh God! Bob! … And with Tara right there in the audience!

Bob C'mon, Izzy, one teensy little orgasm.

Isabel And it's almost 9.30!

Bob It's not 9.30 yet.

A slight pause. **Isabel** *stops resisting for a moment or two. Then:*

Isabel Do you think it's about us?

Bob What is?

Isabel Her play.

This breaks the mood.

Bob Would you stop worrying about the goddamn play?

Isabel I'm not worried! I'm just … I wonder what it says about us.

Bob It probably says nothing.

Isabel It's your goddamned fault she came out the way she did!

Bob What way?

Isabel You know.

Bob No I don't.

Isabel Stop being a fool.

Bob A fool!

Isabel Don't patronise me.

Bob 'Stop being a fool.'

Isabel Stop being a fucking prick.

Bob That's better.

A pause. **Bob** *takes a seat on the couch and begins to flip through his programme again.*

Isabel What time is it?

Bob Almost 9.30.

Isabel The play's on at 9.30!

Bob Then I'm sure it'll be starting soon.

Isabel The play is about us, Bob.

Bob (*not looking up*) Mm?

Isabel Only she's too scared to tell us because she knows … she knows …

Bob Mm.

Isabel It's always like that! The mother has to sacrifice! She doesn't even want us here tonight! She can't mount her play properly until we're dead. She doesn't want to shame us.

Bob Mmhm.

Isabel We're inhibiting her self-expression, we're crippling her with guilt. Oh God! We've crippled our own daughter!

Bob You're getting a bit ahead of yourself …

Isabel We'll have to make the sacrifice, Bob. It's our reputations or our lives.

Bob I never had a great reputation to begin with.

Isabel Commit suicide with me, Bob.

Bob What's that?

Isabel Come on, it's not 9.30 yet. We can do it before the play starts.

Bob Alright.

Isabel Really?

Bob Sure. You go first.

Isabel I'm serious, Bob!

Bob Do I get to pick the way I go?

Isabel Sure.

Bob Then I choose … death by orgasm!

He grabs her again, pulling her onto the couch.

Isabel Bob! Oh, Bob … Bob!

Bob What?

Isabel What time is it?

Bob You're a fucking lunatic!

Isabel Lunatics make great play characters, don't they? She's just itching for the world to have a laugh at my expense. The crazy old mother …

Bob Stock character since the dawn of drama.

Isabel That's all I am to her, material. That ungrateful little bitch.

Bob Let's kill her.

Isabel Yes, let's!

Isabel *starts into the audience for* **Tara. Bob***, seeing this, follows.*

Bob I was kidding.

Isabel *stops.*

Isabel Oh. Me too.

Bob *escorts her back to their seats in the first row.*

Bob Come on. It'll be starting any minute.

They *take their seats.*

Isabel What time is it, already?

Bob Almost 9.30.

Isabel Not 9.30 yet?

Bob Almost. Almost.

In the seats, they resume their original positions. **Bob** *fiddles with the programme;* **Isabel** *crosses and uncrosses her legs.*

Blackout.

THE END

Meeting Venus

BY SIMON O'GORMAN

Meeting Venus was first performed by Fishamble: The New Play Company on 7 May 2003 at Project Arts Centre, Dublin, with the following cast and production team:

Trevor	Eamonn Hunt
Benjamin	Charlie Bonner
Director	Siobhan Miley
Set Designer	Sinéad O'Hanlon
Costume Designer	Niamh Lunny
Lighting Designer	Mark Galione
Sound Designer	JJ Vernon
Artistic Director	Jim Culleton
Producer	Ciara Flynn
Script Development	Gavin Kostick
PR/Administration	Cerstin Mudiwa
	Kathy Scott
Production Manager	Marie Tierney
Stage Director	Tara Furlong
Stage Managers	Pamela McQueen
	Marella Boschi
Photography	Colm Hogan
Graphic Design	Gareth Jones

'how refreshing it is to spend an evening like this … an eclectic collection of new plays written and directed by this country's emerging talent … the theatre will never be the same again'
Dublin Daily

CHARACTERS

Trevor
Benjamin

Two men sit on a park bench. As they sit, there is the sound of birds twittering. **Benjamin** *throws scraps of bread and is perplexed that they do not come to feed.*

Trevor I met Venus the other day. Wasn't very impressed. Mind you I don't think she cared much for me either.

Benjamin Venus, Venus?

Trevor What other Venus is there?

Benjamin Was she very beautiful?

Trevor Well there's a thing. At first I thought she was. Fine-looking woman, I thought. But it's strange how indifference takes the glow out of someone's face. And she had arms. She's not supposed to have arms. I found that very strange.

Benjamin Did you have the chat?

Trevor I wouldn't call it chat. Decidedly reticent with the chat.

Benjamin Did she not say anything?

Trevor She made a noise. A sort of 'Huuh' noise. I said, 'Hello', and she said, 'Huuh'. It doesn't encourage conversation, a noise like that.

Benjamin That's a terrible shame.

Trevor That's what I thought.

Benjamin You'd like an old chat if you met Venus.

Trevor That's exactly what I thought. So I pushed on.

Benjamin Pushed on with the chat?

Trevor Pushed on with the chat, yeah.

Benjamin Fair play. What did you say?

Trevor Well at first I didn't know what to say.

Benjamin Were you a bit intimidated?

Trevor I wasn't, no.

Benjamin A bit scared, maybe?

Trevor No, no, I wasn't scared. But I was aware that I was talking to Venus—

Benjamin Venus! Right—

Trevor And I wanted to make an impression.

Benjamin What did you say?

Trevor I decided to tell her about stuff.

Benjamin Did you?

Trevor I did.

Benjamin What kind of stuff?

Trevor Stuff about the world. I told her why the sky turns red at night. I told her how snowflakes are all unique, like people. I told her about gravity. Newton. The apple, all that.

Benjamin All good stuff.

Trevor She wasn't very interested.

Benjamin What?

Trevor Not interested at all.

Benjamin Snowflakes?

Trevor No interest.

Benjamin Newton?

Trevor Not a flicker.

Benjamin The apple?

Trevor I'm telling you, she wasn't interested.

Benjamin That's good stuff that!

Trevor I think maybe she knew that stuff already. So I pushed on. I told her something that I thought she wouldn't know. I told her that I've never been in love. No reaction. She just looked at me.

Benjamin Have you never been in love?

Trevor I have not.

Benjamin And she had no interest?

Trevor None whatsoever. So then I said it. It just came to me. So I said it.

Benjamin What did you say?

Trevor I said, 'Maybe, I'm in love with you.'

Benjamin Me?

Trevor Venus! You melon. I said, 'Maybe, I'm in love with you,' to Venus.

Benjamin Did she find that interesting?

Trevor She found that very interesting. She wanted to know all about that. She wanted to know how the words 'love' and 'maybe' could live in the same sentence. She asked me what I thought love was. She asked me what I knew about her. We had never met before. How could I love someone I didn't know? She asked me if I knew who she was. I said I did. 'You're Venus,' I said. She asked me if I was sure. I said that apart from the arms I was pretty much certain. She was a bit confused by that but after a brief discussion we both agreed that arms or no arms she was, indeed, Venus. And when she went on to further dispute my claim that I was in love with her, I reminded her that I had said 'maybe'. 'Maybe, I'm in love with you,' was what I had said. I didn't know for sure, I just thought 'maybe'.

Benjamin What did she say then?

Trevor A brief silence followed. In fact she thought about that for quite a while. In order to occupy myself during the lull I attempted to figure out what it was she was thinking. I wondered if she might mention the tiger.

Benjamin What tiger is that?

Trevor They say that if you walk through the jungle and you think you hear a tiger roar, don't worry. You haven't heard a tiger roar. Because when you hear a tiger roar, you'll know you've heard a tiger roar.

Benjamin And did she? Mention the tiger?

Trevor No. After the brief pause had evolved into what I can only describe as a silence, she eventually said, 'Huuh.'

Benjamin And that was it?

Trevor That was it. Very disappointing. Not only would you expect a goddess to have more to say for herself, generally speaking, but this was her specialised subject. Love! You'd think Venus would have some very strong views on that.

Benjamin Gods! I sometimes think they're no better than the rest of us.

Trevor So there we were, me and Venus, just sitting there.

Benjamin Saying nothing?

Trevor Saying nothing.

Benjamin No chat whatsoever.

Trevor Just looking at one another.

Benjamin Would you not just go?

Trevor I could have. I was considering that very option. But there was something about her that made me stay.

Benjamin Ah. that'd be the godly aura. They have a fierce aura about them, gods. I think they learn it in god school.

Trevor It wasn't that at all. It was something else. It was her eyes. She was looking straight at me but I had the distinct feeling that she couldn't see me. As if the workings of her thoughts were getting in the way. A process was occurring. And I wanted to see how it would all end, this process that I had somehow started.

Benjamin So you stayed?

Trevor I did.

Benjamin In silence.

Trevor In absolute silence.

Benjamin You could hear a pin drop.

Trevor You could hear a pin not drop.

Benjamin You could hear the time pass by.

Trevor That's exactly what I could hear. The faintest, most delicate 'tick'. It was the tiniest sound that I have ever heard. Quieter even than a heart beating in another room.

Benjamin Is that the sound that time makes?

Trevor It was the sound of the gentlest, quietest watch ever made.

Benjamin It was that quiet you could hear your watch tick?

Trevor I don't have a watch.

Benjamin … Venus!

Trevor Venus! Roman goddess of love and the sea had a wristwatch.

Benjamin That's remarkable.

Trevor I hadn't noticed it before because it was a very subtle, silver one and it blended in with her skin in a very lovely way. But Venus, renowned across the known universe as the most beautiful and armless woman in creation, was sitting silently in front of me with what I can only describe as two perfectly formed arms, one of which was adorned by a very nice but perfectly ordinary wristwatch. Rarely, in all my years, have I felt so confused. I felt quite dizzy. In fact, it's not beyond the bounds of possibility that I was in a state of medically defined shock. This perilous state of mind was not helped by the realisation that the thought uppermost in mind, at this point, was to ask her the time. A sense of hysteria beckoned at the thought that this mighty goddess would have to lift one of the arms that she wasn't supposed to have, to look at the wristwatch that was quieter than a heartbeat in another room, in order to find out what time of day it was. Fortunately, at this point, I became distracted. I began to notice the arm itself. It was naked from shoulder to fingertips. And it was a beautiful cream colour with shades of healthy brown and white. Her skin curved delicately over her muscles, down to her elbow which came to a perfect round button with a vulnerable little hollow on the inside. Heartbreaking veins coloured the whiteness of her lower arm which flowed down to the band of her wristwatch. And there it was, the most breathtaking, feminine wrist, quiet and caring. Humble beneath the shy ornament of the watch, her hand beyond: gentle, loving and sad. I looked back to her face. She was still watching me. Her eyes were bigger now, all wet and full of pain. I wanted her to kiss me. For both our sakes. We hung there for a moment, both seeing something in the other but not quite knowing what. Then a little tear broke out of the outside of one eye and trickled down her cheek. She spoke then, very quietly, almost a whisper: 'I've never been in love either.'

Benjamin Did you not kiss her?

Trevor No.

Benjamin Give her a hug even?

Trevor No. Something inside her closed when she said that.

Her eyes changed. She could see me again. I think we both kind of pitied each other. Then she did it; she looked at her watch. She looked at her watch and said, 'I have to go now.' She didn't have to go, I'm sure of that. But I understood why she said it. She stood up; she stayed there for a moment, just thinking I suppose, and then she went.

Benjamin Was that it?

Trevor Yes.

Benjamin Nothing else?

Trevor I said, 'Goodbye.' She said, 'Huuh.'

THE END

Twenty-Two

BY JOHN CRONIN

Twenty Two by John Cronin was first presented by Fishamble: The New Play Company in association with Temple Bar Cultural Trust on 13 July 2006 as part of the production *Whereabouts* with the following cast and crew:

Simon	José Miguel Jiménez
Sydney	Dylan Tighe
Director	Roisin McBrinn
Artistic Director	Jim Culleton
Producer	Orla Flanagan
Script Development	Gavin Kostick
PR and Marketing	Cerstin Mudiwa
Production Manager	Rob Furey
Production Designer	Suzanne Keogh
Sound Design	Cormac Carroll
Stage Director	Simon Manahan
Stage Managers	Ailbhe Brennan
	Bianca Moore
Fight Arranger	Paul Burke
Trainee Directors	
(NAYD Mentoring Scheme)	Emma Haugh
	John Taite
For Temple Bar Cultural Trust	Dermot McLaughlin
	Grainne Millar

Whereabouts won the *Irish Times* Special Judges' Award for 2006

'... quite riveting assembly of short site-specific plays ... (performances) weave themselves into the fabric of the city – reality and fiction blur ... Temple Bar becomes vivid and compelling ... wonderfully bizarre, expertly directed ... when it stops, you see the city in a different way: a place teeming with narratives if you just take the time to look' *The Irish Times*

'Jim Culleton and Fishamble Theatre Company are to be praised for putting the promenading back into promenade theatre with *Whereabouts* ... the audience (is) literally on its toes ... the acting throughout is of a high standard ... riveting ... brilliant ... this makes all of Temple Bar a stage and all the pedestrians players on it – one is left assessing everyone, never quite sure who is *real' Irish Independent*

'There were moments that were extraordinary ... there were also moments of well-handled social-realism ... exciting for the way they blurred the division between what was *theatre* and what could have been just somebody on the street ... well realised ... what was special was the way it all worked together, the way it surprised and subverted' *Village*

CHARACTERS

Simon – *twenties, decent guy; easy for the audience to identify with*
Sydney – *slightly hyper-real, brusque, melodramatic*

The play is located entirely in a narrow laneway off East Essex Street beside the Dublin Theatre Festival office and directly opposite the Clarence Hotel. The audience will be positioned in the laneway against the wall, facing the side door of the theatre office. On the first occasion that **Sydney** *leaves the laneway he will re-enter through the front door of the theatre office on East Essex Street, unseen by the audience and re-enter the lane way through the side door. On the second occasion* **Sydney** *leaves the laneway he will enter the front door of the theatre office, pass through to the back door which is at the top of the laneway out of sight of the audience, before entering the laneway as* **Simon** *does at the beginning of the play. There is a window directly above the side door of the theatre office through which the sound of the ambulance can be played at the end of the play.*

Play opens. A man (**Sydney**) *is lying face down towards the street end of the laneway.* **Simon** *enters from the far end talking on the phone.*

Simon Yeah I know. Look it depends, it could take a while. I don't know how hard it's gonna be to … yes OK. Why don't … I can't do that … look you head, I'll meet you there. There's nothing I can (*sees* **Sydney**) Jesus! Babes I'll call you back. Hello? (*Approaches tentatively*) Are you OK? (*Kneels beside* **Sydney**) Hello? (*Gently shakes shoulder*) Fuck. (*Rises, dials phone*) Hello … yeah I need an ambulance and police I guess. Hello I've just found a guy … I think he's dead or nearly, don't know. He's just lying in the street. No I don't think so, he doesn't look. Yeah, I called him, gave him a little shake, nothing. Temple Bar or a laneway … it's opposite Essex Street … I didn't check. OK hold on … (*Goes to* **Sydney**, *gingerly puts hand to neck*) I don't feel anything … but I don't fucking know. Yes, I'll wait. Hold on, I'll tell you exactly, it's opposite the Clarence. Yeah, I'll wait. (*Hangs up*).

Sydney *rises, matter of fact, dusts himself down.* **Simon** *turns.*

Simon Are you …? I just called you an ambulance … What's …?

Sydney Marvellous. Very kind. Must be off. Cheerio. (*Walks briskly out of laneway into street, and disappears*)

Simon Hold on … (*Stops, dials phone*) Yeah … em, ambulance please. Hi, listen, I called two minutes ago … It wasn't you, it was someone else. There was a guy lying in the street. Anyway look he's fine … he just got up and walked away … I don't know … Look I'm sorry … I didn't mean to … I thought he was dead … (*Walks to street*) No, no sign yet

… yes cancel it. Sorry. (*As he speaks* **Sydney** *re-enters laneway and resumes position.* **Simon** *turns*) Hey! What the fuck is this? (*Goes to* **Sydney**) Get up you fucking eejit. This isn't fucking funny. (*Kneels, shakes him roughly. No response*) I'm warning you … (*Rolls him over.* **Sydney** *looks dead.* **Simon** *is baffled; he looks around for a hidden camera. He doesn't know what to do*) Come on, look … I called an ambulance and cancelled. That's messing, it's … you can't … (*Checks pulse. Listens to chest*) Jesus. (**Simon** *dials phone. Doesn't take eyes off* **Sydney**) Hello, ambulance. Look I've called twice. I don't know what the hell is going on. There is a guy … he was dead I thought. He got up … he walked away. I cancelled. I turned around, he was back … He's got no fucking pulse … I don't know … If it's a joke it's not my fucking joke alright? Send the police as well – he should be arrested. Maybe he's nuts. Yes I'll wait; it's the laneway opposite the Clarence.

Hangs up. Sits against wall, watching **Sydney**. **Sydney** *sits up dramatically, then stands up.*

Sydney (*looks at watch*) Good Lord.

Hurries off. **Simon** *sits in baffled silence, takes out phone and dials.*

Simon Hey babes … something mad is going on here. When I hung up on you … there was a guy lying on his face … I thought he was dead …

Simon *continues narrative until interrupted by* **Sydney** *approaching briskly from far end of laneway.* **Sydney** *is on the phone.*

Sydney (**Sydney**'*s speech on the phone is identical to* **Simon**'*s at the opening of the play*) Yeah I know. Look it depends, it could take a while. I don't know how hard its gonna be to … yes OK. Why don't … I can't do that. Look you head I'll meet you there. There's nothing I can … (*Stops, transfixed, staring at the point on the ground where he originally lay*) Babes I'll call you back.

During the following **Sydney** *acts exactly as* **Simon** *did at the opening. He sees and interacts with a lifeless body which is lying in the same positions he himself was in at the start of the play. To* **Simon** *and the audience, there is nobody there.*

Sydney Hello? (*Approaches tentatively*) Are you OK? (*Kneels beside 'body'*) Hello? (*Gently shakes shoulder*) Fuck. (*Rises, dials phone*) Hello … yeah I need an ambulance and police I guess. Hello I've just found a guy … I think he's dead or nearly, don't know. He's just lying in the street. No I don't think so, he doesn't look. Yeah, I called him, gave him a little shake, nothing. Temple Bar or a laneway … it's opposite Essex Street … I didn't check. OK hold on … (*goes to 'body', gingerly puts hand to neck*) I don't feel anything … but I don't fucking know. Yes, I'll wait. Hold on, I'll tell you exactly, it's opposite the Clarence. Yeah, I'll wait. (*Hangs up*).

Simon, *staring in absolute bewilderment, stands, takes a couple of steps, unsure what to do.* **Sydney** *turns, sees him.*

Sydney Jesus Christ! What the hell are you doing?

Simon What are you doing?

Sydney I just called an ambulance for you! Is this your idea of a joke? You scared me half to death. I have a weak heart.

Simon I … I don't understand.

Sydney You don't understand? Are you insane? Lying on the ground like some sort of vagrant …

Simon (*fear, anger and confusion rising*) What are you talking about?

Sydney (*dawning realisation*) Oh I get it, I see it now. Playing possum – draw the sucker in and then strike … (*Rising anger and indignation. Takes out wallet, waves it*) This what you were after, eh? Or maybe it was the phone. You disgust me – taking advantage of the kindness of a man; victimising those who are willing to help another human being. Scum … parasite.

The following becomes an incessant increasingly manic rant from **Sydney** *with* **Simon***'s interjection increasingly panicky.*

Simon Look, stop with this shit.

Sydney Ha, the worm has turned now, me bucko – the hunter becomes the hunted. You picked the wrong man to mess around with today. Yes indeed.

Simon Look, get out of my way, I don't … I can't … (*attempts to leave the laneway;* **Sydney** *stops him*)

Sydney Oh no, no, no, no. You can wait right here and explain to the ambulance men why their time has been wasted in this way. Explain to the police! I hope they charge. Loitering with intent I should think!

Simon Just let me by!! (*Makes another attempt to leave*)

Sydney I should like to hear you explain your little scheme to a judge! You degenerate, you creeping scoundrel, you insidious rat!

Simon Get out of my way.

Simon, *determined to leave, attempts to push past* **Sydney**. **Sydney** *grabs* **Simon***'s shoulders.* **Simon** *reacts by grabbing* **Sydney**.

Simon Just leave me ALONE!!

Sydney Help! Ho! Police … Police!

Simon *shoves* **Sydney** *hard.* **Sydney** *does not release his grip. They swing around in a circle until* **Sydney** *is shoved into the door. He releases his grip; he clutches his chest.* **Simon** *steps back.* **Sydney** *drops to his knees; he slumps forward into the exact position he started in.* **Simon** *steps back to the wall; he slumps against it, watching in horror, disbelief and fear. The audience hears the sound of an approaching siren. The siren grows louder.* **Simon** *half cries, half laughs gently to himself. He closes his eyes.*

THE END

Drapes

BY BELINDA MCKEON

Drapes by Belinda McKeon was first presented by Fishamble: The New Play Company in association with Temple Bar Cultural Trust on 13 July 2006 as part of the production *Whereabouts* with the following cast and crew:

Tim	John Olohan
Anna	Olga Wehrly
Director	Karl Shiels
Artistic Director	Jim Culleton
Producer	Orla Flanagan
Script Development	Gavin Kostick
PR and Marketing	Cerstin Mudiwa
Production Manager	Rob Furey
Production Designer	Suzanne Keogh
Sound Design	Cormac Carroll
Stage Director	Simon Manahan
Stage Managers	Ailbhe Brennan
	Bianca Moore
Trainee Directors	
(NAYD Mentoring Scheme)	Emma Haugh
	John Taite
For Temple Bar Cultural Trust	Dermot McLaughlin
	Grainne Millar

Whereabouts won the *Irish Times* Special Judges' Award for 2006

'… quite riveting assembly of short site-specific plays … (performances) weave themselves into the fabric of the city – reality and fiction blur … Temple Bar becomes vivid and compelling … wonderfully bizarre, expertly directed … when it stops, you see the city in a different way: a place teeming with narratives if you just take the time to look' *The Irish Times*

'Jim Culleton and Fishamble Theatre Company are to be praised for putting the promenading back into promenade theatre with *Whereabouts* … the audience (is) literally on its toes … the acting throughout is of a high standard … riveting … brilliant … this makes all of Temple Bar a stage and all the pedestrians players on it – one is left assessing everyone, never quite sure who is *real*' *Irish Independent*

'There were moments that were extraordinary … there were also moments of well-handled social-realism … exciting for the way they blurred the division between what was *theatre* and what could have been just somebody on the street … well realized … what was special was the way it all worked together, the way it surprised and subverted' *Village*

CHARACTERS

Tim
Anna

The interior of an upmarket boutique in Temple Bar (suggestion: Smock, Smock Alley). As the audience members encounter him, **Tim**, *a man in his sixties, is sitting in a chair in the middle of the store, shopping bags at his feet. He looks around him at the clothes on the rails; he looks down to his feet. The curtain of the changing cubicle to his right twitches, indicating that there is someone inside.* **Tim** *sighs and reaches into one of the shopping bags beneath him. He takes out a woman's cardigan, a garment for a woman his own age, brand new with labels intact, and shakes his head as he looks at it. This is the cue for the audience members to ask their question: do you have something to tell me? As* **Tim** *answers, his gaze may vacillate between the item in his hand, other parts of the room, and the audience. It should not be clear whom or what he is addressing.*

Tim This isn't me.

Anna (*from cubicle*) What did you say?

Tim I should have said something.

Anna Said what?

Tim This isn't me, and this isn't you, this place.

Anna This one is nicer. I like this one, yeah.

Tim But that's not your fault.

Anna Wanna see it?

Tim I should have been straight with you, Anna.

Anna Hmmm?

Tim Should have been straight with her. With myself. (**Tim** *stands up, walks over to the adjacent rack of clothes. He runs his hand along the fabric and picks a garment out. He looks at it. He shakes his head. He takes the price label in his hand and examines it. He shakes his head. He laughs to himself.*) Jesus Christ. Did I bring you here?

Anna *steps out of the cubicle in a striking dress. She is in her early thirties, attractive, but looks awkward in this pose.* **Tim***'s back is turned; he hasn't heard her emerge.*

Anna Daddy?

Tim *turns around and looks at her.*

Anna You like it?

Tim What …

Anna What …

Tim What do you think of it, love?

Anna I love it, Dad. I think it's really …

Tim Really …

Anna Really *me*.

Tim Is this really you?

Anna You don't like it.

Tim I do like you.

Anna What?

Tim I do like it.

Anna *stares at herself in the mirror.* **Tim** *watches her as she twists and turns. He walks up to her, puts his hands on her shoulders, meets her eye in the mirror.*

Tim Anna … love … if you like it …

Anna I do …

Tim That's all, so.

Anna Really?

Tim Of course.

Anna Would you have let me buy this …

Tim You?

Anna Would you have? If this was the old shop. If I were a customer in Dolan's store, standing with the clerk Mr Murphy in front of the little mirror with the tinge of brown? Would you be honest with me then?

Tim That was a good mirror.

Anna It was muddy.

Tim Was it?

Anna Dusty, then. Brown with dust like everything else in that shop.

Tim *moves away from her, towards the rack of clothes. He parts the clothes and looks through them, as though expecting to find something behind. He looks back to* **Anna.**

Tim What kind of place was that, anyway?

Anna A grim place.

Tim What kind of place is this?

Anna This is the real thing, Dad. This is the way it should be. Look at these clothes. Look at them. (*Goes to racks, picks out first one garment, then another*) Feel that, Dad. You ever feel silk like that before? And this? This is 100% virgin wool. You ever feel wool like this before? And this dress. (*Clutches the fabric of the dress she is wearing*) Isn't this incredible?

Tim I know what silk is. I know what wool is. (*Muttering*) I know the price of them, too.

Anna You know the what?

Tim Nothing. Take it off. Get out of it. Get them (*gestures towards the audience*) to wrap it up and we'll go. We have enough bought. We have enough now to fill them. Come on.

Anna They won't be full.

Tim What?

Anna They still won't be full. She had more things than this. She had coats. Lots of coats. And dresses. More dresses than you can see in this whole shop. She had shoes …

Tim She had too much. It'll do.

Anna What did you say?

Tim I said, it'll do.

Anna (*laughing*) She had too much? She had too much?

Tim Come on, Anna. It's time to go home.

Anna To what?

Tim To … (*Sighs*)

Anna There's nothing only empty wardrobes and empty drawers and empty rooms and why …?

Tim We have a house to go home to. We have a home.

Anna That you emptied. That you … that you *scoured* of the bits of her. That you sluiced and doused and rinsed until there was nothing even left of the smell of her. That you *hosed down*.

Tim You're being unreasonable.

Anna What did you do with them?

Tim (*pointing to her dress*) You're starting … Anna, love … you're beginning to perspire.

Anna Did you give them to the neighbours?

Tim That silk stuff … you can't be getting that … damp … it's going to stain …

Anna To the charity shop? Did you give them to the Vincent de Paul?

Tim Come on, love … someone's going to see you … someone's going to say something …

Anna Did you burn them? In the garden? With the Sunday supplements and the margarine wrappers? Did you stand there and watch them fly up? Did you turn your back and turn back to the wardrobe for more? Churn them into the fire until there weren't any more and the jet beads on her winter gown were hot and hard as nubs of coal on the scorched black ground …

Tim Love, love, take it off now, take it off before you destroy it …

Anna Why could you not leave them behind? Why could you not leave them … to wither and rot by the moths' wings … leave them to …

Tim You …

Anna Me … There won't be enough to fill the spaces up, no matter what we gather, no matter what we spend …

Tim Come on, love. Take it off. Take it off, now, like a good girl.

Long pause.

Anna OK, Daddy.

Tim That's the girl.

Anna *unzips the dress and steps out of it. She hands it to* **Tim** *and faces him, braless, wearing only her knickers.*

Anna Go on.

Tim I …

Anna Wrap it up.

Tim *is silent.*

Anna Mr Murphy. Timothy Murphy, Dolan's little clerk. Do you hear me? Wrap it up. Wrap it up and put it with the rest of the parcels. (*Pause*) Come on man, I don't have all day. Come on!

Tim (*snapping to*) Certainly, madam, certainly, madam ... I'll see to that right away (*He hands the dress, bundled, to an audience member*) ... Wrap that up, please, and quickly, no dawdling ... (*To* **Anna**) Would Madam like to see anything else today?

Anna *takes a coat from the rack and puts it on, belts it over her nakedness. She steps into a pair of shoes from the shop floor. She picks up the shopping bags and makes her way through the audience, slowly, handing pieces of clothing from the bags to people as she goes.* **Tim** *follows after her, offering new garments from the racks, calling to her.*

Tim Madam? Madam? Madam looks so well ... Madam needs a home ... Madam comes, Madam goes ... Madam shines ... Madam ... gone? Madam? Madam? (**Anna** *exits, shutting the door in* **Tim**'s *face. He hangs his head. He turns to the audience*) Who did we think we were ... shopping in those places ... spoiling ourselves with those things? She knew as well as I did that we could never go on in that way ... selling rags to the neighbours for a living ... borrowing money back from them to drape ourselves in silks and tweeds and the furs of a rich man ... a rich woman ... nights the child went hungry, even, think I'm proud of that? Nights she went to bed with only a spasming in her belly while we went out in splendour, her mother so lovely with those jet beads at her throat ... Where were we going? We hadn't even places to go ... hadn't even people to see … Used to drive into town, and walk in the square, and maybe a drink in the Royal Hotel, and coming close, maybe, to talking with the doctor, or the solicitor, or the man from the bank … to having a drink with them, to growing into people like them … but never getting there, you know? Never getting there, although we were looking the part. Never getting there. Getting into the car again, the two of us, quieter on the way home, in spite of the wine and the whiskey … and the house was quiet when we got there, you know? That house was always quiet. And her things would rustle as (*going back to the rack, starting to replace the clothes, hanging them back up*) she brushed them and folded them and hung them back in the wardrobe, and stood back to admire them, the way they all seemed so beautiful and elegant and straight all in a line, all the different colours, all the different ways they'd feel … And in the morning, back in our shop clothes, our starched aprons and our grey coats, we'd smile at each other for just a moment, as if to say to each other that we were more than this. More than this. More than what they knew of us. More than what they saw. (*He shrugs. He walks to the door. He stops and looks back at the audience*) Thanks anyway. Goodbye.

Exit.

THE END

BIOGRAPHICAL NOTES

JOHN CRONIN is an actor who has worked on stage, TV and film. *Twenty-Two* is his first play, which was performed as part of Fishamble's *Whereabouts.*

JIM CULLETON is the Artistic Director of Fishamble, for which he has directed many award-winning productions in Ireland and on tour to the UK, USA, France, Germany, Czech Republic and Romania. He has also directed for Amnesty International, Pigsback, 7:84 (Scotland), Project Arts Centre, Amharclann de hÍde, Tinderbox, The Passion Machine, The Ark, Second Age, RTÉ Radio 1, The Belgrade, The Abbey/Peacock, Semper Fi, TNL Canada, Scotland's Ensemble @ Dundee Rep, Draíocht, Barnstorm, TCD School of Drama, Origin (New York) and RTÉ lyric fm. He previously edited *Fishamble/Pigsback: First Plays* also for New Island and has contributed to books for Carysfort Press, Ubu, Amnesty International, European Theatre Convention and NCI.

TARA DAIRMAN's plays include *PB&J* (2007 NY International Fringe Festival), *The Wedding Cake* (Heideman Award finalist, Actors Theatre of Louisville's National Ten-Minute Play Contest), *Tara Has Written a Play* (produced at Project Arts Centre by Fishamble Theatre Company) and *The Question House* (produced at HB Studio and Dartmouth College as winner of the Eleanor Frost competition). She was recently named a finalist for the Jerome Fellowship at The Playwrights' Center and a semi-finalist for the Princess Grace Playwriting Award. Tara studied creative writing at Dartmouth College and Trinity College Dublin and currently lives in New York.

GARY DUGGAN won the Stewart Parker Trust Award for his first play, *Monged* (Fishamble, Project Arts Centre, April '05; Revival tour, Autumn '06; UK production, Belgrade Theatre, Coventry, Nov '07). Gary's other plays include *Dedalus Lounge* (Pageant Wagon, 2006 Dublin Fringe Festival and national tour '07/'08), *Trans-Euro Express* (Pageant Wagon & Mill Theatre, Nov '08), *Stop/Over* (part of Abbey Theatre's 20:Love season, March '08) and *Mission* (Part of an anthology show *End of Lines*, Origin Theatre Company, New York, Sept '08). Both *Monged* and *Dedalus Lounge* have been translated into Romanian and produced in Bucharest.

STELLA FEEHILY's writing includes *Duck*: Royal Court, Peacock Theatre and English Tour; *O Go My Man*: Royal Court, Cork Everyman, English Tour; *Catch*: Royal Court; *Think Global, Fuck Local*: Rough cuts, Royal Court. Radio Plays: *Sweet Bitter*: Fishamble Theatre Company/Lyric fm, *Julia Roberts' Teeth*: BBC 3. Short plays include *Game*: Fishamble Theatre Company and *Happy*. She is under commission from Out Of Joint, The Royal Court, The Royal National Theatre, Soho Theatre and Manhattan Theatre Club.

ROSALIND HASLETT was winner of the Fishamble Playwrighting Competition in 2002 and her winning play *Still* was performed as part of the Diversions Festival in Temple Bar. She also contributed the monologue *Slips* to Fishamble Theatre Company and Amnesty International's *She Was Wearing…* in celebration of International Women's Day in 2005. Rosalind received her BA in Drama and English from Trinity College Dublin and her MA in Creative Writing from Queen's University Belfast. She is currently completing a Ph.D thesis on the subject of dramaturgy and new play development in the anglophone theatre.

Dublin journalist RÓISÍN INGLE has been a reporter with *The Irish Times* for over ten years and writes a weekly column in that newspaper's Saturday magazine. She is the author of *Pieces of Me*, a collection of the columns with some extra bonus material gathered in book form. She rollerskates (badly) and gets her kicks playing Scrabble online with strangers. She has never in all her thirty-something years visited a Chinese herbal medicine shop seeking help with her sex life. *Suspenders* is her first play.

RODNEY LEE was born in Dublin in 1975. He completed a BA in UCD and studied film in DLIADT. In 2004, he won the Tiernan McBride Screenwriting Award for his first feature script, *69*. He followed this with *Autograph*, a radio-play, and *The Gist of It*, produced by Fishamble. In 2005, he won the WYD-Eye competition for his script; *Nun More Deadly*. The subsequent film went on to win Best Irish Short at the Galway Film Festival and the Audience Award for Best Short at the Cork Film Festival, both in 2006. Rodney lives and works in Dublin.

BELINDA MCKEON was born in Co. Longford in 1979. She studied English and Philosophy at Trinity College, Dublin and at UCD, and has recently completed an MFA in Fiction at Columbia University, New York. As well as *Drapes*, which was produced by Fishamble as part of its series *Whereabouts* in 2006, her plays include *Word of Mouth*, which won a P. J. O'Connor Award in 2005, and *Two Houses*, originally commissioned by the Abbey Theatre as part of its 20:Love series and co-produced by the Abbey Theatre and thisispopbaby at the Dublin Fringe Festival 2008. She lives in Brooklyn, New York and works as an arts journalist and curator.

As a young boy, SEAN MCLOUGHLIN wrote compulsively, winning many awards for his poetry and short stories. Sean started writing seriously when he was twenty-eight, much due to the encouragement of the award-winning playwright Aodhan Madden and theatre director Jimmy Fay. *Noah and the Tower Flower* is his first play, which was commissioned by Fishamble. It was directed by Jim Culleton for Fishamble in Axis Arts Centre in 2007 and won both the *Irish Times* Best New Play Award and the Stewart Parker Trust Award for that year. Sean's play, *End Time*, was produced by the Gaiety School graduation students at Project Arts Centre in June 2007. He has been commissioned to write *Gone for Bread* for Fishamble, *French Park* for Druid, *Monkey No Mates* for the Abbey Theatre and *St. Martin in the Fields* for Samson Films.

SIMON O'GORMAN has worked in theatre, film and television as an actor for many years. He also works as a voice artist and is currently writing his first full-length play.

A writer-director for television and theatre, JIM O'HANLON's plays include *The Buddhist of Castleknock*, *Pilgrims in the Park* (both Fishamble), *My Bonnie Lies*, *Dinner with Duck*, and *Ready or Not* (Edinburgh Festival Fringe). Other work as a writer includes *Coronation Street* (Granada TV), *Casualty* (BBC), *The Boy Who Became Prime Minister* (BBC Radio 3) and *Even the Olives are Bleeding* (BBC Radio 4). Jim's credits as a director include the BBC/HBO mini-series *House of Saddam, Mutual Friends* (BBC), *Shameless* (Channel 4), *Waking the Dead* (BBC), and the controversial Channel Four drama *All in the Game* starring Ray Winstone.